TEACHER EDUCATION
AND
NATIONAL EDUCATION POLICY 2020

VOLUME ONE

About the Editors

Professor P.K. Sahoo, hailing from Asureswar, Cuttack, Odisha, is a distinguished Educationist and Teacher Educator in India. Professor Sahoo has previously served as the Vice-Chancellor and Dean of the Faculty of Arts at the University of Allahabad, Allahabad. Presently, he is engaged as an ICSSR Senior Fellow in Education, leading a project focused on Developing a Blended Learning Package on Education for Sustainable Development. Additionally, Professor Sahoo holds the position of Lok Pal at UPRT Open University, Prayagraj. Professor P.K. Sahoo has held various significant roles throughout his career, including Chairperson of Digital Education in Social Sciences at the University of Allahabad. He has been an active participant in shaping educational policies, serving as Hon'ble Member of the Northern Regional Committee, NCTE from 2012 to 2019, and has been Hon'ble Member of the Teacher Education Standing Committee of UGC, New Delhi. His expertise has contributed to the formulation of the National Education Policy 2020 particularly in the domain of Teacher Education. With over three and a half decades of teaching experience, Professor Sahoo has held administrative positions, such as Head of the Education Department, Director of the Institute of Correspondence Courses at the University of Allahabad, and Director of Academics at Kota Open University, Kota and prior to this he taught at Institute of Education, Centre of Excellence at Devi Ahilya Vishwavidyalay, Indore over a decade. He began his research journey as a UGC Junior Research Fellow at the Centre of Advanced Study in Education, M.S. University of Baroda, and later served as a Research Associate. Professor Sahoo's contributions extend beyond academia; he has been actively involved in national and international level professional activities, collaborating with various institutions, universities, and government bodies. He is renowned for his pioneering contribution to Open and Distance Learning in India and across Asian countries, as well as for his work in Future Studies in Education, Management, and Teacher Education. With a notable publication record, including 10 books and over 100 research papers in many international and national journals, Professor Sahoo has also mentored numerous scholars, guiding 29 Ph.D. students, one post-doctoral project, and 25 M.Phil. students. He has led more than 20 research projects sponsored by prestigious organizations such as UGC, IGNOU, ISRO, NIEPA, MHRD, and NIOS. His academic contributions have been recognized internationally, receiving awards for paper presentations at conferences in countries such as the UK, China, Hong Kong, Thailand, Malaysia, the Philippines, Nepal, Pakistan, and Vietnam. He played a pivotal role as the coordinator of the MOOCs Programme in Education and has contributed significantly to the development of e-PG Pathshala modules in Education in collaboration with CIET, NCERT, which are accessible to students on SWAYAM. Furthermore, Professor Sahoo served as the President of the Indian Association of Teacher Educators (IATE) and has been the recipient of numerous national and international awards, showcasing his dedication and excellence in the field of education.

Dr. B.C. Das is Assistant Professor of Education, Department of Education, Ravenshaw University, Cuttack, Odisha. He has also served Faculty of Education, Banasthali University, Rajasthan, Rani Bhagyawati Devi Women's PG College, Bijnor and has been the Programme In-charge of IGNOU B.Ed. Programme Study Centre. He has owned the distinction of being a National Research Fellow of the Ministry of Tribal Affairs, Government of India at University of Allahabad. His teaching and research interest zeroes-in-on teaching skills, constructivist and digital pedagogy, tribal education, development education and education for sustainable development. Dr. Das is currently engaged with his research focus on Development Education and Empowerment of Tribal Communities which may be recognized as pioneering effort in India. Dr. Das has published seven reference and textbooks: Tribal Education: Trends and Future Scenario; Education for Tribals: Participation and Effectiveness; co-edited four volumes: *Professionalism in Teacher Education: Contemporary Perspectives; Quality in Higher Education: Issues and Practices; Quality Education in India*: Vol. 1; *Problems and Prospects; Quality Education in India*: Vol. 2; *Inputs and Initiatives*; Lead Author of the Textbook titled *Critical Understanding of ICT*; published more than 50 research papers and undertaken three research projects; guided M.Phil. and Ph.D. research students; and innovated K-4 Learning Transaction Model for teaching practice. Recently he has completed a TPACK based Research Project funded under PMMMNMTT, Government of India. Dr. Das has been elevated to the prestigious position of Hon'ble Member of NCTE (ERC), New Delhi.

TEACHER EDUCATION
AND
NATIONAL EDUCATION POLICY 2020

VOLUME ONE
Development and Technology Integration

Edited by

P.K. Sahoo
B.C. Das

CONCEPT PUBLISHING COMPANY PVT. LTD.
NEW DELHI - 110 059

ISBN: 978-93-6344-587-1 (Set)
ISBN: 978-93-6344-083-8 (Vol. 1)
ISBN: 978-93-6344-700-4 (Vol. 2)

First Published 2025

Published and Printed by

Concept
Since 1974

Concept Publishing Company Pvt. Ltd.
A/15-16, Commercial Block, Mohan Garden
New Delhi-110059 (India)
T: +91-11-41101460
E: publishing@conceptpub.com, *W*: www.conceptpub.com

Cataloging in Publication--Courtesy: D.K. Agencies (P) Ltd. <docinfo@dkagencies.com>

Teacher education and national education policy 2020 / edited by P.K. Sahoo, B.C. Das.
volumes cm
Includes bibliographical references and index.
Contents: volume 1. Development and technology integration -- volume 2. Research and quality assurance.
ISBN 9789363445871 (set)
ISBN 9789363440838 (vol. 1)
ISBN 9789363447004 (vol. 2)

1. Teachers--Training of--India. 2. Curriculum change--India. 3. Educational technology--India. 4. Teachers--Professional ethics--India. 5. Teachers--Training of--Government policy--India. I. Sahoo, P. K., editor. II. Das, B. C., Dr., editor.

LCC LB1727.I5T43 2025 | DDC 370.71154 23

Dedicated to

Professor M.B. Buch

Father of Teacher Education and Research in India

Preface

Teacher Education remains at centre stage in catering education for sustainable development as the priority of the global society. Quality education with emphasis on equity, inclusiveness and excellence is to be ensured for every child in the knowledge society. Blending indigenous knowledge base with modern technology in the socio-cultural milieu of every human being can lead the path of self-reliance. While generalised discipline oriented knowledge system helps us to generate universal understanding of natural and behavioural phenomena, the understanding of life world and its worth is deeply rooted in grassroots level life experiences. Therefore, education for life is imperative and its future must integrate the context specific experiences with universal understanding. The multiple realities concerning meaningfulness of individual and social life must be reflected in the curricular experiences. Teachers' role in promoting such experiences is to be valued duly in the preparatory teacher development programmes and in various kinds of professional development practices as well.

The National Education Policy, 2020 (NEP 2020), emphasises on the basic principle of "teachers as the heart of the learning processes". It spells about their preparation, professional development, and positive working environments. It also focuses on encouraging innovation through autonomy, good governance and empowerment indicating professionalism in teaching. Professionally competent teachers can do justice to the emerging concept of holistic education for a multidisciplinary world, with due emphasis on conceptual clarity, creative inquiry process, critical thinking and practice of morals and constitutional values (NEP 2020). Teachers' role is not just restricted to transaction of teaching activities inside the classroom, rather, they must have respect for the local context in all curriculum and pedagogy. Teachers' respect for equity and inclusion must be reflected in the whole school environment. Such principles have a lot of bearing for reforms in school curriculum as well as for teacher development programmes. Restructuring of school system has also implications for reforms in teacher education curriculum. Development rooted in NCF-2005 and NCFTE-2009 took a long path for bringing structural changes in Teacher Education. As per recommendations of Justice Verma Commission Report, 2012 and NCTE Guidelines, 2014 & 2019, integrated teacher education programme in composite higher education institutions has been a component of higher education institutions. The emphasis on professional skill development programme in the form of internship and longer duration exposure to teaching-learning practices in real school situation is a significant deviation from traditional teacher training practices. In this respect, the discourse on quality in teacher education and school education draw major attention of the stakeholders of the school system. Even, such debate is extended to the relationship between teacher inputs and teaching-learning process at higher education level. These issues have been discussed elaborately in these volumes through the contributions of reputed scholars, experts and the researchers in the field of education in the country.

The theoretical discussions on education, teaching, learning and assessment with multidisciplinary perspective of teacher education have been corroborated in the form of conceptual papers in these volumes. The write-ups reflect on compositeness, continuity and contemporary expressions on teacher education system in India and abroad. Moreover, the efforts on curriculum reforms in teacher education and its practices, even though it is a recent phenomenon, reveal openness of the system in Indian context. Teacher education programmes for pre-service teachers and in-service teachers in a wider framework of operation draw special attention of regulatory bodies and governance of the institutions. The Indian experiences of multiplicity and newness in teacher education talk about inclusiveness of teacher education. The system caters to the diversified professional needs of teachers of different stages of school system. Effort on innovative practices in teacher education is related to different institutional factors. The emergence of privatisation and unplanned growth of teacher education institutions in the country have a lot of negative bearing on professional orientation and innovations in teacher education. The empirical evidences on curricular practices of teacher education reveal multiplicity and variations in different practices in institutional context. The phenomena of technology use and technology integration in education are of a recent origin. Teacher education system has dual position in this regard.

The foremost requirement is to make teachers competent in suitable integration of pedagogy, content and technology in meeting the curricular objectives of school system. There have been integrated efforts to link teacher education programmes with online platforms, open distance learning programmes and blended learning approach. Some such disconnected efforts must be placed in the form of consortium for generation of e-resources, integration of technology inputs with innovative pedagogic principles and promotion of online education for teachers. The role of national level, state level and local level bodies in education for promotion of academic excellence and resource generation like NCERT, CIET, IGNOU, NIOS, EMRCs, SCERTs, SIEMATs, IASEs, CTEs, DIETs, etc. is very much meaningful in this regard. The chapters devoted to innovations, quality upgradation and technology integration in school education and teacher education ponder on different issues and practices concerning technology orientation of teachers. The nature of research in education, particularly in the context of teacher education needs a different orientation. The traditional approach of theory practice divide and dominance of generalised knowledge orientation of behavioural science in education are found obsolete to educational reforms, particularly, in the context of teacher development practices in the ground reality.

The teachers need to be oriented towards educational action based reforms through research. Their participation to interlink hands on reflective practices in education with broad- based knowledge framework must be encouraged through teacher empowerment programmes in decentralised form. The Schools of Education at university level must explore the quality enhancement oriented institutional possibilities on different aspects of education.

Professionalism is considered as the core of teacher development programmes. The globalised world has generated complexities in the role of teachers in current educational setup. Various issues have been raised about teachers' morals in the context of life in the ground reality and perception of a universal view of professional ethics. The teachers' position in quest of universal mission with critical reflection on day-to-day professional practices is very much significant in the current scenario. There is little scope for centralised code of conduct approach in generation of discourse on professional ethics among teachers, especially in the context of autonomous role of teachers and learners in teaching-learning process.

The discussions on different areas of professional ethics become more significant, when teacher is placed in the centre of school system, as per NEP, 2020. The concept of autonomy with accountability needs to be addressed in the form of dialogues among teachers at institutional level as well as in different forums of teachers through suitable networking. This will pave the way for promoting deep involvement of teachers in evolving professionalism in teaching. Thus, professionalism in teaching will be very much meaningful with inclusive perspective. As a whole, the experiences shared by the eminent scholars on different dimensions of professionalism in teacher education, policy orientation and reforms in teacher education curriculum, quality issues and technology integration research and development of professional ethics of teachers shall contribute meaningfully to development of contemporary knowledge on teacher education among teachers, students and scholars of education.

P.K. Sahoo
B.C. Das

Acknowledgements

We take immense pride in receiving the guidance of revered mentors Professor Y.P. Agarwal, former Emeritus Professor of Education, Kurukshetra University, Professor Murmur Mukhopadhyay, Chairman, ETMA Society and former Director, NIEPA, New Delhi and cooperation of senior colleagues. Professor R. Govinda, former Vice-Chancellor, NUEPA, New Delhi, Professor Mohan B. Menon, former Deputy Vice-Chancellor of Wawasan Open University, Penang, Malaysia and Chairperson DISHA Global Trust, Cochin, Professor D.N. Sansanwal, former Director, IOE, DAVV, Indore, Professor Santosh Panda, former Chairperson, NCTE and Professor S.S. Jena, former Chairperson, NIOS as source on inspiration for this outcome. Contributors were specifically urged to prepare write-ups on various themes covered in this volume. The list of authors encompasses a wide spectrum of young researchers, seasoned academicians, and experts in the field of education across the nation. We extend our heartfelt gratitude to each one of them.

Our sincere thanks go to esteemed colleagues Professor Shyam B. Menon, founding Vice-Chancellor of AUD, Delhi, and Professor Mohd. Miyan, President of IATE and former Vice-Chancellor of MANUU, Hyderabad, for their unwavering moral support and encouragement that could bring forth these volumes on Teacher Education, enriched with contemporary insights, policy perspectives, and research on the implementation of new guidelines for Teacher Education in India. We are deeply thankful to the most distinguished professors of education in the country for their generous contributions. Special acknowledgment is due to Professor M.S. Lalitha, Former Vice-Chancellor and Dean of the School of Education, Pondicherry Central University; Professor D.R. Goel, UGC Emeritus Professor, M.S. University of Baroda; Professor N.K. Dash, former Director of the School of Education, IGNOU, New Delhi; Professor A. Muthumanickam, Former Dean of the School of Education, M.K. University, Madurai; Professor Sunil Behari Mohanty, President of AIAER, Puducherry; Professor S.C. Panigrahi, CASE, MSU Baroda; and Professor Sushma Sharma, DDUGU Gorakhpur, for their invaluable contributions to these volumes.

The authors express their gratitude to senior colleagues from the University of Allahabad, including Professor Dhananjai Yadav, Head of the Education Department, and Professor Vidya Aggarwal and Professor Usha Mishra, former Heads of the Education Department, for their insightful write-ups. The editors owe a debt of gratitude to the young contributors from various universities and colleges, including Professor Sujeet Kumar from GGD Central University, Bilaspur; Professor Gyanendra Kumar Rout from IGNTU, Amarkantak; Dr. Ashok Dansana and Dr. Praveen Bobby Binjha from NCERT, New Delhi and formerly with Ravenshaw University, Cuttack; Dr. Meenakshi Biswal from Basanta Women's College, BHU, Varanasi; Professor Namita Sahoo from K.P. Training College, AU; Dr. Rama Gupta from JTGDC, AU; Dr. B.S. Gupta from CMPDC, AU; Dr. Surendra Kumar from UPRTOU; Dr. Subhash Chandra from DN PG College, Gorakhpur; Dr. Hemant Mistry from MSU, Baroda; and Dr. Prerna Mandhyan from D.S. College, Katihar.

We also acknowledge the contributions of promising scholars from the University of Allahabad and Ravenshaw University, including Dr. Priyanka Sharma, Dr. Chandan Prasad, Smt. Manju Kumari, Dr. Brijesh Kumar, Dr. Ashok Kumar, Dr. Uzma Khanam, Ms. Usha Devi, Shri Bijay Kumar Das, Shri Gulsan Behera, and

Ms. Debajani Sahoo, for their research-based articles on emerging areas of Teacher Education. Special recognition is extended to Dr. Priyanka Sharma for her consistent cooperation in word processing and editing tasks.

Our heartfelt gratitude goes to Shri Ashok Kumar Mittal, Managing Director of Concept Publishing Co. Pvt. Ltd., New Delhi, for timely publishing these volumes for our target stakeholders.

P.K. Sahoo
B.C. Das

Contents

Section II
Curriculum Reforms in Teacher Education

Section III
Technology Integrated Teacher Education

VOLUME 2

SECTION IV
Research Innovation in Teacher Education

SECTION V
Professional Development of Teachers

SECTION VI

Quality Assurance in Teacher Education

Introduction

P.K. Sahoo

Professionalism in teaching and Teacher Education has been a significant discourse in the era of globalization and liberalization. The imperative of cultivating high-quality human resources in teaching, equipped with professional knowledge, skills, and ethics, holds paramount importance in the education policy frameworks of both developed and developing nations. The core principle of the National Education Policy, 2020 underscores the pivotal role of teachers and faculty as the cornerstone of the learning process. It emphasizes the necessity for their rigorous recruitment, preparation, continuous professional development, positive work environment, and assured service conditions, advocating for a "light but tight" oversight and regulatory system to uphold the integrity and transparency of the educational system.

Teacher Education is valued in the context of quality professional education within the organized service sector, playing a crucial role in shaping the future of children and, consequently, the nation as a whole (NEP 2020). Furthermore, contribution of education to sustainable development, guided by principles of equity and inclusion, stands as a central agenda in global development discourse. Enhancing educational inputs is contingent upon strengthening the quality of teacher inputs. Effective teaching and learning practices hinge on the professional knowledge, attitude, and skills of teachers. Consequently, teacher development programmes, starting from the preparatory stage, are meticulously designed to address curriculum design, implementation, and assessment, adhering to guidelines and standards set by statutory bodies in Teacher Education and other educational authorities at national and state levels.

Recent years have witnessed a heightened emphasis on the professional development of in-service teachers, often encouraged on a voluntary basis. Centralized efforts are being made to disseminate knowledge and facilitate skill development exercises for teachers and other school functionaries, albeit within limited scopes. The growing concern for the teaching profession is further accentuated by the influence of liberal economies and private management in school and Teacher Education sectors, which have elevated expectations from teachers and accentuated their role in market-oriented endeavours within a globalized society.

Teachers' roles and responsibilities, *vis-à-vis* students, parents, communities, governance systems, and the broader global landscape, are undergoing a re-evaluation compared to the latter part of the last century. The Teacher Education community, particularly researchers and experts in the field of education, are compelled to explore various avenues for fostering professionalism among teachers in alignment with educational objectives and sustainable development goals. This book endeavours to shed light on new perspectives and avenues for the professional development of teachers, encompassing both theoretical frameworks and practical applications of Teacher Education, with a specific focus on the Indian context. It incorporates contributions from seasoned experts, leading teacher educators, and emerging researchers across different volumes, with Volume 1 focusing on "Development and Technology Integration", progressing to Volume 2 on "Research and Quality Assurance".

There are six sections in these volumes, viz.

I. New Perspectives in Teacher Education,
II. Curriculum Reforms in Teacher Education,
III. Technology Integrated Teacher Education,

IV. Research and Innovation in Teacher Education,
V. Professional Development of Teachers, and
VI. Quality Assurance in Teacher Education.

The first section of Volume 1 delves into the presentation of a conceptual framework for teaching and Teacher Education from a fresh perspective. While the conventional approach to fostering professional ethics, knowledge, and skills among teachers remains prevalent in pedagogical discussions, the incorporation of open distance learning methods and blended learning systems into Teacher Education practices is gaining traction. **Professor Shyam Menon's** article critiques the National Education Policy (NEP) of 2020 within the context of Teacher Education, particularly relevant in India's market economy landscape. Professor Menon evaluates the trajectory of Teacher Education, examining three key national education policy documents in India. His analysis reveals a lack of sustained commitment to instigating reforms aimed at future directions. He highlights the intricate role of the National Council for Teacher Education (NCTE), particularly concerning initial Teacher Education programmes governed by statutory provisions. It appears that continuous professional development programmes may fall outside the purview of the NCTE. Professor Menon advocates for structural reforms, emphasizing the critical integration of preparatory Teacher Education programmes with ongoing professional development initiatives under the dynamic leadership of university education departments. He expresses concerns about the growing influence of market-oriented approaches in school education, suggesting a potential dilution of focus on quality education, particularly regarding social inclusion and equitable access.

The chapter on Teaching and Professional Development of Teachers by **Professor P.K. Sahoo** focuses on conceptual analysis of teaching with different perspectives. Accordingly, different perspectives of teacher development have been discussed at length in this chapter.Different approaches of development of competencies, teaching skills and multiple models of teaching among student teachers and working teachers have been discussed. This chapter consolidates the participatory approach, ICT based information processing models and holistic framework of teacher development in real school situation. The integration of theoretical understanding, stakeholders expectations, training objectives, teachers and students aptitudes and abilities and skilful human interaction in conducive learning environment and feedback mechanism have been highlighted for continuous development of teachers in real school situation. **Professor N.K. Dash** has thrown light on the conceptualisation of teaching by taking into consideration different factors such as transaction and indirect engagement of teacher, learning outcome orientation, planned and unplanned activities of teachers. Professor Dash elucidated the relationship between different concepts like teaching and learning, teaching and instruction, teaching and training, teaching and indoctrination. He has extended the discussion on emerging concept of teaching in the era of open learning society and information and communication technology. He has aptly sited the view of Professor S.B. Menon that didactic teaching is the segment that is largely amenable to online and digital forms of transaction. It is to be extended to interaction between teacher and learner as well as to peer interactions for development of analytical and other intellectual skills through deconstructive approach. Professor Dash has focused on creating a hybrid model of teaching or blended learning approach through combination of digital learning and face-to-face teaching.

Education must be linked with core values of human life and societal system. The issues are, of course, context specific in nature. Keeping in view emerging issues of education, Teacher Education need to be restructured and reoriented with a larger scope of multistage schooling. Many such issues have been focused well by **Professor D.R. Goel** in his write up "Education in Quest of Identity: Role of Teacher Education" has raised concern about Teacher Education's identity. He has alarmed that, "soul of education is being killed through ruthless expansion and privatisation leading to marketization of education". Professor Goel has listed various issues in detail concerning digitalisation, peace and health. He has also listed a number of capacity building programmes in the context of Teacher Education and has given a number of suggestions for strengthening teachers professional development. Different themes concerning teachers' personality development, digitalisation in education, development of technology competencies and reorganisation of professional bodies in Teacher Education have been elaborated through the write up of Professor Goel.

Constructivist paradigm of teacher development has been proliferated in different policy documents like NCF 2005, NCFTE 2009 and NEP 2020. **Dr. Biswajit Behera** a pioneer has thrown light on humanistic teacher development practices in an inclusive setting. He emphasises on the collaboration roles of teachers and learners in constructive classrooms having a shift from teaching for teaching sake to teaching for learning sake. Thus, Teacher Education programmes must gear up for incorporating reflective collaborative and constructive practice in teacher preparation. To him, learners should involve themselves in talk, dialogue, public reasoning and shared problem-solving. Classroom environment is counterproductive to learning. Therefore, teachers should illustrate collaboration between and among the teachers and students.

The emphasis on education for teachers in Higher Education Institutions (HEIs) has been duly projected in NEP 2020. **Professor S.B. Mohanty** has made a comparative study of provisions for Teacher Education for HEI teachers in different developed countries of the world. He has highlighted the major attributes of teaching-learning system of HEIs as per NEP 2020, such as inclusive curriculum, flexibility, learner support and learning resources, community engagement and projects. The role of e-learning platforms for continuous professional development of HEI teachers occupies key position in teacher development. The on-going practices for Teacher Education through different schemes of UGC like HRDC programmes and Mahamana Madan Mohan Malviya Mission for Teacher Education need to be revamped with online blended learning approach and promotion of original contribution of resource persons in such programmes. There is a need for strengthening the quality inputs of online programmes for teachers of HEIs. In this context, the Inter University Consortium for Teacher Education (IUCTE) may be redesigned as National Centre for Teachers Excellence for Higher Education (NCTEHE) and treat HRDCs as regional centres for teachers' excellence for higher education. The Centre must develop appropriate learning materials for the mentors as well for newly-recruited teachers of HEIs.

The Second Section of the book has a wide coverage of issues concerning structure and process of Teacher Education curriculum in India. Curricular perspectives of Teacher Education have been discussed in the context of National Curriculum Framework (2005) National Curriculum Framework for Teacher Education (2009), Justice Verma Commission Report (2012) and NCTE Curriculum Guidelines 2014 as referred in NEP 2020. This has highlighted indigenous knowledge based curriculum at school stage. Mother tongue has been considered as basic medium of instruction to school children. The principles of plurality, multilingualism, cultural diversity and Indianness have been the major focus of curriculum. Accordingly, Teacher Education is to be geared towards such transformation. In his chapter on Gandhian Perspective of School Curriculum **Professor P.K. Sahoo** has made a review of national system of education as proposed by Gandhiji, while throwing light on the provisions of NEP 2020. **Dr. Akha K. Mao's** chapter on "Policy Conscious Teachers and Their Perception Towards Teacher Education Programme" reveals, worth reforming conclusion that "Teacher Education institutions should be embedded in universities as they provide more conducive and democratic environment for academics, scholars and practitioners not only engage with their parent disciplines but also carry a continuous intellectual dialogue across disciplines." In addition to the academic perspective the author has focused on collective participation of teachers to carry out reformation in education through "carrying forward a pollicised intellectual intervention with the system."

The essence of Teacher Education curriculum lies on making teacher development practices relevant to school system and development of professional quality of teachers. Several initiatives have been made during last decade to bring reform on structural and process dimensions of Teacher Education Curriculum. A major emphasis have been laid on bringing Teacher Education to the fold of higher education and provision for integrated Teacher Education programme (ITEP) with general education at undergraduate and postgraduate level. Pedagogic principle based practices in real school situations has been integral part of Teacher Education curriculum for elementary and secondary level Teacher Education programmes respectively. Similarly, master's degree programme in education has changed its focus to preparation of teacher educators with required competencies to deal with Teacher Education programmes.Internship practices at school level and Teacher Education institution level have been incorporated with emphasis on encouraging hands on experience based teacher training. A detailed discussion has been done on reforms in Teacher Education Curriculum by **Dr. B.C. Das** and **Professor Namita Sahoo** in their chapter titled "Reshaping Teacher Education Curriculum" especially in the context of NCTE guidelines and NEP 2020. They have portrayed the global vision as well as national level priorities of Teacher Education. They talk about the educational goals and shifting role of higher education institutions.

The programme evaluation study on integrated B.Ed. Programme of Central universities, as per NCTE Guidelines (2014) have been conducted by **Professor P.K. Sahoo** and **Dr. Priyanka Sharma** at all India level. In their study, Sahoo and Sharma have explored favourable perception of Arts and Science background student teachers on perspectives in education, curriculum and pedagogic studies, practicum and school internship components of Teacher Education curriculum. Similarly, in their chapter on the students and teacher educators' perception of M.Ed. programme, Sahoo and Sharma have found positive opinion of the stakeholders about new curriculum structure and implementation. The

Teacher Educators, of course, were comparatively less enthusiastic about reforms concerning M.Ed. programme's structure and its implementation strategies.

School internship practices have been considered as on integral component of Teacher Education curriculum. School internship builds a sound base to develop inclusive understanding of professional skills and its application in real School Situation with sustained involvement of would be teachers and mentors. **Professor P.K. Sahoo** and **Dr. Ashok Kumar** in their chapter on School Internship have deliberated on different empirical evidences regarding school internship practices in Teacher Education Institutions of India. Encouraging experiences were revealed regarding such practices. However, the private institutions did not take such programme as seriously in comparison to that of their government (aided) counterparts. Moreover, the lacunae concerning academic programme management and mentoring were very much prevalent in implementation of school internship practices. Linkage of theory and practice and *vice versa* could not be established well through school internship.

A good curriculum with proper implementation emphasises on stakeholders' involvement in it at different stages. In Teacher Education curriculum especially in Open Distance Learning (ODL) system learner autonomy is considered as the key feature. Hence, student teachers of ODL system are expected to get priorities in decision making in curriculum design, implementation and evaluation. There may be variations in students' involvement in the context of background factors like gender, locale and discipline. The research evidences gathered by **Professor P.K. Sahoo and Dr. Chandan Prasad** revealed that different components of ODL mode Teacher Education had significant effect on student teachers' decision making in different components of curriculum. Students' involvement was very high in curriculum transaction and assessment and evaluation components and low in teacher support system and curriculum design components. There was significant interaction of locale and ODL components on student teachers involvement in ODL mode Teacher Education programme.

Section Three of the book is devoted to Technology Integrated Teaching Learning and Teacher Education. Quality enhancement in Teacher Education is mainly linked with technology use and integration. The digital India campaign has gone into the ground level functioning of school education. This is high time to focus on development of technology competency among teachers for making teaching flexible, learner friendly and constructive in nature. On quality enhancements of Teacher Education several initiatives have been made at institutional level for promotion of blended learning approach. Of late, NEP 2020 has highlighted promotion of blended learning technology at different stages of education. At Teacher Education stage technology integration aims at developing competencies of teachers in pedagogy, course content and technology applications to achieve the objectives of curriculum. In this context Dr. B.C. Das and his colleagues have reported about their experiments on effectiveness of TPACK based internship practices at B.Ed. level. They have elaborated on the competency development of pre-service teachers using such package. **Professor A. Muthumanickum** has made a conceptual analysis of Blended Learning in Teacher Education highlighting its role in process and product of teaching learning system. He has focused on integration of offline and online learning in education. Different approaches of blended learning like instructor led e-learning facilitated e-learning and self-paced e-learning have been discussed in detail. The role of teachers in blended learning in the context of development of competencies, creation of learning environment, exploring learning needs, research competencies and evaluation strategies are considered key components of blended learning approach. He also talked about appropriate management of technology in Teacher Education programmes. **Dr. Sujeet Kumar** has highlighted the key features of hybrid model of teaching-learning through traditional face-to-face mode and advanced digital technology at school stage. He has presented how traditional face-to-face mode teaching has been replaced by smart classroom activities and virtual learning environment in Teacher Education.

Several efforts have been made to promote e-learning opportunities for teacher development. The SWAYAM portal has been devoted to MOOCs at higher education stage. Professor P.K. Sahoo *et al.* have focused on their experiences of developing e-PG Pathshala Programme in Education and its operationalization. The authors have found that majority of learners of MOOC course in education appreciated its quality and utility. This was noticed that the course was very useful in enhancing professional understanding of students. The students were motivated to join in more numbers of MOOC courses in the field of education.

As stated above technological skills, pedagogic competencies and Content Knowledge mastery must be well knitted for development of professionalism among teachers. **Dr. B.C. Das and B.K. Das** have done an analysis of the status of Technological Pedagogical and Content Knowledge in Teacher Education curriculum of different Teacher Education institutions of Odisha. Most of the student-teachers of integrated B.Ed. programme reported that they had minimum knowledge of Teacher Education system. They have highlighted on quality improvement with technology inputs in Teacher Education programme has a better scope in four-year integrated B.Ed. programme. The chapter on a study of uses of ICT by doctoral research scholars by **Professor P.K. Sahoo** and **Dr. Uzma Khanam** revealed no significant effect of faculty background on ICT use in different stages of research. However, there was significant effect of gender on use of ICT in research. The women scholars had an edge over their men counterparts on use of ICT in different stages of research. As a whole, the research scholars made optimum use of ICT in different stages of research.

Section IV of the book as included in Volume 2 deals with research and innovation in Teacher Education. Research in Teacher Education is one of the major areas of educational research. Teacher education research highlights different practices aiming at professional development of in-service and pre-service teachers. Of late, there has been emphasis on strengthening the base of teacher research. This section includes empirical studies concerning teacher development practices. Most of them belong to evaluation research category. Current researches on Teacher Education system have focused on study of perception/attitude of stakeholders about the outcome of different kinds of currently introduced pre-service and in-service Teacher Education programmes. Such programmes aim at development of professional competencies in different areas like personality development through *yoga* practices, computer education, decision making, action research etc. Teacher research has gained momentum as a tool for professional development of teachers. In this context, research competencies among working teachers need to be identified with top priority. There is a need to encourage context specific in-depth teacher research studies leading to development of research competencies among working teachers. Of late, there have been efforts by the teacher educators to emphasise on process based competencies of teachers. In their chapter **Dr. B.C. Das** and his team have focused on a study of application of K-4 learning model in pre-service teacher development practices.

In his article on developing research potential of elementary teachers through action research, **Professor Dhananjai Yadav** highlights the effectiveness of action research module as experimented over school teachers. The study found significant effect of action research module on improving research skills of elementary school teachers. **Professor Vidya Agarwal** and **Professor Sushma Pandey** conducted an extensive study on impact of teacher training programmes on teaching learning environment and student achievement at elementary level. They noticed that teachers are not using training experience in natural classroom situations and teaching. This was also reported that use of appropriate teaching methods and techniques have significant effect on enhancement of achievement of learners.

A study conducted on effectiveness of online Teacher Education programme of National Institute of Open Schooling (NIOS) by **Professor P.K. Sahoo** revealed that there was positive impact of online programme on attitude of the in-service elementary teachers. The online programme was found more effective among rural area teachers, especially teachers with longer teaching experience. The teachers' attitude towards different components of online programme was found to be of very positive in nature.

Dr. Subhash Chandra and **Professor P.K. Sahoo** conducted a study on learning style of traditional mode and ODL mode student teachers. The article revealed significant association between the modes of Teacher Education and participatory learning style of student teachers. It was noticed that the open distance learning mode student teachers were of higher participatory category than that of their face-to-face mode counterparts. As a whole, the student teachers had adopted high competitive as well as high collaborative learning styles in their studies.

Dr. H.K. Mistry and **Professor S.C. Panigrahi** had conducted an extensive study of "Inclusion of Students with Disabilities in HEIs". The findings revealed a meagre (0.56%) enrolment of students with disabilities at higher education. Among them there was predominance of students with orthopaedic background. The vocational skills training facility was very poor among them. The authors have discussed about the role of teachers in tackling challenges of inclusive education at higher education stage.

The Fifth Section of the book is devoted to "Professional Development of Teachers". Professional ethics has been a matter of discussion for teachers in the context of globalisation and liberal economy. The standard code of conduct for teachers and standard framework of assessment of educational institutions include professional component in Teacher Education system. The NEP 2020 talks about teachers' accountability towards students, institution and teaching profession. It highlights that teachers must be grounded in Indian values, languages, knowledge, ethos and traditions, while also being well-versed in the latest advances in education and pedagogy. These points have been discussed in the context of development of disciplinary/multidisciplinary knowledge, pedagogic knowledge with hands on experiences and theoretical understanding and professional ethics. Professional ethics is related to welfare of learners, own personality, critical reflection on teaching-learning practices, building conducive learning environment and leadership for innovative practices. It also includes institutional growth and continuous pursuit for equity, excellence and sustainability in academic endeavours. Thus, professional ethics is understood as the nerve system of teaching profession. It is imperative to ponder upon applied ethics in teachers' personality and teaching functions. How ethics can be evolved through continuous collective dialogue among experienced teachers and the experts has been the major concern of teacher development. Different approaches of nurturing ethics with special reference to empowerment of teachers have been presented in the chapter written by **Professor P.K. Sahoo**. Different group-based collective participatory models of teaching ethics have been projected for development of ethics.

Since professional ethics is a relative concept, "encouragement must be given to working teachers for continuous professional development activities on ethical issues concerning development of self, appropriate decision making and ethical approaches on students' development, institutional practice and eco-friendly approach to teaching." On Teachers Professional Development: Emerging Issues, **Professor G.K. Rout** writes on reforms in subject matter teaching (standards, curriculum and pedagogy), equity concerning heterogeneous student population; nature of learners' assessment and its application; social organisation of schooling; and professionalization of teaching. He focuses on professional development models and the tasks ahead, "teachers' autonomy may be intensified by various circumstances surrounding collegial and institutional life, the norms underlying peer acceptance and admiration, and the fabric of relationship between teachers and administrators."

Dr. Rama Gupta highlights content competencies for professional development of teachers at primary school stage. She found significant association between teaching competencies and students achievement in Hindi language at primary stage. She suggested the in-service programme must cover both the concerns—"how to teach and what to teach to whom". In this respect, professional development programmes must be a continuous part of working language teachers' career. While different responsibilities of teachers can be attributed to committed behaviour of teachers, human resource development orientation to Teacher Education must be in the forefront of Teacher Education policies. These ideas have been proliferated in the chapter of **Professor Usha Mishra** and **Dr. Prerna Mandhyan**. They have done a conceptual analysis of accountability of pre-service Teacher Education programme in relation to teachers' quality and student outcomes. To them "teaching quality in practice constitutes a set of actions and activities that improve student outcomes." They focus on the approach for influencing human capital pool in the form of context—specific intervention through teaching. This chapter discusses in detail about multiple teacher evaluation criteria. The chapter on Professional Development of Teacher Educators, written by **Professor P.K. Sahoo** and **Dr. Brijesh Kumar**, highlights the relevance of empowerment of teacher educators to prepare better teachers. The institution-based professional development programme models have been discussed in detail. The authors have presented empirical evidences on needs prioritised by the teacher-educators of elementary and secondary education on different areas, such as professional development, discipline, Teacher Education policy, research competencies and personality of teachers.

In her chapter on Inclusive Education and Development of Professional Ethics of Teachers, **Professor Minakshi Biswal** throws light on innovative teacher preparation model having input, process and output for development of professional ethics among teachers. Collaborative teaching and attitudinal change are considered as the training inputs, whereas the process is identified with strategies, methods and techniques. The outputs are listed in the form of professional ethics as reflected in teachers' behaviour for effective inclusive education.

Section VI of the book is devoted to quality assurance in Teacher Education. Professional education for teachers must be of quality oriented nature. The NEP 2020 has focused on equity and excellence in education.The global society expects high quality output of teachers to be absorbed in the school system. Quality enhancement concept is directly linked with internal efforts of quality management of institutions with regard to curriculum design and curriculum transaction process. Participatory management for quality enhancements must be promoted through stakeholders' committed involvement in planning and decision making, execution, assessment and feedback functions of the system. Quality appraisal by external body is done according to centralised parameters applicable to professional institution programmes. The role of statutory bodies is very much significant in formation of assessment and accreditation norms, procedures of institutional evaluation, grading of institutional performances. In the Indian context, such responsibility is vested with the regulatory bodies like NCTE for Teacher Education Programmes. Issues involved in accreditation practices and quality assessment mechanisms in different contexts of Teacher Education system have been elaborated on different forums of Teacher Education. A new development is witnessed for quality appraisal of different issues concerning Teacher Education quality and technology intervention. Major reform is expected in promoting different professional institutions under one Umbrella of National Higher Education Regulatory Authority.

Professor Lalitha in her chapter on "Teacher Education towards Excellence focuses" on various challenges of Teacher Education like qualitative experience in school education, technological interventions in school curriculum and its transaction and global context of schooling in the current society. She has thrown light on various issues concerning quality of Teacher Education covering curricular objects, management of content and process, professional development of teachers and teacher educators and research output. She talks about shift from pedagogical content knowledge to technological pedagogical content knowledge of teachers. She also emphasises on the competencies of teacher educators to produce teachers with twenty-first century skills, there is a need for continuous professional development among teacher educators. This is very much in tune with NEP 2020. She highlights that research should be built into process dimension of Teacher Education. The teacher educators must be inspired to innovate, and execute differently practices even based on intuitive judgement for improving Teacher Education. The role of networking technology for sharing of research experiences among teacher educators must occupy top priority quality enhancements in Teacher Education System.

The community orientation in Teacher Education has been highlighted in NEP 2020. A study conducted by **Professor P.K. Sahoo** and **Dr. Surendra Kumar** on curricular practices of open distance learning mode B.Ed. programme revealed that community awareness programme is an essential component of Teacher Education. Such kind of awareness programmes are encouraged through project-based activities. These experiences reveal different practices being promoted through alternative forms of Teacher Education in the country.

Research has been conducted by **Dr. B.S. Gupta** on yogic activities in quality enhancement in primary education in the context of intelligence of boy and girl students. The study confirmed significant effect of yogic activities in enhancement of intelligence of students. **Dr. Ashok Dansana** and **Mr. Gulsan Behera** have written on Resource Management and Challenges in Teacher Education on the basis of an empirical study in Teacher Education Institutions of Odisha. They concluded that different kinds of resource supports are essential for successful functioning of Teacher Education programme at institutional level. They suggested that learning resources should be made more effective and amenable to all the student-teachers.

Inclusion is one of the Principles of National Education Policy, 2020. The chapter on Inclusive Teacher Education by **Dr. S.K. Panda** focuses on the characteristics of Inclusive Teacher Education as highlighted in different policy documents. Dr. Panda discusses at length on institutional provisions and suitable strategies for implementation of Inclusive Teacher Education Curriculum. He emphasised on improvement of teaching practices and school-based experiences of special education students.

Dr. Subhash Chandra and **Manju Kumari** have deliberated at length about open distance learning mode and its role in professional development of teachers. They have visualised the significance of technology facilitated open learning strategies with high coverage of student population and cost-effectiveness. **Dr. B.C. Das** and **Debajani Sahoo** in their chapter on Need Level Assessment of Research Competencies focused on the assessment of research competencies which encompassed five dimensions: research review, proposal writing, research methodology, ICT utilization, and research publication and ethics. Findings revealed no notable correlation between various research competencies and the gender of the scholars. Nonetheless, scholars articulated differing levels of requirement, with the majority expressing a desire for further competencies although the Ph.D. coursework is tailored to pinpoint and fulfil these competency gaps.

The conceptual analysis of various factors associated with Teacher Education in India has a lot of bearing on understanding the policy perspectives as well as research priorities in education. Such understanding can prepare a sound base for visualising the nature and scope of Teacher Education in the contemporary India. The experiences reveal that integration of technology with pedagogical principles can deal very well with multidisciplinary knowledge base, subject to development of appropriate professional competencies of teachers. In this context, research evidences presented in the book will act as a beacon of light for rejuvenation of Teacher Education in Indian Subcontinent. The complexities arising in the context of provision of quality Teacher Education as envisaged in NEP 2020 need to be tackled with proper understanding of contextual realities of the school system and appropriate decision making. Moreover, such phenomenon is to be understood in the context of pluralistic factors linked with socio-economic and political developments taking place at national level as well as global level. Hence, multiple strategies need to be evolved for teacher development programmes. The chapters contributed by the eminent scholars in the book will inspire teachers and researchers to explore different perspectives of Teacher Education and work accordingly. This is anticipated that the students of education, researchers, teachers and the policy makers of education will be benefited a lot from this compendium of two volumes.

List of Contributors

A. Muthumanickam has been Former Professor & Head and Dean, Faculty of Education, Madurai Kamaraj University, Madurai. Professor Muthumanickam is a distinguished Syndicate Member of Tamil Nadu Open University, Chennai. His areas of expertise are Teacher Education, Quality and Teacher Management Issues in Education.
Email: professormuthumanickam@gmail.com

Akha Kaihrii Mao is an Associate Professor in the School of Vocational Studies, Ambedkar University Delhi (AUD). Dr. Mao's areas of research interests are in Traditional and Indigenous System of Education among the Nagas, Teacher Education, History of Education, Sociology of Education and Vocational Education. **Email:** kaihriimao@gmail.com

Ashok Dansana is Associate Professor in NCERT, New Delhi and formerly with School of Education, Ravenshaw University, Cuttack. Dr. Dansana is a scholar of Sustainable Development in Education. His research and publication interests include Policy Perspectives in Teacher Education and Development issues in Education. **Email:** dansana.cie@gmail.com

Ashok Kumar has been UGC Research Fellow, Department of Education, University of Allahabad, Allahabad. Dr. Ashok Kumar is currently working as Assistant Professor in the field

of Teacher Education. His research interest includes Teacher Education Programmes and Curriculum Reforms.
Email: ashokllbau@gmail.com

B.C. Das is Assistant Professor in the Department of Education, Ravenshaw University, Cuttack. His areas of interest are Teacher Education, Educational Technology, Development Education and Empowerment of Tribes. He has recently completed a project on TPACK Experiment in Pre-service Practice Teaching Programme in Science and Social Science under PMMMNMTT, Government of India.
Email: dasbcbu@gmail.com

B.S. Gupta is Assistant Professor in the Department of Education, CMP Degree College, University of Allahabad, Prayagraj. Dr. Gupta's areas of research interest remain on Teacher Education, Yoga and Well-being Education.
Email: bsguptaedu@gmail.com

Bijay Kumar Das is Assistant Professor in Education at Dharanidhar University, Keonjhar, Odisha and formerly has been Project Assistant, School of Education, Ravenshaw University, Cuttack. His areas of interest are Teacher Education and Educational Technology. He is currently engaged in a research on blended learning in higher education.
Email: dasbijay12345@gmail.com

Biswajit Behera is Associate Professor, NCERT, New Delhi and formerly with the Department of Education, Central University of Punjab, Bathinda. Dr. Behera is a scholar of Constructivist Pedagogy. His research interest remains on Technology Integration in Constructivist Pedagogy.
Email: biswajit.b@ncert.nic.in

Brijesh Kumar has been UGC Junior Research Fellow in the Department of Education, University of Allahabad, Allahabad. Dr. Brijesh Kumar is currently an Assistant Professor in Teacher Education. His research interest includes professional development of teachers and quality management in education.
Email: bk34855@gmail.com

Chandan Prasad has been UGC Research Fellow in the Department of Education, University of Allahabad, Allahabad. Dr. Chandan Prasad is a scholar in the area of ODL Mode Teacher Education. His research interests are curriculum design and teacher education programmes in open universities.
Email: cprasadald@gmail.com

D.R. Goel has been the Professor of Education and the Director of Centre of Advanced Studies in Education, The M.S.University of Baroda, Vadodara. Professor Goel has also been the Chairman of Western Regional Committee, NCTE, Bhopal. Professor Goel has been awarded UGC Emeritus Fellowship. Professor Goel has been significantly engaged in the field of Teacher Education and substantially contributed to teacher education researches and technology integration in education.
Email: goel_d_r34@rediffmail.com

Debajani Sahoo is Assistant Professor in Teacher Education in Bhadrak Government College, Bhadrak, Odisha. She is currently engaged in a research work on Quality of Ph.D. Coursework in Education and Need level Research Competencies of Scholars. She has been a Gold Medalist in her postgraduate studies from Ravenshaw University, Cuttack.
Email: debajanisahoo2000@gmail.com

Dhananjai Yadav is Professor of Education and Head in the Department of Education, University of Allahabad, Allahabad. His areas of research interest include Philosophy of Education, Teacher Education Policies and Practices, Science Education and ICT in Education.
Email: dhananjaiyadevedu@gmail.com

Gulsan Behera has been a Postgraduate Scholar in School of Education, Ravenshaw University, Cuttack. His areas of interest are policies and practices in teacher education programmes and curriculum reforms. **Email:** gulsanbehera95@gmail.com

Gyanendra Kumar Rout is Professor in the Faculty of Education, Indira Gandhi National Tribal University, Amarkantak. Dr. Rout is a scholar of Curriculum Studies in Education.

His areas of interest include Curriculum Reforms in Teacher Education. **Email:** gkr75@yahoo.com

Hemendra S. Mistry has been ICSSR Postdoctoral Fellow in the Department of Education, Faculty of Education and Psychology, The Maharaja Sayajirao University of Baroda, Vadodara. Dr. Mistry keeps on his interest in Teacher Education issues and developments. **Email:** mistryhemendra@yahoo.com

M.S. Lalitha is Professor of Education and Former Vice-Chancellor of Pondicherry University, Puducherry. She has been Head and Dean in Faculty of Education, Pondicherry University. Professor Lalitha is an eminent expert in the field of Teacher Education. She has significantly contributed to the development of Teacher Education in the country.
Email: nandakumarlalitha02@gmail.com

Manju Kumari is Research Scholar, UGC-JRF, Department of Education, University of Allahabad, Allahabad. Dr. Manju Kumari is currently engaged as Assistant Professor in the field of Teacher Education. **Email:** manjucret10@rediffmail.com

Minakshi Biswal has been Associate Professor in the Department of Education, Vasanta College for Women, Banaras Hindu University, Varanasi. Dr. Biswal has been a scholar of value education. Her areas of interest include Teacher Education, Value and Peace Education. **Email:** sanima11@rediffmail.com

N.K. Das is Professor of Education in the School of Education, Indira Gandhi National Open University, New Delhi. He has been Director of the School of Education, IGNOU. Professor Das has been involved in the development of several courses under different programmes of School of Education like PGDHE, B.Ed., D.El.Ed., PGDET and M.A. (Education). He is currently the Programme Coordinator of M.A. (Education) Programme. **Email:** nkdas123@gmail.com

Namita Sahoo is Professor of Education in K.P. Training College, University of Allahabad, Allahabad. Dr. Sahoo is a scholar of Educational Media and Technology. Her areas of interest are

Educational Technology, Teacher Education and Social Science Education. **Email:** drnamitasahoo@gmail.com

P.K. Sahoo is the Former Vice-Chancellor of University of Allahabad. Professor Sahoo has been the Director, Institute of Correspondence and Continuing Education, University of Allahabad. He has been Head, Department of Education and Dean, Faculty of Arts, University of Allahabad, Allahabad. Professor Sahoo is the Former President of Indian Association of Teacher Educators. Currently Professor Sahoo is engaged in ICSSR research project focusing on Education for Sustainable Development. **Email:** pksahooald@rediffmail.com

Praveen Bobby Binjha is Associate Professor at CIET, NCERT, New Delhi and formerly with School of Education, Ravenshaw University, Cuttack. Her area of interest remains in constructivist and ICT integrated pedagogy.
Email: bobby452@gmail.com

Prerna Mandhyan has been D.Phil. Scholar in the Department of Education, University of Allahabad, Allahabad. Her research interest includes emerging issues and quality improvement practices in teacher education.
Email: prernamandhyan@gmail.com

Priyanka Sharma has been a Senior Research Fellow in the Department of Education, University of Allahabad, Allahabad. Her research interest includes Teacher Education Curriculum and Issues, Integrated Teacher Education Programmes and Education of Teacher Educators.
Email: priyankasharmaedu.au@gmail.com

Rama Gupta is Assistant Professor in the Department of Education, Jagat Taran Girls' P.G. College, University of Allahabad. Dr. Gupta is a scholar of Quality Management in Elementary Education. Her research areas of interest include Elementary Teacher Education and Management issues.
Email: ramagupta81@rediffmail.com

Shyam B. Menon is Professor of Education in CIE, University of Delhi. Professor Menon is Former Vice-Chancellor of

Ambedkar University Delhi (AUD). He has been Head and Dean, Faculty of Education, University of Delhi; Professor and Director, School of Education, Indira Gandhi National Open University (IGNOU); and Professor of Educational Technology and Head, Department of Evaluation, Research and Training, Central Institute of Educational Technology, National Council of Educational Research and Training.
Email: shyambmenon@gmail.com

S.C. Panigrahi is Professor of Education, Former Director of Centre of Advanced Studies in Education, Coordinator of UGC-CAS, Department of Education, Faculty of Education and Psychology, The Maharaja Sayajirao University of Baroda, Vadodara. Professor Panigrahi is a renowned expert in the field of Education of Deprived. He has been engaged in many research projects in his field of expertise.
Email: panigrahi24@gmail.com

S.K. Panda is Associate Professor in the Department of Education, University of Jammu, Jammu. Dr. Panda is an emerging scholar in the field of Teacher Education. His research interest includes equity, quality and inclusion issues in teacher education.
Email: drpanda77@gmail.com

Subhash Chandra is Assistant Professor in the Department of Teacher Education, Digvijay Nath PG College, Gorakhpur. Dr. Subhash Chandra has worked upon teacher preparation through ODL Mode. He keeps on his research interest on the learning styles of student-teacher and imperative issues in ODL Mode teacher education programmes.
Email: subhash84au@gmail.com

Sujeet Kumar is Professor in the Department of Education, Guru Ghasidas Vishwavidyalay, Bilaspur. Professor Sujeet Kumar is a well known scholar for his innovations in teaching and research. His areas of interest include Skill-based Teacher Education, Application of Constructivism in Teacher Education and Blended Learning Approach to Higher Education Delivery.
Email: sujeetmishraedu@gmail.com

Sunil Behari Mohanty has been Professor of Education and served as the Principal in the Institute of Advanced Studies in Education in Odisha. Dr. Mohanty has been the President, All India Association for Educational Research. He is the Founder of International Forum of Researchers in Education, Puducherry and the Editor of the Journal of AIAER.
Email: sunilmohanty@gmail.com

Sushma Pandey is Professor in the Department of Education, DDU Gorakhpur University, Gorakhpur. Her research interest includes Teacher Education Policies and Initiatives.
Email: pandeysushma94@gmail.com

Usha Devi has been a Postgraduate Scholar in the Department of Education, University of Allahabad. Her research interest includes Teacher Education and Development Issues.
Email: ushachaudhary798@gmail.com

Usha Mishra is Professor of Education and has been Head, in the Department of Education, University of Allahabad, Allahabad. Her research interest includes School Education and Teacher Education. **Email:** ushamishraau@gmail.com

Uzma Khanam has been a PG Scholar in the Department of Education, University of Allahabad, Allahabad. Her areas of research interest include ICT in Education Research, Teacher Education and Emerging Issues.

Vidya Agarwal has been Professor and Head in the Department of Education, University of Allahabad, Allahabad. Her major areas of interest remain Educational Administration and Management, Teacher Education and Quality Management issues. **Email:** profvidyaagarwal@yahoo.com

Section I
NEW PERSPECTIVES IN TEACHER EDUCATION

1

Teacher Education

Practice, Policy and Market

Shyam Menon

This chapter is about exploring cursorily how Teacher Education (TE) has meandered through the contours of practice, policy initiatives and the dynamics of market in the post-Independence India. The main arguments that I intend to put forth through this chapter are built around the contention that the policy pronouncements related to TE in India and the complex manner in which the multiple realities related to the practice of TE have unfolded in the country do not have a functional cause-consequence relationship as one would expect. This is explored through a historical overview spanning from the year of India's independence to the present.

In fact, TE has had a trajectory not entirely determined by policy, a contention that has intertwining strands:

1. Practice has often been determined by administrative actions not necessarily emanating from policy. Several new initiatives in terms of structures and institutions in TE have happened in the interstices or interludes between policies, and some of them have changed course midway equally abruptly.

2. It is also the case that policies have often treated TE in an instrumentalist manner, often not with the intention of investing in teachers to develop as a community of professionals who would have the agency to reflect on the direction, content and approach of school education and to participate proactively in its development and transformation. Policies have mostly looked at teachers and teacher educators as assembly-line workers merely to implement policy directives, not just in school education but also in other related areas like adult education.
3. Unlike in some other major countries, a substantial volume of TE in India was left to the private sector to operate in with weak regulatory structures. Resultantly, the major streams of institutional processes and practice in TE have been as much a function of the market forces as they have been of policies and administrative fiats.
4. The tension between federalism as a part of the basic structure of the Constitution and the transfer of school education from State to the Concurrent List under the 42nd Amendment in 1976 at the behest of a strong centre, has made policy making in education increasingly a contested terrain, which has had its repercussion in TE as well.

The Early Years

The colonial India's bequeathal to us in 1947 was a deeply unequal society with a miniscule upper and middle class (comprising largely the upper castes, the land owning class and those in the professions, the government service and in medium-size business) forming a thin upper crust of society, geographically concentrated in and around urban locations. The colonial education system that we inherited mirrored this layered social structure. It was an anemic and inadequate education system—both school and higher education. This applied to TE all the more since it was located in the intersection between the two. What we inherited was a disparate and under-resourced system of TE.

Only children of the upper and the middle classes accessed education up to high school and beyond. Presumably, as a result of this skewness, this stage of schooling received more attention from the perspective of quality. Consequently, high school teachers' qualifications and training were perched at the university degree level, and their salaries also reflected this. This was in sharp contrast with those envisaged for teachers at the primary and upper primary schools. TE programmes differed in entry qualifications, duration, content and nature of institutions, and had major variations across provinces (Menon and Mathew, 2016).

At the two ends of spectrum of school system, however, there was considerable anomaly. In schools in remote locations, particularly in certain provinces and in the erstwhile princely states, teachers had hardly any TE qualification. At the other end, as regard to the "princes' schools" and "public schools" which were residential schools meant for the elite, there was considerable leniency about TE qualifications, so long as the teachers themselves hailed from backgrounds with social proximity to the elites.

The Initial Commissions

The University Education Commission also known as Radhakrishnan Commission (1948) articulated:

1. Giving legitimacy to education as a university discipline;
2. Bringing about some standardization to the disparate BT, LT programmes that were being offered by the various secondary teachers' colleges;
3. Laying emphasis on the school-practice component in the TE programmes;
4. Ensuring that teacher educators were firmly rooted in the profession of teaching; and
5. Highlighting the importance of research in education, particularly through collaboration among university departments of education.

Its recommendations indirectly impacted TE through an elevated status and additional resources made available to some select university departments of education.

The Secondary Education Commission popularly known as Mudaliar Commission (1953) recommended:

1. The consolidation of disparate structures of teacher education into two tiers, viz. one-year programmes for graduates leading to a university degree and not a diploma awarded by departments of education of state governments, *and in the long run, two-year degree programmes,* and two-year programmes for those who have school leaving certificates or higher secondary school certificates;
2. Emphasis on practical training including school-based practice teaching and in scholastic test construction and on an array of other organisational activities that a teacher was involved in;
3. Emphasis on in-service training of teachers; and
4. Tasking TE Institutions (TEIs) with research.

The emphasis on strengthening research in TEIs that one finds special mention in both University Education Commission and Secondary Education Commission ironically tapers off in subsequent policy documents. It is, as though after the establishment of NCERT in the early 1960s, research in education would become the preserve of this institution and the university departments of education.

As an apparent deviation from the recommendations of the Mudaliar Commission, in 1959 it was proposed that the Central Institute of Education (CIE) would experiment with a "combined course of general education and professional training on the lines of the teacher education courses in the USA and the USSR" (Ministry of Education, 1959). However, this proposal would soon be abandoned and the programme would instead be instituted in the Regional Colleges of Education (RCEs) under the NCERT, its curriculum hinging on the multi-purpose secondary school model recommended by the Mudaliar Commission. The irony however was that by the time the four RCEs were established and were fully functional, the multi-purpose secondary school model had been as a consequence of the Kothari Commission and NPE 1968.

The Education Commission (1964-66), popularly known as Kothari Commission, had the following recommendations as regard TE:

1. A greater thrust be made on getting TEIs out of their "Cinderella" status by breaking isolation from sister departments in universities, from schools and from between themselves;
2. Measures be taken for improving quality of TE in terms of subject knowledge, professional studies, methods of teaching and evaluation, student teaching, curricula for primary and secondary teacher education;
3. Correspondence, evening and part-time courses in TE be strengthened to meet the training need for the large backlog of untrained teachers in schools; and
4. Emphasis be made on in-service education for school teachers.

NPE 1968 and Its Consequences

The National Policy on Education (1968) or NPE 1968 was supposed to be consequence of the countrywide deliberations and parliamentary debates based on the Education Commission (1964-66). However, when it came to TE, it was as though there was nothing substantive about TE that NPE 1968 found fit for inclusion. The entire set of recommendations of the Education Commission pertaining to for TE eventually got distilled into just one sentence in the NPE: "Teacher Education, particularly in-service education, should receive due emphasis". On the other hand, the national system of education that the Policy promulgated would give rise to a large number of private schools proliferating under the CBSE; and it is this that would have a major impact on teacher education in the next couple of decades.

The NPE 1968 with its emphasis on a national system of education around the 10+2+3 system, made it possible for the Central Board of Secondary Education (CBSE) to affiliate a large number of schools all over the country with a uniform structure and curriculum. The Kendriya Vidyalaya Sangathan was the flagship organization through which this was initiated, targeting predominantly at the children of the employees of Government of India. However, the aspirations of a growing middle class that included the motivation to make lateral movements across the country to pursue work and studies created an enormous demand for more schools under the common national curriculum. This steadily manifested in the proliferation of private schools affiliated to CBSE in the 1970s and 1980s. Such a sudden expansion of schools in the private sector created a huge demand for trained teachers, much beyond the capacity of the TEIs in the government sector. Resultantly, private colleges of TE proliferated in large numbers. Given the inadequate and ineffective regulatory mechanisms for assurance of quality and legally permissible fee structures, the uncontrolled proliferation of TEIs in the private sector gave rise to large scale commercialization. This was largely the scenario in the 1980s and the early 1990s.

Meanwhile, several universities would offer TE programmes through correspondence. Although it was the University of Delhi that for the first time in India in 1964 started a B.Ed. correspondence programme as a pacesetter, it soon discontinued this programme. Subsequently, it was largely the state universities that continued to offer B.Ed. through correspondence throughout the 1970s and 1980s. Several of these programmes would cross-subsidize other programmes. Thus, B.Ed. through correspondence would become "milch cows" for these cash starved universities.

Much of the proliferation of TEIs in the private sector and through correspondence happened in B.Ed. programmes which were catering essentially to initial teacher preparation for secondary schools. However, a large number of private schools pursued the practice of hiring B.Ed. graduates as primary school teachers. With the governmental priority on universalization of primary education to begin with and subsequently on universalization of elementary education, primary and upper primary school system expanded considerably through the establishment of new schools, expansion of existing schools and through nonformal schools in geographically remote areas and in urban slums, right through the 1980s. Non-availability of trained teachers for primary and upper primary schools would thus become a major challenge. Initial preparation, often as a condensed programme for elementary school teachers, and their Continuing Professional Development (CPD), would become a major preoccupation in policies and programmes of action in the 1980s and early 1990s.

Introspection, Self-Criticism and NPE 1986

The Challenge of Education (1985) was a remarkable document, quite unusual for a government document in its bold self-criticism. Challenge of Education was formulated in response to an assessment of the implementation of the NPE 1968 and the recommendations of the National Commission for Teachers (NCT)—1 of 1983. Challenge of Education offered a comprehensive critique of TE in terms of its relevance, quality, selection and admission process, inadequate preparation on spirit of inquiry, scientific temper, promoting national integration, cultural cohesion, humanitarian values etc. It also offered a critique of in-service training as unimaginative, one-way teaching routine.

Unlike its predecessor of 1968, NPE 1986 had an entire section on TE that had a certain vision and perspective. NPE 1986 recognized that TE is a continuous process involving initial professional preparation and CPD. CPD had an emphasis on continuing education of teachers also to prepare them to implement the new policy. The mainstay of NPE 1986 was the institutional architecture in TE at the state and district levels that included:

1. Setting up DIETs with an ambitious mandate, although in many cases it amounted to rehashing old institutions and old professional resources to carry out new mandates;
2. Creating a network of training colleges, university departments and SCERTs with a focus on CPD of teachers; and
3. There is a mention of NCTE with additional resources and capacities, but with no mention of a statutory status.

As a consequence of a change in government at the centre, the NPE 1986 was subjected to review through the Acharya Ram Murti Committee, 1990. The Committee recommended some fundamental shifts in the emphasis of the NPE 1986 and reiterated the recommendation of the common school system and neighbourhood schools, and also on the integration of "head, hand and heart". These recommendations in retrospect appear to be more rhetorical than substantive. The Report had no mention whatsoever of TE.

With another change of government came the Programme of Action (POA) 1992, which was a way to go back to NPE 1986. POA 1992 clearly chalked out the way to finance and monitor the institutional structures of TE.

1. POA set out the schemes of DIET, CTE, IASE and SCERT as Centrally Sponsored Schemes (CSS).
2. It roped in NCERT (and to a limited extent even NIEPA) into the CPD programmes for Teacher Educators, viz. P-MOST and SOPT which was designed in a "cascade model".
3. It also clearly brought out the plan to establish NCTE with full statutory status.

The NCTE Effect

National Council for Teacher Education (NCTE) was enacted and established in 1993. The provisions in the NCTE Act were structural and meant to control the "commercialization menace" that was plaguing TE. The NCTE Act provided for an elaborate and complex nationwide structure with distributed powers in regional committees to accredit and disaccredit TEIs through due process. These structures and bodies were, however, populated largely by the very set of people who had themselves been custodians of the pre-NCTE institutional arrangements in TE. Several of them sneaked into the new system the old institutional and professional cultures that they brought with them as their legacy.

NCTE came down heavily on the TE programmes through correspondence. However, the pressures for drastically increasing the number of trained teachers to cater to the expanding school systems were too real that NCTE and Distance Education Council (DEC), under the aegis of the Indira Gandhi National Open University (IGNOU), together had to put in place an accreditation protocol for TE programmes through Distance Education (DE). This facilitated a contained expansion of teacher education in those sectors and geographical regions which had greater need for trained teachers. This arrangement arguably put a check to substandard TE programmes through DE.

Having said that, commercialization of TE through private institutions offering substandard TE degrees and diplomas persisted to be a hardy perennial problem. There have been several back-and-forth in NCTE regulations over the years. Some of them pertaining to qualifications for becoming a faculty in a TEI. Some issues (e.g., M.A. *vs.* M.Ed.) have gone on over many years, often involving judicial interventions.

When the universalization of primary education (UPE) and later universalization of elementary education (UEE) assumed project modes under the District Primary Education Programme (DPEP) and Sarva Shiksha Abhiyan (SSA) in the 1990s and in the early 2000s, a large number of Alternative Schools came into being, particularly in geographically remote and educationally backward areas. This was considered essential as a part of ensuring greater access to school for unreached habitations and for those in the economic and social margins within a limited timeframe. A cadre of parateachers or *shiksha sahayak*s were raised for this, with matriculates, intermediates or graduates with no TE qualifications except for special training ranging from a few weeks to a few months. This "exceptional" situation diluted a great deal of what should have been NCTE's legitimate domain of ensuring pre-service TE qualifications as a prerequisite for anybody permitted to teach at school.

Similarly, the structures created as a consequence of the NPE 1986 and POA 1992, viz. SCERT, DIET etc. got somewhat robbed of their role of providing in-service education to teachers because parallel project structures that got created under DPEP and SSA, viz. District Project Offices (DPO), Block Resource Centres (BRC) and Cluster Resource Centres (CRC). DIETs and SCERTs gradually came to be restricted to their pre-service teacher preparation functions.

The Right to Education (RTE) Act of 2009 was meant to bring the qualifications of elementary school teachers within a legal framework based on fundamental rights. This was expected to add some "bite" to NCTE's "bark" by way of enabling greater effectiveness to NCTE's regulatory functions.The phenomenon of Alternative School was legally delegitimized because of RTE, and so did the deployment of untrained or undertrained para-teachers. However, enormous unevenness in this regard across regions and states continues to be the case.

There has been a mushrooming of private, "English medium", low fee charging schools, particularly in the urban and peri-urban areas. These schools still do not come under any serious public or regulatory scrutiny. The indications are that there is a large deployment of underpaid (some of them untrained) teachers in these private schools. Evidently, there is a market for this genre of schools, especially among the immigrant working class and the lower middle class who find that they have been let down badly by the municipal schools and other government schools operating under suboptimal conditions. The link clearly established in the minds of the public between upward social mobility and English language is an important factor here.

It is very clear that the "rights" perspective that RTE brings upfront has been put to very little use over the years by way of seeking legal redressal for non-provision or sub-optimal provision (by governments) of conditions that support elementary education of acceptable quality. This matter is still to be fully understood or assessed. One hypothesis to explain this would be that civil society activism as a phenomenon that used to serve to mobilize and ventilate public demand and advocacy for quality education is on the decline in recent years. Another factor would be the aspirations for English medium education that is driving the lower middle class all over the country to private schools.

The National Curriculum Framework for Teacher Education (NCFTE), 2009 and the Justice Verma Committee (JVC), 2012 together served to bring back into the public discourse the necessity for increasing the duration of TE programmes and locating all such programmes within the higher education system, thereby assuring a professional degree status to TE qualifications. This was clearly against the interests of those who controlled the market of private TE who were always in favour of the perpetuation of short duration TE programmes (like one year B.Ed.). The NCTE regulations of 2013-15 eventually gave a seal of authority to the regulatory stipulations for a two-year B.Ed., two-year M.Ed., three-year B.Ed.-M.Ed., Four year B.A./B.Sc.B.Ed. and BEl.Ed. There has, however, been a loud murmur of disagreement about these regulations in the market and among a subset of TE community who have been giving voice to it.

NEP 2020: Critiques and Promises

The tone that NEP 2020 takes on, so far as TE is concerned, is that of critiquing the existing practices and distancing itself from the past policies, structures and institutional processes that have presumably been responsible for the present state. The policy document starts with some severe indictments:

1. On stand-alone TEI, quoting JVC, that about 10,000 of them are "selling degrees for a price". (15.2: 42); and
2. On NCTE:

> "Regulatory efforts so far have neither been able to curb the malpractices in the system, nor enforce basic standards for quality, and in fact have had the negative effect of curbing the growth of excellence and innovation in the sector. The sector and its regulatory system are, therefore, in urgent need of revitalization through radical action, in order to raise standards and

> restore integrity, credibility, efficacy, and high quality to the teacher education system". (15.2: 42)

The way out that NEP 2020 is prescribing along the following lines:

> "In order to improve and reach the levels of integrity and credibility required to restore the prestige of the teaching profession, the Regulatory System shall be empowered to take stringent action against substandard and dysfunctional teacher education institutions (TEIs) that do not meet basic educational criteria, after giving one year for remedy of the breaches. By 2030, only educationally sound, multidisciplinary, and integrated teacher education programmes shall be in force". (15.3: 42)

This assertion, however, begs the question that while despite the NCTE Act of 1993 having the teeth to enforce such a rigorous regulatory regime it still has not worked satisfactorily all these years, how do we expect that a new set of initiatives (which are still to be specified) under NEP 2020 would be more effective, energized as they seem to be just by the good intentions behind them? In other words, the question is: NCTE, even in its present form, is adequately empowered. Despite this, why is it that it has not been able to perform? Would the structure that will replace NCTE in the promised new regulatory architecture going to be any different? The devil as they say is in the details. NEP 2020 has not gone into these details. Also, the full armature of the institutional structures and legal provisions to implement the policy are yet to unfold. Evidently, we will have to wait longer.

The strategy of the NEP 2020 for salvaging TE from what it has diagnosed as its present maladies are examined in the following two paragraphs:

> The Policy document talks about multi-disciplinary universities and colleges as the location for TE

> programmes and stand-alone TEI to be phased out. There is nothing very new here; it is along the lines of the JVC recommendations. The question again is about the way in which this will be implemented. The amendment to the NCTE Act in 2022 has changed the definition of composite institution that would now hopefully enable the starting of the four-year integrated programmes. What do we do with existing stand-alone TEIs? The 2022 amendment seems to clear the possibility of their collaborating with nearby multidisciplinary HEIs within the same affiliating university (Sharma *et al.*, 2023). How this would eventually pan out is to be seen.

The Policy document also about the following programmes:

1. Four-year integrated dual major bachelor's degree programme;
2. Two-year B.Ed. for those who are already graduates; and
3. One-year B.Ed. for those who have a four-year undergraduate degree in a specialized subject.

What is not clear is how the add-on one-year B.Ed. be made equivalent to the two-year programme? How far can an "add-on" programme be compared with an "integrated degree" model in the four-year programme? How can the one-year programme be considered equivalent to the two-year programme? Answers to these questions are awaited, as the programmes for implementation of NEP 2020 are still in the process of unfolding.

In the meanwhile, there are several alternative systems of private schooling that is proliferating in the education ecosystem for the privileged and the affluent, viz. the IB schools, ICSE schools, and those following the Cambridge programme. For such schools, the teacher qualifications do not seem to be governed by the NCTE stipulations. Some of such Boards and school systems have their own distinct and separate TE programmes. In some cases, there are structured and arguably rigorous initial teacher preparation and certification programmes, as well as CPD programmes. And these do not seem even to blip on NCTE's radar. Also, in several private school systems even with the CBSE, separate continuing professional development for teachers have been in operation for many years. On the other end of the spectrum, in several states and regions, the system of alternative schools and para-teachers reportedly still exist, particularly in remote and educationally backward areas and communities. RTE seems to have diminished in its importance and have regressed to being an increasingly ineffective instrument to check such lapses.

Conclusion

The historical overview of TE in India that we have attempted in this chapter reveals the following:

1. A lack of long-term commitment to a planned course of action. There seem to be too many abrupt mid-course corrections and too much meandering.
2. NCTE has been a mixed bag. While there has been some obvious advantage of NCTE's presence in terms of reining in the overdrive of unscrupulous commercialization of TE at the cost of even minimum acceptable levels of quality, there are insidious ways in which market continues to influence the accreditation and regulatory processes.
3. The very philosophy underlying the national accreditation and regulatory architecture, that uniformity and standardization are the principal ways for assurance of quality, is itself highly fallacious. This whole matter merits a comprehensive scrutiny, analysis and debate.
4. CPD as a strategy has not taken roots in the public systems. SCERTs and DIETs are too preoccupied with initial teacher preparation programmes that they have been tasked. Some private school systems have their own CPDs. Some state governments have outsourced to corporate institutions through CSR the entire teacher monitoring and CPD systems in their states. The effect this will have on their

own resource institutions is yet to be fully understood or assessed.

5. The new regulatory architecture envisaged in the NEP 2020 suffers from the basic contradiction that rehashing old institutions with new roles or building a new architecture of institutions recycling the debris of the old is often a problem and it does very little to transform the default regulatory culture which is highly bureaucratic and mindless.
6. University departments of education are likely to continue to be caught in between school, teacher education and their academic peer group from other disciplines within higher education, even as envisaged under NEP 2020. The question to ask is: Wouldn't TE (or even Education as a discipline) continue to hold its "Cinderella" status?
7. Our gaze towards future reveals to us a critical question: Amidst possible intensification of ideological contestations in TE, both in terms of curricula and institutional composition, isn't it likely that on the one hand, the social margins will be left more and more to their own devices, and on the other, the doors would get opened wider by the day for the private market-oriented system of TE to play a dominant role, particularly in those school systems meant for the affluent and the aspirant middle class?

REFERENCES

Menon, S.B. and Mathew, R. (2016). "Teacher Education in Universities: A Case from India". In Bob Moon (Ed.). *Do Universities have a Role in the Education and Training of Teachers?: An International Analysis of Policy and Practice.* Cambridge: Cambridge University Press.

Ministry of Education, Government of India (1959). *Annual Report 1958-59*, p. 33.

Sharma, G., Mittal, R. and Zayan (2023). "Teacher Education in India's National Education Policy 2020: Knowledge Traditions, Global Discourses and National Regulations". *Contemporary Education Dialogue. 20*(2), 256-82. Sage.

2

Professionalism in Teacher Education Programme

P.K. Sahoo

Teaching is considered as a profession. Profession has certain specific characteristics, viz. (i) an organised body of intellectual theory with strong research base; (ii) an intellectual technique serving a bridge between theory and practice; (iii) an application of intellectual technique to practical affairs; (iv) a long period of formal training and certification sets of codes of ethics; (v) ability to provide its own leadership; (vi) an association of members with high quality communication among members; (vii) recognition as a professional body; (viii) professional concerns for its own work in the society; and (ix) an established relationship with other professions (Hitchens, 1985). A general understanding of any profession is developed in the context of four characteristics, viz. a sound knowledge base, high level specific skills with sound linkage of theory and practice, professional ethics to be evolved and ensured by its own guild, accountability to the stakeholders or the clientele in specific and society in general. Professionalism in education enables the teachers to develop knowledge, skills and values concerning teaching profession. It is very much essential to focus teaching into the category of profession. There have been debates over professional credentials of teaching job in organised sector, particularly with regard to its knowledge base, development of professional skills and maintenance of professional ethics at par with other professions. However, there have been serious efforts to work on teaching theory and practice with broad perspectives of a profession.

Especially, professional education for preparing teachers and upholding their professional standards during teaching career has been the concern of educationists of current era. It is more relevant in the national and global perspective, in view of shaping the quality of schooling and its outputs. Hence, every scholar in the field of teacher education must be sensitive about professionalism, in attributes of teaching and teachers' role in it. A cursory view of professional attributes of teaching, and teacher development programme especially in the Indian context has been highlighted in this chapter.

Understanding Teaching

In formal education, teaching occupies significant position. There have been serious efforts to conceptualise teaching in the modern age. Since the concern for quality in education is the main focus of the society, quality of teaching draws major attention of the stakeholders of the system. Teaching is understood as activities of a teacher that lead to learning of students. All kinds of relevant activities performed by a teacher in a formal education institution leading to student's development as per curriculum can be considered as teaching. From this point of view, teaching is linked with teacher behaviour, student's behaviour and learning, curriculum, and the school or college where teaching activities are organised. Teaching is considered as a process. Since, teacher carries out such process, teaching is linked with teacher competencies, expectations, ethics and other personality factors. Teaching activities are purposeful. Such purposes are mainly guided by curricular aims as well as inherent knowledge base of instruction.

Different curricular expectations are reflected in teaching process. Simultaneously, the knowledge base of teacher regarding pedagogy, its applications, and mastery of teaching skills, decision making tactics and value orientation are very well noticed in behaviour of teachers in dealing with various kinds of activities performed to attain curricular objectives. Since, individual differences are associated with teachers' behaviour, we may notice teacher factor dominating teaching process. Of course, theoretically teaching process can be understood in a systematic form, by categorising them in the context of intended actions and competencies of teachers. Different kinds of tasks are carried out by teachers to enable learners to achieve expected learning. In this regard, nature of learning, especially, different schools of thoughts related to students learning are very much associated with conceptualisation of teaching. Moreover, the philosophical, social, cultural and psychological perspectives contribute to understand the concept of teaching, teacher behaviour, teaching-learning evaluation and learning outcome more inclusively. The knowledge base of teaching has subscribed to understand teaching from different kinds of learning perspectives. A teacher takes responsibility of transmission of knowledge, skills and values to students through systematic presentation of learning experiences. Such kind of teaching process is considered structured and externally doctored by the experts. Another kind of teaching process takes learners' cognitive potentials into conceptual clarifications through teachers' help. In the recent past, there has been a movement to encourage students experience based learning in the socio-cultural context with scaffolding practices of teacher. Such kind of learner oriented teaching-learning process enables the learners to be accountable for their own learning being engaged in different kinds of learning experiences created by themselves. In this context, teaching-learning process is conceptualised with the facilitator role of a teacher, where teachers and students mutually influence each other to create conducive environment of learning.

Teaching and Related Terms

One can witness activities performed by a teacher as done in the case of a preacher, a trainer, a coach, or a supervisor. The focus on the concept "teaching" remains on the action of a teacher to bring about learning in student. The human interaction taking place between teacher and student is purposeful. The expected learning outcome of a student is the central point of teaching activities. Hence, teaching activities including a range of activities of a teacher like demonstrating, questioning, giving examples, narrating, guiding etc. are performed to enable the students to gain new knowledge, skills and values. The relationship between teacher and student appropriate the conditions in which human interaction takes place; and the varieties of activities carried out by teacher and students are all purposeful. The teacher plays a key role in managing the teaching-learning activities with a view to create conducive learning environment, systematic delivery of teaching-learning inputs, own engagement in different activities, students' participation to gain various learning experiences, assessment of student behaviour, students involvement in teaching-learning process and their progress in learning. Since, the teaching takes place in a formal condition to deliver goods to a group of students as per their cognitive dispositions and instructional objectives; it becomes more complex on the part of a teacher to plan, act and progress in professional sphere. Teaching cannot be considered as a set of formal activities to be adopted by any person. Teachers' role in teaching is very much unique, in the sense, it requires teachers' judgement potentials in deciding what is worth to be considered for expected learning outcome in given context and what is educational worth of the content and what is appropriate method to be employed in classroom and outside classroom conditions. Teachers' role in teaching is directly linked with quality output, quality input and relevant process. The learning in conditions very specific to the students and the institution where they work are also very much significant for teaching. Teaching leading to transformation of thought, feeling and action of students is a planned job. Such job is to be planned and executed by a teacher judiciously taking into consideration the quality of learning among students, it requires professional ethics among teachers.

Teaching is not considered training since teaching encompasses various forms of human engagement in learning. **Training** refers to conditioning or indoctrination. Teaching may include training to develop certain expected skills. However, it encompasses more critical process for development of intellectual skills, which are not continued to just observe, practice and proceed in a chained form.

Conditioning is adopted as a process of teaching where major emphasis is led on external inputs and sensory participation of students in learning. However, conditioning has its limitations with regard to attainment of higher order cognition, skills and creative expression. A teacher may not continue to conditioning, since it serves little purpose to quality learning.

Similarly, the notion of **indoctrination** has little relevance to teaching because of its vagueness and insistence on beliefs. Teacher's activities encourage the journey to create meaning to the experiences among students through lively participation. Even though, some philosophers emphasise on "indoctrination" as synonym to education, in ground reality a teachers' activities are valued differently. The nature of teaching involves humanistic approach. Indoctrination may have some place to understand a doctrine. However, there are varieties of approaches to enable students to analyse and assess the belief critically. Above presentations make it clear that teaching is not just training, conditioning or indoctrination.

Teacher's activities need to be rationalised in the context of student's cognitive faculties, socio-cultural experiences and initiatives to explore and create new meaning of life and its surroundings. Teacher's preparedness, commitment and competencies to perform various activities make "teaching" more meaningful and relevant to student's learning. Such activities not restrict itself to a set of rules. It expands its scope to support learners' initiatives in identifying problem, gathering evidences and evaluate its relevance in generating new meaning to concepts and solving problems which may be of cognitive, emotive and practical nature. Teachers' role in performing various kinds of humane activities leading to discovery and creative learning requires a different approach, which are not of just mechanical skills based nature or **craftsmanship**. Teachers encouraging students in discovery of truth for themselves and others require more rationale and creative approach of teaching. Empowering students to make optimum use of their cognitive skills and emotive spirit in education process become the forefront of quality teaching of the day. Students' participation in different kinds of learning experiences incorporating reflective thinking and creative expressions require teachers' activities very much different from programmed and conditioned nature. This is the age of information. Teachers promoting information processing skills among students lead to different kinds of teaching-learning activities. Valuing plurality and fluidity in information processing approach in teaching-learning can contribute to teaching of humanistic, liberal and open in nature.

Everything cannot be pre-decided for teaching every group of learners. Teachers employing approaches to enable students to decide their own expected learning outcome and plan their engagement in different kinds of learning experience becomes a part of quality teaching. This has been seen in the wider context of life skills where students must be empowered to "develop their own rational life plans rather than simply acquiring the patterns of thought, feeling and action possessed by the elders" (Robertson, 1987). However, there is scope for rationalising the ideas and thoughts of the elders through exercise of students reasoning and evaluation abilities. The concept of teaching is more wide and complex. Teacher as a performer of teaching activities has skilful, thoughtful, value ridden and dynamic role in teaching. In this context, one cannot confine the meaning of teaching to just reproduction of set of skills to achieve predetermined objectives of instruction. Long back John Dewey had stated that teaching is not seen as services of predetermined and presequenced procedures but as context-sensitive action grounded in intellectual thought. Hence, conceptualising teachers' multifaceted role in teaching is very much intricate in this respect.

Teaching Objectives and Teaching Outcome

Teaching as action of a teacher is irrelevant, unless it is directed to achieve specific instructional objectives, which are arrived at by analysis of teaching-learning standards as well as by teachers' critical reflection on curriculum. Thus, restricting the meaning of teaching to a particular course of development is very much limited to signify the real intention of teaching. Learning may occur without teaching; such serendipitous learning is understood as change. The practice of teaching comprises thoughtful action of teachers in achieving the curricular objectives. Teaching can be differently shaped in the context of instructional objectives relevant to the curriculum.

As presented in above section, teacher activities and learning experiences are correlated in the context of expected learning outcome of students. Teacher's behavioural outcomes are judged in the context of students' learning what is being taught. Hence, teacher "task verb" is to be correlated with learning achievement verb. A good teachers' behaviour (task verb) must correspond to students' learning outcome (achievement verb). The task verbs are to be reflected in teacher behaviour, which may be done skilfully, successfully or effectively. Its worth is judged not only in terms of skilful performance of teacher, but also it is valued in terms of intended outcome of students' behaviour. It is logical to state that effective interaction will lead to effective learning. However, all effective learning may not be attributed to effective teaching-learning activities performed through teaching. In this context, teaching objectives and learning outcomes must be associated with judicious approach. This is argued that although learning may be gained through various sources, the intentionally designed activity reduces chance factor and increases the probability that students will attain specific intended goals. Deoborah & Francesca (2009) stated that teacher behaviour must be effective and successful in terms of enabling students to intended behavioural transformation, even though anything and everything can be associated into the control of teacher behaviour.

Teaching is intentional in nature. The teacher does not restrict his behaviour to revelation of a set of general rules or maxims irrespective of contextuality. A teacher makes continuous efforts to learn with a view to improve on his/her performance in context of learning situations. A teacher remains vigil about what he does, how he does, what leads to what, what is more relevant, what changes are expected, how to adopt such changes, what are the sources of learning. What are more meaningful experiences of teaching etc. Teachers' curiosity and commitment to perform intended behaviour is more keenly linked with the approaches of "inducing" learning. It emphasises on teachers' own intellectual meta-cognitive exercise to improve on their own performances. It is guided by their intentions. Such intentions, of course, are based on their own values and thoughts about teaching. Teachers' continuous exposure to varieties of day-to-day teaching experiences in real school situation as well as sound knowledge of pedagogy build solid ground for transformation in teaching behaviour.

Scientific Nature of Teaching

The scientific nature of teaching is understood in the context of observable acts of a teacher in teaching-learning situations. Teaching is "implicated in the sentences where it occurs" (Smith, 1987). The empirical evidences about teaching activities are useful to understand what is meant by "teaching". Different terms like "competency", "competence", "performance", "skills" etc. are referred in the context of teaching. Subsequently, the characteristics of effective teaching are exemplified with the help of such terms. It leads to arrive at the theories, models and principles of teaching. "Teaching" becomes a subject of pedagogical discourse, depending on the nature of science in it. That is, how understanding teaching becomes a subject of scientific and methodological inquiry.

Research on "teaching" can facilitate the generation of knowledge on "effective teaching" focusing on "teacher performances" in varied teaching-learning contexts. Different teacher preparation strategies are evolved following the scientific nature of teaching. Appropriate teacher education models can emerge scientifically by analysing relationship between different factors associated with teaching. Moreover, the concept of effective teaching can be evolved following the theories of teaching. Hence, it becomes imperative to throw light on scientific background of teaching and teacher education in the endeavour of professional development.

Teaching as Art and Science

Considering the nature of education as quality oriented interventions to development of human life, this is well understood that teaching cannot be understood as a matter of pure scientific investigation. Teaching is considered as an art on the ground that it involves human efforts to achieve the goals of life through interaction between human beings (Dunkin, 1987). It is a value ridden concept. A teacher acts as per his own values and to act "as oneself". Such standpoint is, of course, countered by the professionals. Teaching is not ordinary behaviour of helping others, rather teachers' behaviour is rooted in professional justified knowledge and on moral imperatives of the role (Deborah & Francesca, 2009). There have been debates whether teaching can be explained scientifically by validating different theories through empiricist approach or not. Consistent endeavours are on progress to conceptualise teaching from scientific perspectives. Such efforts are made to strengthen knowledge base of teaching. Teaching may be considered as art. In this respect, very few persons with artistic ability of teaching may deliver good to the students. However, in the context of identifying major patterns of teaching behaviour for expected learning outcomes, the phenomena of teaching can be understood by applying scientific investigations. There is also large scope for conducting scientific researches on teaching and theorising teaching by accommodating intuitive expressions, emotional intelligence, critical reflections, creative action and contextuality in teaching-learning situations. In addition to scientific explanations of causal relationships, there have been strong initiatives to understand knowledge base of teaching through qualitative research paradigms.

Even though teaching is not fully considered as science implying laws, controls and predictions as applicable to pure science, there is ample scope to explore scientific bases in interdisciplinary form so that the scientific explanations can be applied by human being (teacher) to bring development among fellow human beings (students). N.L. Gage (1975), a propounder of theoretical understanding of teaching, was of the view that even though teaching is a kind of art, the scientific basis of teaching can be developed by establishing "relationships between variables on teaching and learning." He emphasised on exploring and establishing causal relationships through experimentations in teaching-learning situations. Hence, strong scientific explanations of factors associated with teaching will provide better opportunities to improve teaching. Towards the last quarter of 20th century, there have been consistent efforts to expand the scientific bases of teaching, considering multivariate relationships and validating different models of teaching with generalisation.

Of late, priorities are made to broaden the scope of scientific explanations to teaching by promoting mixed method paradigms (quantitative and qualitative) to understand the complex nature of teaching, such efforts highlight process oriented decision making variables in the context of teaching-learning outputs. The socio-cultural and technological factors have also been incorporated with the concept of inclusive teaching and teacher development. This may not counter the scientific explanations rather they can enlarge the scope of understanding teaching from multidisciplinary perspectives. Such practices have been escalated by emphasising multi-method paradigms in teaching and teacher learning.

Theorisation in Teaching: Knowledge Base of Education

A theory is understood as a set of interrelated constructs, definitions, propositions which present a systematic view of the phenomena by specifying relations among variables with the purpose of explaining and predicting (Kerlinger, 1973). In this context, research efforts have been made to explain relationships among teaching variables with the purpose of controlling teaching tasks and predicting the causal relationship between different variables. Such kind of investigations has adopted scientific inquiry to expand the scope of understanding teaching. There has been predominance of psychological concepts and measurement theories in this direction. In such kind of investigations, the theoretical explanations on teaching do not yet match to scientific theory based explanations to other branches of knowledge. The contributions of other cognate disciplines like psychology, sociology, political science, geography, economics and informatics have a lot bearing on education theory. The role of information and communication technology in teaching has brought a forceful shift to understand the concept of teaching and teacher behaviour. In this regard, a multidisciplinary approach has been considered more essential to theorisation of teaching in the dynamic context of individual and social values, socio-cultural environment and technological advancements. There is a lot of scope to develop sound theoretical understanding of teaching.

There have been debates on epistemological issues concerning development of knowledge base in education, especially, teaching. Different disciplinary perspectives have been amalgamated to build knowledge base of education like psychology, neuroscience, sociology, anthropology and philosophy. It also makes use of different approaches drawn from social sciences, humanities and physical and natural science. However, the major focus remains on generation of theoretical knowledge of education taking into consideration of different internal and external factors. Hence, teaching theories, even though appear to be restricted to behavioural dimensions of teachers and students, different philosophical, sociological, linguistic and communication perspectives influence the framework of understanding teaching (Furlong, 2014). Many educationists like Becher (1989) highlighted that knowledge bases of education are 'soft'. It is mainly derived from reinterpretations of the human and social sciences. Of course, there has been a tradition of conducting scientific enquiry as a matter of studying educational phenomena. Contradictions may remain about the approaches of investigation of educational phenomena and building a distinct theoretical base of education. However, its significance is recognised in conceptualisation of education with its uniqueness. Many educationists project professional dimension of educational knowledge in the context of teaching-learning practices. There has been focus on practical conception of knowledge in education, i.e. knowing-in-action within professional life (Schon, 1983). The concept of tacit knowledge, having its root in exploring knowledge embedded in practice. When enquiries in broad concept of education still continue to answer knowledge base questions in education, teachers' pursuit to know the practical dimensions of 'teaching' is of paramount significance to deliver the goods of education to students' development. That is, how the concept of teacher knowledge and teacher research is gaining ground to develop theoretical base of 'teaching' in a unique form. Simultaneous efforts need to continue enquiry on theoretical knowledge as well as professional or pragmatic knowledge concerning education in general and teaching in specific.

As a professional, a teacher must have discipline based knowledge of education. While understanding of educational theories and pedagogic principles play significant role in application level, teachers' experience based interventions and understanding shall strengthen practical knowledge base of teaching. The theories and rules governing teaching practices must be the background of every teacher education programme. Hence, development of theories, research activities and experiential knowledge generated through continuous professional engagement must be integrated with professional orientation of teachers.

Teacher Development Practices

There have been efforts to educate teachers about their professional role to carry out teaching-learning functions in educational institution. The teacher education system focuses on enabling the novice teachers to acquire knowledge, skills and values to fulfil their professional obligations as per expectations of education system. There are different approaches to deal with this mission. The core concern refers to enable aspirant teaches to acquire knowledge and skills on how to teach to achieve the curricular objectives. Development of necessary values linked with teaching job is also the focus of such endeavour. An integral framework of teacher development as developed by National Institute of Education (NIE) Singapore called values, skills and knowledge (VSK) model takes into account interlink age of Professional skills with Education knowledge jointly associated with professional values of teachers. Different skills of teachers like pedagogical, interpersonal, reflective, personal and administrative and management are interlinked with disciplinary knowledge of self, students, pedagogy, curriculum, content and educational context. These aspects are based on teacher values on the notion that all children can learn, teacher must have care and concern for all pupils, he must respect for diversity with full dedication and commitment to the profession collaboration, sharing and team spirit and desire for continuous learning, excellence and innovation. All these factors contributing to development of personnel in teaching profession require systematic preparatory teacher education programme for different levels of education (Chong & Cheah, 2009).

A comprehensive teacher education curriculum focuses on these areas of teacher development based on theoretical and practical knowledge approaches of teacher education classified under five areas, viz. traditional role model approach; discipline based approach; competency based approach, personalistic approach and ecletic approach. Hutchinson (2008) summarised different orientations of initial teacher education taking into consideration five areas, viz. Academic orientation, Practical orientation, Technical orientation, Personal orientation and Critical enquiry orientation. Emergence of disciplinary approach to teacher education assumed that understanding of different theoretical bases of education will form foundation for applying such knowledge in the classroom. The practical orientation is very much dominated to depend on expert teachers' knowledge and skills to be transmitted to the student-teachers through rigorous practices in classroom teaching. The common framework of technical orientation highlights achievement of competencies of teaching by developing knowledge and behavioural skills. This orientation has gained ground during the latter half of the 20th century on extensive contributions of behaviourism to the field of teacher development. The personal orientation emphasised on development of teachers' personality through human interactions and learning to bring reforms in own self-through sensitisation, reflection and progressive action. The critical enquiry orientation is rooted in socio-cultural context based learning theories, where the teacher development practices take care of inclusiveness in school system, teachers and students development oriented collective action. Teachers' role in contextual framework are analysed by the participant student-teachers and intervention based experiences in real school situation are useful for development of knowledge and skills of pupil-teachers to deal with problematic aspects of teaching. Current system of teacher education accommodates different orientations in teacher learning.

Competency Development Approach in Teacher Education

There have been serious efforts to concentrate on professional competency development programmes for would-be teachers as well as working teachers. The research based evidences have formed the ground for competency development practices with sound rationale. Competency development strategies are adopted in real school situations as well as in simulated conditions. Modelling facilitates competency development programmes with the help of technological gadgets and facilities. Competency development approach assumed that the student-teacher develops "performance tendencies and capabilities that promote students' achievement of educational objectives" (Gage & Phillip, 1975). In this regard, scientific principles of teaching played prominent role in competency development practices. The researches identified hundreds of competencies. However, the pre-service teacher education covered some core competency areas. The in-service programmes, of course, covered many competency development training packages for school teachers. Such programmes were of centralised as well as decentralised nature.

Teacher competency is directly associated with different observable tasks to be performed by a teacher informal education institutional set-up (Houston, 1974). They are known as task related competencies. In general term competency means application of knowledge, attitude and skills to perform expected tasks for facilitating intellectual, social, emotional and physical growth in children. Competency has knowledge dimension, i.e. a teacher must have clear understanding of different tasks and required skills. He must be aware of quality parameters of different tasks. Competency has attitude dimension, a teacher must have commitment and positive attitude for involvement in different tasks. The third dimension is skill of carrying out different activities. Competency consists of teaching skills which can be assessed by performance of teachers. Hence, proficiency in skills will enable a teacher to deliver well in the workplace.

The competency based teacher education focusses on attainment of required behavioural changes among teachers for successful completion of a teacher education programme or a package. There are five classes of competencies, viz.:

- **Cognitive based competencies** involving knowledge and intellectual skills for teaching functions;
- **Performance based competencies** involving teaching skills and overt actions;
- **Consequence based competencies** involving demonstration of competence to bring out desired change among students taught by a teacher;

- **Affective competencies** incorporating change in attitude and values among teachers; and
- **Exploratory competencies** highlighting passion of teachers to learn, engagement of teachers in community welfare measures, participation of teachers in personality development programmes like *yoga*, meditation, artistic expositions. Unlike first four categories of competencies exploratory competencies cannot be measured with structured standard (Houston, 1987).

The NCTE listed ten competencies categories, viz.: (1) Contextual competency; (2) Conceptual competency; (3) Content Competency; (4) Transactional competency; (5) Competency related to other educational activities; (6) Competency related to develop teaching-learning materials; (7) Evaluation competency; (8) Management competency; (9) Competency related to working with parents; and (10) Competencies related to working with community and other agencies (RIE, Mysore, 1998).

RIE Mysore (1998) categorised school teachers' competencies in 12 categories: (1) Preparation for instruction; (2) Development, preparation and utilization of instructional material; (3) Motivation of children; (4) Communication in classroom; (5) Methods of instruction; (6) Evaluation of learning; (7) Diagnosis and remediation; (8) Classroom management; (9) Co-curricular activities; (10) Community participation; (11) Special education; and (12) Institutional planning.

Yadav and Lakshmi (2003) categorised teacher competencies on three headings, such as: (a) Instructional competencies comprising verbal and non-verbal competencies, (b) organisational competencies, and (c) evaluative competencies. While such competencies are general in nature keeping in view of teacher's role in different functions of school system, UNESCO document on increasing teacher effectiveness (Anderson, 2004) focused on specific areas of teachers' interventions in curriculum, classroom environment, teaching and students' learning. Area-wise classification of teacher's competency is stated as follows:

1. Curricular Understanding

- Teacher must have a sound understanding of standards expected in the form of student learning.
- Making use of their understanding of standards, they should design effective learning units.
- Teachers must be capable to establish linkage between curriculum standards, instructional units, assessment of learning outcome and the instructional activities and learning materials.

2. Classroom Environment, Climate and Culture-based Competency

- Attractive and functional classroom environment should be created by teachers.
- Teachers must play significant role in making classroom climate warm by taking into consideration students' socio-cultural background.
- The classroom culture must be nurtured through teacher's efforts. Teacher should build such culture by encouraging students' participation in value-based activities.
- Classroom organisation: Small group or individual activity-based instructional activities should be promoted by the teacher.
- Teacher should take lead to form co-operative learning groups within the classroom on the basis of students' characteristics.
- Teacher must facilitate learners' engagement in different activities and assignments.

3. Classroom Management Competency

- Teacher should present appropriate standards for pro-social behaviour expected from students.

- Teacher must be sensitive about problem children and give appropriate feedback to make them pro-social.
- Inappropriate student's behaviour should not be tolerated by the teacher. Appropriate discipline steps are taken in this regard.
- Teacher must implement meaningful rule and routines remaining present in class, during non-instructional situations.
- Teacher should communicate to students that they are aware of different activities and learners' responsibilities for their learning.

4. Instruction Competency

- Teachers and students must understand the large unit of instruction and its components.
- Intended outcome of each unit of instruction must be clarified to students. Teacher makes students prepared for achieving such outcome.
- Teacher must facilitate meaningful learning by interlinkage of different components of content.
- Teacher must provide ample opportunity for learning of students through exercise of students' intellectual skills.
- Teacher should assist student to remain engaged in learning activities productivity.

5. Classroom Communication Competency

- Teacher's presentation should be clear and comprehensive to students.
- Teachers must provide appropriate reinforcement to students' response.
- Teachers must be fluent in communication with oratory and demonstration skills.

6. Student Learning and Assessment Competency

- Proper techniques to be used by teachers to maintain

attention towards learning and sustaining students' involvement in learning appropriately.

- Assignments must be given to students by teachers taking into consideration learning units and students' background. Standards of assignments must be communicated to students.
- Teachers should ensure students' learning through assessment of assignment.
- Appropriate feedback should be given by teacher on students' performance in assignments. Guidance must be provided to improve further in learning.
- Students' involvement in learning must be monitored on continuous basis through appropriate means.

Development of Teaching Skills

N.L. Gage (1968) defined teaching skill as "specific instructional activities and procedures that a teacher may use in his classroom." There are different kinds of instructional skills very much common to any kind of teacher behaviour was analysed in different segments. The common skills identified in teaching were skills: (i) writing instructional objectives, (ii) introducing a lesson, (iii) questioning, (iv) probing, (v) explaining, (vi) illustrating with examples, (vii) stimulus variation, (viii) silence and non-verbal cues, (ix) reinforcement, (x) increasing pupil participation, (xi) using blackboard, (xii) achieving closure, and (xiii) recognising attending behaviour (Passi, 1976). During the last quarter of the 20th century, teacher training programme named as 'microteaching' was introduced as an essential strategy of training teaching skills. It followed behaviouristic model of learning by emphasising SR theory. The professional experts were engaged in training teacher educators and pupil-teachers following three phases of microteaching, viz. (i) Modelling, (ii) Practice, and (iii) Transfer of different types of modelling like perception modelling (demonstration by expert), symbolic modelling (textual) and audio/video modelling were used for understanding the nature of teaching skill. The skill acquisition phase involved plan-teach-feedback-replan-reteach-feedback. It gave emphasis on repeated practice of different skill components. It was followed by self-feedback, peer feedback and tutor feedback. As a special feature of microteaching, the practices took place in simulated condition where a small group of peer trainees (5 to 8 in numbers) practised each skill one by one for 3 to 5 minutes duration. It followed by observation based discussions. The third place involved integration of various skills to teach a lesson called 'mini-teaching' (Ray, 2014). After practice of integration of skills, the trainees proceed to real classroom teaching.

Similarly, another model of training for classroom interaction analysis was adopted following behaviouristic paradigm to improve communication abilities of teachers and students. In such trainings, emphasis was given on verbal and non-verbal communication in effective and cognitive areas. It contributed to shape classroom teaching language of teacher trainees. The application oriented teacher training practices covered observation, assessment and re-practice of skills for mastery in small group situations. Scientificity of such kind of training can be attributed to definition of skills, identification of components of skills, planning lesson, observation of behaviour, recording formative evaluation, discussion and practices. A series of training activities were arranged in sequential order. First, the pupil-teachers read about the skill and its components. Second, they observe a demonstration lesson on a skill through video presentation. Third, the pupil-teachers plan a lesson on use of skill in a mini teaching session. Fourth, the pupil-teachers' lesson is observed as well as recorded. Fifth, the pupil-teacher analyses a playback and tick the performance on a checklist and finally, the analysis is discussed with the peer and supervisor. If needed, further practice takes place. Such practices provided great scope for application of scientific principles in shaping teachers' behaviour. The mastery of teaching skills contributed significantly to develop general teaching competencies as reported in the above section. Of course, because of time consuming behaviouristic applications in teacher training, such practices were criticised. In spite of several criticism of competency development approach, its "Concerns for accountability and the premises underlying the movements persists" (Dunkin, 2020). As a result, to accommodate student-teachers' experiences and knowledge base more comprehensive models of teacher development were promoted in teacher education system.

Teacher Learning on Multiple Models of Teaching

Joyce & Weil (1990), focused on educating teachers about using different models of teaching to achieve different objectives belonging to cognitive, affective and skill domains. Instead of training of teachers on one by another skill separately and integrating them during real classroom teaching, they focused on use of a set of interrelated skills in the form of a coherent model. They had reviewed different models of teaching and presented 25 models for teacher education purpose. The models were categorised under four families. Each family considered classroom from different perspectives of teaching. The models were categorised under the heading of (i) Information processing models, (ii) Personal models, (iii) Social interaction models, and (iv) Behaviour modification models.

The model of teaching is described in four sections: orientation, teaching model, application and instructional and nurturing effects. The orientation highlights goals, theoretical assumptions and principles. The model is described in four contexts: syntax. Some models are teacher centric ones whereas some are learner centric ones. The models of teaching based teacher education enables a teacher to take appropriate decision on designing teaching-learning activities keeping in view instructional objectives. It takes into account teaching input, teaching output, interaction among teachers, students, subject-contents and technology support and arrangement of the structure suiting to the feedback.

Teacher education programme making use of models of teaching highlights the following requirements (Flander, 1987):

(i) The trainees are exposed to theoretical background of teaching. It helps them to justify the use of an instructional strategy as model of teaching.

(ii) Demonstrations and modelling related to theoretical images. Demonstrations in real classroom situations shall enable the trainees to identify appropriate and inappropriate situations to use model. Several practical examples for each concept in the model of teaching is clarified with the help of demonstrations and video presentations.

(iii) The teacher trainees practice different models of teaching in simulated situation. Initial training in real classroom situation may distract the functioning of real classroom teaching. Hence, simulative teaching has been preferred at initial stage of training.

(iv) Feedback is essential to improve on teaching practices. Unstructured feedbacks are sought through informal discussion with peers. It builds confidence among teacher trainees. Structured feedback is derived on the basis of data gathered through checklist.

(v) Coaching is essential in planning, delivery and assessment phases of teaching, especially in real classroom situation. Teacher trainees decision making abilities, skill mastery and uses interaction with different components of teaching and his/her leadership in carrying out different models of teaching enable them to be skilful in adopting appropriate models of teaching in day-to-day teaching practices.

The practice of models of teaching in teacher education was based on the premise that teachers must follow flexible styles of teaching. They must be exposed to variety of styles of teaching. The teachers learning a few models from each family can be empowered to use them in routine teaching adopting flexible approaches. The researches on teacher education programmes during models of teaching practices revealed that the teachers can be skilful to adopt them in dealing with variety of teaching objectives in classroom teaching.

ICT based Information Processing for Development of Teacher Competencies

The teachers make use of information resources for knowledge construction regarding teaching-learning practices (Corno & Edelstein, 1987). They make use of his cognitive thought process with experiences gained through daily teaching situations and information resources available through different forms of ICT based learning. The teachers are engaged in learning from the ICT, learning about the technology and learning with the technology. Learning from the ICT is directly linked with the acquisition of knowledge and skills through ICT mediated learning system. The user teacher makes use of computer software for acquiring conceptual knowledge and skill in simulated form through repeated practices.

Initially, the first category of ICT was noticed when pupil-teachers made use of computer assisted instruction (CAI), computer based tutorials, and assessment software in teaching-learning process. Online teacher education texts were used by the distant teacher learners. The working teachers adopted CAI and integrated learning systems in traditional classroom teaching situations. Such kind of technology supported learning enabled teachers as well as students to acquire more knowledge with flexibility and economy of time.

The second category of ICT application in teaching was to enable teachers to make appropriate use of computer in teaching-learning practice. Hence, the focus was on learning ICT skills. The students' and teachers' acquaintance with skills to use ICT was given prominence through different training packages, especially through Open University programmes.

The third category of ICT use in education was learning with technology. The information processing model of teaching-learning is reflected in such category of technology supported learning.

Technology is used as a tool for both teachers and students to make use of variety of sources of available information for inter-relating their knowledge with a view to create knowledge for them. Different cognitive tasks are accomplished by the teachers and students through information processing activities with the help of ICT. Learners generate their own representation of subject content and also generate own cognitive skill about representation of information about their learning strategies and their own participation in the same.

Jonassen (1996) highlighted that learning environment created through ICT and its facilitating role in development of knowledge in interactive form make intellectual development process more small and flexible. Different software like data bases, spread sheets, email, multimedia and hyper media facilitate students and teachers learning in constructivist learning environment (Senapaty, 2014).

ICT Use in Competency Development of Teachers

The teacher professional models (TDP) focused on three kinds of ICT based teacher education programmes (Gaible and Burns, 2005), viz. standard TDP, site-based TDP and self-directed TDP. The standardised TDP aimed as disseminating information and skills among teacher participants. In the case of site-based TDP efforts were made to promote profound and long-term changes in teaching process focusing on teachers belonging to a specific region/location. The third category of TDP promoted independent learning, giving emphasis on teachers' own initiative to learn by making use of learning resources available through ICT. In other words, it promotes the concept of learning with technology as stated in above section. By making use of ICT, different kinds of teacher competencies can be developed, viz. content and pedagogy competencies, collaborating and networking competencies, social competencies and technical competencies.

Teacher competency on fusion of ICT in teaching-learning process and acquisition of contemporary knowledge related to curriculum is promoted through development of ICT skill among teachers. ICT promotes autonomy of teachers to acquire current affairs and integrating information processing approach to teaching, learning and assessment process.

ICT facilitates collaborative projects among teachers. Teachers get opportunity to share experiences on transformation in workplace with other teachers at local as well as global level. ICT supported interaction system contributes professional development of teachers. Networking of professional groups promote refinement of practical knowledge of teachers.

Teachers' accountability towards community welfare and the role of school system becomes stronger through ICT. Teachers disseminate transformative measures for upliftment of awareness of parents and other community members on burning issues like health hazard, environment preservation, scientific orientation to problem solution, parental education and social values.

Technical competencies to integrate various sources of knowledge with education are essential among teaching-learning in school system. It requires enhancement of teachers' ability to search and identify wide range of ICT resources (including OER) for teaching ICT skills among teachers are needed to trap advanced technology know-how in education field.

Integrated Approach of Teacher Competencies Related to Technology, Pedagogy and Content Knowledge (TPACK)

A framework of integrated approach of teacher competencies was developed by Mishra & Koehler (2006). Educational technology covers teacher competence in content knowledge, pedagogy and technology areas. Teachers' mastery of knowledge domain of curriculum covering concept clarity, theoretical explanations, application of principles in problem solution, establishment practices etc. are promoted through ICT. ICT enabled knowledge development process involves inquiry approach and validation of knowledge through cross-examination of different sources of knowledge. Teachers' inquisitiveness to acquire valid contemporary knowledge through ICT on timely basis make them continuous learners. Different areas of ICT-based knowledge and skills as highlighted by Mishra & Koehler (2006) have been presented in the following:

- Pedagogical Knowledge (PK) of teacher require teachers' readiness to proper integration of ICT in teaching-learning practices in view of supporting autonomous learning. Teachers' competency in adopting appropriate pedagogical principles for flexible learning of students. Teachers' knowledge and skills of facilitating enquiry based approach of learning among students is strengthened by use of ICT.
- Teachers' knowledge of theories and principles of teaching and learning is of multidisciplinary nature. Pedagogical Content Knowledge (PCK) involves transformation of subject content for teaching. Such transformation occurs through teacher competence in dealing with the nature of concept, teaching objectives, appropriate instructional material knowledge sources and encouraging students' participation in teaching. Teachers' knowledge of pedagogical content deals with the areas of teaching, learning, curriculum assessment and their interlinkage.
- Technology Knowledge (TK) is associated with mastery of knowledge concerning information technology, its role in information processing, communication and problem solving. Teachers used to be oriented about computer literacy programme at the initial stage of use of ICT. Since, knowledge concerning ICT develops in a faster speed, teachers' knowledge must be updated regarding ICT and different tasks associated with ICT on information processing.
- Teachers' Knowledge of Technological Content (TCK) refers to the manner in which technology and content are interconnected with each other. Teacher must be acquainted with different approaches of technology for clarification of a concept and constructing new meaning of a concept contextually. Suitability of alternative technology must deal with conceptual understanding and its applications in the context of cognitive structure and experiences of learners.

- Technological Pedagogical Knowledge (TPK) refers to the strategies of using technology in different manners for allotment of different kinds of instructional objectives. Different applications of technology require management of support system in the context of learning specific concepts. Different kinds of software developed for wide purpose can be identified and used for education purpose depending on their relevance and suitability to achievement of instructional objectives. Moreover, available resource support and the technological knowledge must be understood by the teachers in specific learning environment.
- Technology, Pedagogy and Content Knowledge (TPACK) is a broad concept to deal with teacher competence on interaction among content, pedagogy and technology knowledge. Fusion of three concepts: content knowledge, principles of teaching and application of technology: takes place in managing teaching-learning in different situation. A three dimensional perception of teaching-learning system on the nature of concept presented in the form of technological representation, level of operation of mind while dealing with such concepts with the help of technology or learning resources and the skill of using technology in the context of teaching-learning by the user teachers and learners can create constructive learning environment for teacher education. Integrating different factors associated with content knowledge and pedagogical competencies can be useful to develop context specific teaching-learning models for teacher development. Application of TPACK framework can be useful for individualized efforts as well as group efforts in development of competence of teachers. The approach seems to be flexible and dynamic from the point of view of tackling teaching-learning problems by teachers especially in the context of their efforts for continuous professional

development. Several studies conducted in this area have proved effective in such model in teacher education.

Application of ICT in Teacher Development Programmes

As presented above, technological support to teacher education has a lot of potential for enabling teacher in decision making process, i.e. to cope with the information "overloads" in classroom to consciously structure and direct the flow of classroom information and to analyse the pedagogical theories and making use of pedagogical principles in practice. Technology plays a major role of mediator or facilitator to teachers in designing (pre-teaching) implementing (interaction phase) and evaluation (post-teaching phase) of teaching-learning with a pursuit of quality instruction. Interaction among students and teachers in ICT enabled teaching-learning situations contribute to constructive learning environment in teacher education. This assumption has led to inclusion of ICT education as curricular provisions in the current teacher education programmes.

Practicum Experience

Teacher education focuses on practice oriented professional curriculum. One of the approaches adopted in this regard is the approach of decomposition or breaking down the complex practices into constituent parts to make it possible for teacher learning. The training of such parts in the context of integrated practice is focused on practical based activities of teacher preparation. In a good teacher education programme, the most meaningful practices for beginner teachers are identified in the initial stage. The pupil-teachers are engaged in carrying out those practices which have highest leverage for them. The practices highlighting such essential components of teaching are nurtured under the expert supervision of teacher educators. The scaffolding takes place in the initial stage of teaching practices. On successful completion of initial practices, the pupil-teachers take up complex practices through their own initiatives.

The practice of specific instructional activities include teacher educators' role in a cycle of presentation-demonstration-scaffold planning-coached rehearsal-teaching-debriefing for promoting of skilled practice by the pupil-teachers.

Settings for Learning Practice

Creation of setting for pupil teaching and learning practice is a key element of teacher development. There are instances of 'Virtual Settings' or digital environments that help in observation of practices, analysis of recorded data in visual and audio form with hints for improvement. Such practices focus on specific teaching practices before taking the pupil-teachers for training in real school situations. There are different practices adopted in teacher preparation like model school practices or experimental school practices, demonstration lessons or critique lessons, or laboratory classes. Such practices may have limitations in their utility for real classroom experiences, however, they are promoted in teacher education programme from the pragmatic perspectives. Real school based practicum as promoted in teacher education programmes are highlighted in the following sections:

Guided Inquiry Based Teaching Practices

Since internship based teacher preparation is flexible and context-specific in nature, a framework of human interaction in practice teaching and competency development of teachers is considered with great significance. In this context, a model for teacher inquiry developed by Flander (1987) has been very much relevant for strengthening pupil-teachers practice teaching experiences. Its major focus was on human interaction based activities through practice teaching can be associated with students' learning outcome. Similarly, human interaction based activities among pupil-teachers and supervisor leads to teacher learning on the basis of student-teachers' classroom interaction and classroom teaching outcome.

To clarify human interaction based teaching-learning, Flanders highlighted that the objectives, subject content, and instructional materials, students' and pupil-teachers' abilities and their expectations played a major role in practice teaching, i.e. in the form of human interaction between pupil-teachers and students. Such human interaction oriented practices lead to achievement of students' learning. Similarly, the nature of teaching competencies, training objectives, pupil-teachers' abilities, supervisors' abilities and their expectations and students' learning through practice teaching influenced interaction between pupil-teachers and teacher educators. Such interaction leads to pupil-teachers' learning. Hence, students learning through classroom teaching practices were linked with pupil-teachers' learning through their interaction with mentors and teacher educators. This model has a lot of implications for internship based teacher preparation. It indicates that understanding student's abilities, expectations, and classroom context must be taken into consideration by pupil-teachers. They must understand their own abilities and expectations from teaching and training. The pupil-teachers' involvement in deciding instructional objectives, organising course content and preparation of instructional materials is very much crucial to teaching and training. Similarly, the teacher educators understanding their own abilities and expectations from practice teaching are also considered significant in the context of pupil-teachers' learning. Hence, more opportunities for human interaction among school students, pupil-teachers, mentor teachers and supervisors can contribute significantly to development of pupil-teachers' professional qualities. It also signifies that pupil-teachers and supervisors self-development is very much linked with their understanding of own abilities and expectations from teaching and training. The human interaction leading to learning outcome of students taught by pupil-teachers are subject to reflection of pupil-teachers and supervisor. Such interaction may lead to context-specific teaching practices by encouraging student-teachers' engagement in effective classroom teaching.

School Internship

The value of teacher training to deal with real classroom situation is to be linked with training practices in real school environment. Hence, the concept of school internship is considered as an essential component of current teacher preparation programme. The provision of practice in laboratory/experiment at schools and internship play a significant role in teacher education. The would-be teachers get familiarised with the school situations. They are engaged in instructional practices which involve pupil-teachers competencies in identifying instructional objectives, selecting content of learning experiences, choosing appropriate methods and approaches, doing classroom organisation, development of instructional and evaluation materials, making decisions about assessment of learning outcomes during the progress of teaching units and at the end of course etc. Teaching practice need proper observation of effective classroom teaching and conducting teaching practices with appropriate plan in the understanding of teaching. Such activities are promoted through internship programmes.

The internship based teacher learning is more close to reflective model of teaching-learning unlike applied science model, where the theoretical knowledge is applied through teacher practices. The applied science model projects application of scientific knowledge and experimentation to achieve clearly defined learning outcome. The pupil-teachers' reflective practice is minimised in such approach. Wallace (1991) developed reflective model where both scientific basis of profession is integrated with practical experience based knowledge. Teachers' content knowledge, pedagogic understanding, skills, and language clarity give shape to professional knowledge. Experience of teachers in dealing with varied teaching-learning situations also form a knowledge base for teaching. Theoretical knowledge combined with practical knowledge leads to teachers' action in complex situation. A reflective teacher focuses on his action and search new meaning out of it. In other words, through reflection teacher understands and explains the relationship between the process measures with learning outcome. It further leads to refinement of competencies of teachers and changes in student learning.

Theoretical Perspective of School Internship

The theoretical base of school internship is linked with learning taking place at teacher education institutions (TEI) and activities carried out at neighbouring schools. The collaboration between teacher education institution and practising school provides sound field experiences to the teacher trainees. At first, teacher education institutions equip teacher trainees with knowledge and skills necessary to work in school situation. Second, teaching practices takes place in practising schools. Teaching learning at TEI and practicing schools must be interrelated with each other. The experiences gained through school internship strengthen pupil-teachers' understanding of school system. Simultaneously, student-teachers' multiple exposures to theoretical understanding and its application in context specific situation enable them to construct new meaning to knowledge generated through practical experiences. Hutchinson (2008), highlighted school based learning of teacher trainees and teacher education institution aim at a common objective, that is dealing with learning of students in the classroom. While theoretical understanding of pedagogy is covered as course activity in TEI, the practical experience based understanding of pedagogic principles takes place in the schools. School internship must facilitate socio-cultural learning of students' teachers working in collaboration with the functionaries of school system, with available resource support and shared practices in school set-up.

There have been discussions over innovative approaches of teacher education from socio-cultural behaviour perspective of teaching. Korthagen *et al.* (2006) focused on the concept of teacher learning as multidimensional in nature since cognitive, affective and motivational sources of behaviour are intertwined and socially embedded. Teacher learning must involve meaning-oriented reflection on different practices carried out in teaching-learning situations. Teacher learning need not be viewed as acquisition of pre-decided skills; rather, it should gear towards adoption of knowledge for problem solving in real classroom situations. Teachers should not only focus on use of new techniques and approaches for enhancement of students' learning, rather, they must understand why the practice worked and what conditions are necessary and sufficient for success (Frank *et al.*, 1998).

Hence, during internship, there must be opportunity for reflective inquiry by student-teachers on their own teaching practices in the context of students' learning. This should lead to practitioner student-teachers to construct meaning on their own rather than just following a schedule designed by the supervisors and mentors, so that the student-teacher grows through development of new knowledge and images during internship.

Development of student-teachers identity with the role of a teacher requires appropriate exposure to conducive environment of school community. Better the opportunity provided to student-teachers to interaction with school community better result is perceived in inculcation of identity with teaching community. It requires social approach of learning in real school situation. Identity is understood as an evolving process. It should be nurtured by continuous exposure of student-teachers' classroom practices and other related activities in a school, for a longer duration. During school internship, the situated learning practices are emphasised through legitimate peripheral participation of student-teachers in the company of experienced school teachers. Initially, they practice peripheral activities of the school. Such activities may be simple as well as productive in nature. The teacher trainees must get acquainted with the tasks, language and organising principles of teaching community during internship. Through social interaction over time the teachers learning can take place in real situation (Lave & Wenger, 1991).

Another significant perspective of school internship is reflective learning of teacher trainees. Reflective learning perspective opposes predetermined and pre-sequenced procedures of teaching practices.

It highlights context sensitive action on the part of teacher trainees grounded in intellectual thought. Teacher trainees are not passive transmitters of techniques in solving problems. On the contrary, they are considered as problem solvers through context specific planning.

Farrel (2012) highlighted "the nature of reflective practice enabling teachers to stop, look and discover where they are at the moment and then decide where they want to go (professionally) in future." Participatory approach of learning encourages problem solution and self-evaluation of the participant teachers. Reflective teaching encourages teacher trainees' collaborative learning with context sensitivity. The teacher trainees' involvement in the practices of reflection on their action in routine activities can orient themselves on their future role as teachers. Hence, reflective practice is considered as the basis of school internship. Behera (2018) concluded that by embracing reflection in learning, the student-teachers will be in a position to accept responsibility for own growth, link efforts with experts with benefits, see value in each learning experience and add new skills over time.

On the basis of NCFTE 2009, the NCTE formulated norms and guidelines for school internship programmes. It highlighted provision for sustained engagement of student-teachers with learners and school, thereby, creating a synergy with schools nearer to TEIs. The student-teachers need to be equipped through internship to cater to needs of diverse learners in schools. The teacher education programme shall also include visits to innovative centres of pedagogy and learning, innovative schools, educational resource centres and teaching-learning centres. The duties of the teachers and their community involvement as highlighted in Rights to Education of Children will also be focused especially as school internship practices of elementary teachers.

School internship includes classroom observations, observations of activities organised in the school campus, participation in preparation of school timetable, planning of school activities, maintenance of school records, library management etc. The major focus is on experiencing the school on its entirety, inclusive of classroom teaching, organisation of activities outside the classroom and parent interaction. The student-teachers' engagement in planning, conducting and assessing meaningful classroom teaching and other activities should be motto of school internship. Observation of classroom activities, record keeping, maintaining reflective journals, preparing comprehensive evaluation reports and continuous interaction with peers, mentors and supervisors are some of the key features of internship. Such practices promote reflective thinking of student-teachers on the practices adopted during internship. For successful outcome, there must be suitable mechanism for mentoring, supervising, tracking and assessing the student-teachers by the teacher education institutions and the participating schools. Of course, it depends on the initiatives of TEI for quality enhancement of teacher education programme.

The experiences of Indian teacher education programmes reveal very much hazy picture of internship programmes that is mainly linked with its management component, TEI school commitment and collaboration, building resource centre based learning environment, collaborative approach of learning, supervision system monitoring, feedback and evaluation mechanism etc.

Professional Quality Oriented Teacher Education

In view of making teacher education effective and relevant to the need for quality schooling, proper emphasis must be laid on development of professional competencies of teachers. In this regard, integration of general education and teacher education must be reflected in the structure and functions of teacher education. Equal emphasis must be led on mastery of own discipline, strong theoretical background of education cutting across the varied fields of cognate disciplines, curriculum, pedagogic principles and applications, and hands on experiences through school internship. Even though 4-5 year duration is allocated to teacher preparation, such exposure cannot suffice to cope up advanced knowledge and applications in education. Therefore, initial teacher education must not be considered as end itself. At international level this has been recognised that professional development is a long-term process. Regular opportunities must be provided in a planned manner to promote professional development among teachers. Pre-service teacher education and professional development practices among working teachers must be perceived with inclusive approach. Many kinds of activities like study groups; action research and portfolios need priority in such process. The NCTE curriculum framework for teacher education (2009) insisted on development, of courses, of short and long duration on development of specific skill or areas of interest of teachers. There can be different strategies of developing need based teacher education curriculum in decentralised form. One of such strategies can focus on blended learning approach to link experiential learning in support of advanced information system back up through ICT. Collaborative efforts must encourage for engagement of teachers' forums in design of need based curriculum, its implementation and evaluation for enrichment of knowledge and skills of working teachers. Open Distance Learning mode professional development programmes have been considered as internal component of teacher education system. There is an urgency to encourage workplace based teacher development programmes on a continuous basis through this mode. This will promote ICT support base for experiential and constructive learning of teachers. Professional experiences can be nurtured through wider networking of teachers, teacher educators and experts from other disciplines and professions. This requires a change in attitude towards the potentials of ODL mode in teacher development both at initial level as well as at post-employment stage of teachers. A suitable combination of ICT based knowledge resources, exposures to practical experiences concerning teacher competency development and hands on experiences of school internship can promote professional development among teachers. Opportunities for sharing of experiences and feedbacks through interaction with peers, supervisors, practicing school mentors and school students must be available through proper management of teacher education programmes. In this context, it is worthwhile to refer Justice Verma Commission Report on Teacher Education (2012) that "the national professional standards for teacher education programmes delivered through purely face to face mode and blended mode should be adhered to across both modes, ensure enabling conditions."

In continuation to this, the National Education Policy draft (2019) appears to be meaningful to promote flexible and modular approach of continuous professional development for teachers. Such courses may be available in blended and online form. The provision for multiple models of integrated teacher education programmes at preparatory stage must have sound discipline background along with exposure to professional experiences in real school situation. Teacher education programmes must be linked with proficiencies needed to deal with real school system with inclusive approach. The integration of knowledge base with school based practice can enhance professional quality of teacher learning.

REFERENCES

Anderson, Lorin W. (2004). *Increasing Teacher Effectiveness* 2nd ed. Paris: UNESCO.

Becher, T. (1989). *Academic Tribes and Territories: Intellectual Enquiry and the Cultures of Disciplines*. Buckingham: Open University Press.

Behera, B. (2018), *Readings in Constructivism*. New Delhi: Mittal Publications.

Chong, S. and Cheah, H.M. (2009). "A Values, Skills and Knowledge Framework for Initial Teacher Perception Programmes", *Australian Journal of Teacher Education*, Vol. 34(3).

Corno, L., and Edelstein, M. (1987). "Information Processing Model" in Dunkin, M.J. (eds.) (1987), *The International Encyclopaedia of Teaching and Teacher Education*, Oxford: Pergamon Press.

Deoborah, L.B. & Francesca, M.F. (2009). "The Work of Teaching and the Challenge for Teacher Education", *Journal of Teacher Education*, November 9.

Dunkin, M. (2020). *Teacher Education: Historical Overview,* New York: College Teacher Education Encyclopaedia. Accessed on 12.5.2020. Press https://www. Encyclopedia.com

Dunkin, M.J. (ed), (1987). *The International Encyclopaedia of Teaching and Teacher Education.* Oxford: Pergamon Press.

Dunkin, M.J. (1987). "Teaching: Art or Science?" In Dunkin, M.J. (eds.) (1987), *The International Encyclopaedia of Teaching and Teacher Education.* Oxford: Pergamon Press.

Farrel, T.C.S. (2012). "Novice-Service Language Teacher Development: Bridging the Gap Between Pre-service and In-service Education and Development". *TESOL Quarterly, 46*(3).

Flanders, N.A. (1975). "Human Interaction Models in Dunkin", M.J. (eds.) 1987, *The International Encyclopaedia of Teaching and Teacher Education.* Oxford: Pergamon Press.

Franke, M.L. *et al.* (1998). "Understanding Teachers Self-sustaining Generative Change in the Context of Professional Development". *Teaching and Teacher Education, 14*(1).

Furlong, J. (2014). *Education—An Anatomy of the Discipline,* New York: Routledge.

Gage, N.L. & Winne, Phillip (1975). *Performance based Teacher Education* in K. Ryan (eds.) Teacher education, 74th Year Book of the National Society for the Study of Education. Part. II, Chicago, IL: University of Chicago Press.

Gage, N.L. (1968). "Can Science Contribute to the Art of Teaching?", *Phi Delta Kappan,* 49.

Gage, N.L. (1987). *The Scientific Basis of the Art of Teaching,* New York: Teacher College Press.

Gaible, E., & Burns, M. (2005). *Using Technology to Train Teachers: Appropriate Uses of ICT for Teachers Professional Development in Developing Countries.* World Bank: Washington DC.

Hitchens, H.B. (1985). "Educational Technology: Professional Associations" in Husen, T., and Poslethwaite (eds). *The International Encyclopaedia of Education,* Vol. 3. Oxford: Pergamon Press.

Houston, W.R. (1987). "Competency based Teacher Education in Dunkin", M.J. (eds.)(1987), *The International Encyclopaedia of Teaching and Teacher Education,* Oxford: Pergamon Press.

Houston, W.R. (eds.)(1974). *Exploring Competency Based Education,* California: McCutchan.

Hutchinson, S. (2008). *Boundaries, Bricolage and Student Teacher Learning.* Unpublished Ph.D. Thesis, The Open University, U.K.

Jonassen, D.H. (1996). *Computers in the Classroom Mind Tools for Critical Thinking,* New Jersey: Prentice Hall Inc.

Joyce, B.R. and Weil, M. (1990). *Models of Teaching,* New Jersey: Prentice Hall (Indian Reprint).

Kerlinger, F.N. (1973). *Foundations of Behavioural Research*, 2nd Edition, New York: Holt, Rinehart & Winston.

Korthagan, F., Loughran, J. & Russel, T. (2006). "Developing Fundamental Principles for Teacher Education Programmes and Practices". *Teaching and Teacher Education, 22*(8).

Lamdsheere, G.D. (1987). "Concepts of Teacher Education", in Dunkin, M.J. (eds.) (1987), *The International Encyclopaedia of Teaching and Teacher Education*, Oxford: Pergamon Press.

Lave, J. & Wenger, E. (1991). *Situated Learning: Legitimate Peripheral Participation*. New York: Cambridge University Press.

MHRD, Government of India (2020). *National Education Policy*, New Delhi: MHRD.

MHRD, Government of India (2012). *Justice Verma Commission Report on Teacher Education*. New Delhi: MHRD.

Mishra, P. & Koehler, M. (2006). "Technological Pedagogical Content Knowledge: A Framework for Integrating Technology in Teacher Knowledge", *Teacher College Record, 108*(6).

NCTE (2009). *National Curriculum Framework for Teacher Education*, New Delhi: NCTE.

Passi, B.K. (1976). *Becoming Better Teacher: Micro Teaching Approach*, Ahmedabad: Sahitya Mudranalay.

Ray, P.K.S. (2014). *Technology of Instructional Design*, Part 1, New Delhi: Dominant Books.

RIE, Mysore (1998). *Identification of Essential Competencies for Primary Education Teacher*, Mimeograph.

Robertson, E. (1987). "Teaching and Related Activities", in Dunkin, M.J. (eds.) (1987), *The International Encyclopaedia of Teaching and Teacher Education*, Oxford; Pergamon Press.

Schon, D. (1983). *The Reflective Practitioner: How Professionals Think in Action*, London; Temple Smith.

Senapaty, H.K. (2014). "Technology Mediated Constructivist Learning", in Sahoo, P.K. *et al.* (eds.) *Quality Education in India*, Vol. 2, New Delhi: Concept Publishing Company Pvt. Ltd.

Smith, B.O. (1987). "Definitions of Teaching", in Dunkin, M.J. (eds.) 1987, *The International Encyclopaedia of Teaching and Teacher Education*, Oxford: Pergamon Press.

Yadav, M.S. and Lakshmi, T.K.S. (2003). *Conceptual Input for Secondary Teacher Education*. NCTE: New Delhi.

3

Concept of Teaching

N.K. Dash

Teaching is a familiar term to most of us. It is majorly understood as a process of interaction between teacher and learners in a schooling system. It means that all those activities performed by a teacher both inside and outside the classroom legitimately constitute teaching. Such a notion of teaching is not only widely accepted but also is given a legitimate value by both the society as well the nation. One cannot disagree with such a well accepted notion of teaching, however, conceptually and philosophically the meaning of teaching transcends beyond what goes in a schooling system. Conceptually, teaching has a broader connotation than what it is understood in schooling context. Teaching starts right from the infancy stage of an individual. A child is introduced to several concepts by her mother. For example, a child is introduced to the concepts of father, grandfather, brother, sister (concepts dealing with family relationships) and concrete concepts like cat, dog etc. by her mother during infancy. The child learns many of these initial concepts through a cognitive process which establishes a connection between visual message and verbal message. For example, whenever a cat passes through the cradle wherein the child is placed, the child receives the visual image of the cat along with the verbal message of the mother about cat when she says cat is passing by.

This is the first stage of what constitutes teaching in an individual' life. Very aptly, therefore, mother is called the first teacher of a human being. As the child moves on, she encounters several social environments which act as great teaching agents. She learns from neighbourhood, peer group, community members. Therefore, teaching can be understood as a broad social phenomenon.

The very fact that family plays a great role in teaching is evident from several examples of intellectuals who reportedly did not attend formal schooling. Rabindranath Tagore did not prefer to attend school. James Stuart Mill was taught at home. Our first education minister Abul Kalam Azad was taught at home. Perhaps great Sanskrit Scholar Kalidas did not attend a formal school.

Although, several social institutions play a significant role in moulding human beings through their teachings, the society has created a structured social system, namely, school, to impart its well established knowledge to its members through a contrived teaching-learning environment.

A child before entering the schooling system develops a good repertoire of conceptual knowledge through her encounters with several social as well as natural settings which forms the basis of her engagement in further intellectual discourse in a schooling system. Henceforward, we will deliberate on understanding teaching in schooling context.

Teaching in schooling context has several understandings or connotations. Majorly, teaching in schooling context is understood as planning and delivering a lesson on a topic from a particular subject area. Classroom teaching involves delivering a lecture, engaging students in question-answers, providing feedback on students' responses, managing classroom ecology, assessing learners' progress etc. All these activities pertaining to teaching characterise the features of teaching. Let understand the characteristics of teaching.

Characteristics of Teaching

1. *Teaching is essentially an act of transacting the learning experiences*

Teaching is essentially an act of transacting the learning experiences which have been codified in the form of curriculum or syllabus prescribed by a centralised governmental agency like Board of Education or a University. In most school teaching, a teacher is expected to transact contents in a given subject within the calendar year. This means that if a teacher has completed the syllabus of a subject, she has done her job of teaching that subject. This seems to be understanding of teaching as equivalent to completion of a syllabus. Teaching is much more than completing a given syllabus. It involves providing all those leaning experiences both codified and not codified in a given syllabus.

2. *Teaching is an art as well as a science*

Teaching is considered as an art as a good teacher can lead his students with his inborn abilities like imagination, creativity, critical thinking, motivation, inspiration etc. on the trajectory of student learning. Along with the innate abilities, a teacher follows the scientific steps of both planning and delivering teaching. Most teachers are familiar with Herbartian steps of planning and executing teaching. Of late, most teachers follow 5e or 7e model of constructive lesson planning and delivering classroom lessons. In either case, a teacher follows a systematic process of delivering lesson. Therefore, it is rightly called a science as science follows systematic process to arrive at a solution.

3. *Teaching can be direct as well as indirect*

In classroom, when a teacher teaches her students, she is directly engaged with them. She delivers lectures to them, asks questions, provides feedback on students' responses, maintains eye contact with them, motivates them, manages their behaviours and assesses their progress through her teaching. This can be understood as direct teaching.

Very often, the teacher plays an indirect role in teaching her students. For example, when a teacher gives students some assignments, project work or fieldwork, she is not directly teaching them as students learn on their own, of course, supported by her. Similarly, many co-curricular activities like organisation of school annual day, school exhibition, sports day, cultural functions etc. teacher plans the activities along with students but students execute such activities. Therefore, such teaching is considered as indirect teaching.

4. *Teaching results in desirable learning behaviour*

It is widely presumed that any act of teaching leads to some changes in human behaviours. These changes may pertain to cognitive or affective or psychomotor domains of human abilities. Therefore, in schools it is ensured that students' abilities in all three domains are developed. Apart from classroom engagement, students are involved in sports, dramas and social service activities.

5. *Teaching can be vertical as well as horizontal*

When a teacher teaches a topic and goes deep into the various aspects of the topic navigating students thinking processes from knowledge, understanding levels to application, analysis and evaluation levels, she is essentially involved in vertical teaching. On the other hand, if she is more focused on completing several topics without deliberating deeply on them, she is apparently engaged in horizontal teaching.

6. *Teaching can be planned as well as unplanned*

In a structured learning environment like classroom, teaching is considered as a planned activity. This is the basic premise on which all teacher education programmes are conceptualised and delivered to prospective teachers. Student teachers are taught how to prepare lesson plans and carry out practice teachings so that they are made ready to teach in a school system. Hence, school teaching is done with prior planning by the teacher. But during classroom teaching, a teacher may face several situations which force the teacher to deviate from her plans and engage students as per their learning requirements. This is because a class comprises students with diverse socio-cultural backgrounds, cognitive abilities, emotional intelligence etc. Students with these diversities bring several prior learning experiences which make the teacher scrutinise her own plan and effect required changes. Hence, teaching deals with planned and unplanned, expected or unexpected, predicted or unpredicted structured or unstructured learning situations.

Let us now understand the relationship between teaching and learning, teaching and instructions, teaching and training, teaching and indoctrination.

Teaching and Learning

There is a close relationship between teaching and learning. All teaching activities are primarily organized to bring in some kind of learning or desirable behaviour in the learners. If teaching does not yield desirable behaviour, it is not considered as teaching even though the basic processes of teaching and learning are involved. The manifested behaviours must be socially desirable and acceptable. Hence, anti-social behaviour may not come under the scrutiny of teaching.

Although teaching leads to learning, learning may occur independent of teaching. It may be a necessary condition for learning but is not an absolute condition. Learning may occur due to unique innate dispositions of the learner. It may occur due to other sources. There are instances where many students exhibit better performances even though they have not attended to lectures of their teachers.

Of late, there has been increasing understanding of the role of a teacher as a facilitator of learning. In fact, the scrutiny of all learning theories also point out to the fact that learning is a gradual progression towards achievement of desirable behaviour wherein teacher acts as a facilitator.

If we closely examine Thorndike's theory of trial and error, Skinner's operant conditioning, Ausubel's advance organiser, we find that all these theoreticians are essentially engaged in navigating the action of learners towards achievement of expected behaviour.

With the wide acceptance and implementation of constructivist method of teaching and learning, there is increasing pronouncement of the role of a teacher as a facilitator of learning. Lev Vygostky, the pioneer of social constructivism, clearly demarcates the role of a teacher as a facilitator of learning than a cause of learning. To him, learning is acquired when a child constructs her own knowledge. He underlies the importance of socio-cultural context and language in the construction of new knowledge. In his famous 'Zone of Proximal Distance', he clearly delineates the role of a teacher who facilitates learner to navigate from potential leaning stage to desirable learning stage. Moreover, he broadens the concept of a teacher by talking about More Knowledgeable Others (MKOs). To him, whoever or whatever facilitates a leaner to reach learning goals can be considered as a teacher. To conclude, we can say that teaching facilitates learning.

Teaching and Instruction

Teaching and Instruction is interchangeably used as the same. Not only in practice, but also in literature, both terms are used as synonyms. However, there is certain subtle difference between these terms. Instruction takes place in a controlled and contrived environment with proper planning, execution and assessment. The same thing also happens in the case of teaching in a schooling system. But teaching is not confined to controlled and contrived learning environment. It can happen even in an uncontrolled and natural learning environment. For example, in day-to-day life, human beings learn a lot from different sources which are informal, and natural. In peer group, neighbourhood, market places, historical places etc. we learn a lot without any kind of pre-planned and structured learning experiences.

Teaching and Training

Teaching and training also are considered to be on the same scale in the context of formal education system. Training is essentially concerned with skill development. For example, when we talk of training courses in typing or in computer, we mainly focus on the requisite skills to be developed in typing or in computer. But teaching, although involved in various skills development, goes beyond in its scope and operation.

It aims at holistic development of human personality. It addresses the concerns of developing abilities in all three domains. Therefore, conceptually teaching is broader than training.

Teaching and Indoctrination

In indoctrination learner confirms to the predetermined instructions without raising any questions to such information. Non-conformity is considered as rebellion. There are examples such as how a learner has to abide by what has been instructed to him/her; and s/he has to follow them. In Communist governmental system, a leaner has to follow what is decided by the state. Even such things happen in other governmental systems, where political ideologies play a critical role in influencing education system. Even in different cultural systems, this seems to manifest very often. But, this conformist behaviour does not happen in teaching as there is a lot of scope to question what a teacher teaches. A learner can refute the teachings of a teacher. A learner assumes the role of an equal partner in the teaching-learning process. However, reformers and intellectuals very often bring in changes in an indoctrinated social environment. For example, Galileo and Socrates brought in changes in the then established notions prevailing in the Greek society. Even in the Indian context we know how Raja Ram Mohun Roy brought social reforms in the then conformist society.

Distance and Online Teaching

Teaching has been considered as a face-to-face engagement between teacher and learners in a formal learning environment right from the beginning of human civilization. During the last century due to several pressing reasons like unable to attend regular classroom due to joining jobs in early age of life, democratization of educational opportunities to masses etc. teaching is being imparted through distance learning mode. It started with correspondence education and later on graduated to distance education during the past decades. In distance education, students are taught through self-learning materials developed by teachers and supported with a variety of technologies like audio-video programmes, radio and television broadcast, teleconferencing etc.

Of late, with advancement in digital technologies like computer, internet, mobile etc., there has been increasing focus on teaching through different Internet tools. This teaching, popularly called as online teaching which has been gaining momentum during the past few years. Several educational institutions, both public and government, have been vigorously engaged in developing online courses and offering them to prospective learners across the globe. With the development of several software and mobile apps, online teaching is reaching billions of learners throughout the world. Online teaching attempts to embody all the characters of face-to-face teaching like delivering lectures, engaging learners in live interactions, providing feedback on their responses, assessing their performance through several digital tools like email, discussion forums, chat groups, and different types of social media. Although there have been attempts to provide the same kind of learning experiences as those provided through face-to-face mode to learners through online teaching. Menon (2020) states that didactic teaching is the segment that is largely amenable to online and digital forms of transaction. He further states, "Learning in higher education means much more than this. It involves development of analytical and other intellectual skills, the ability to deconstruct and critically evaluate given knowledge." Therefore, he emphasizes, "All these assume direct human engagement, not just student-teacher interaction, but also peers' interaction. The above analysis point out the limitations of online teaching and learning, though he has not discarded the potential of online learning. We may agree that digital technologies or digital platforms have been created to perform designated functions. Therefore, a digital technology or digital platform needs to be used for those teaching functions which can be performed satisfactorily. The dynamics involved in face-to-face teaching is certainly different from virtual teaching and learning. Hence, there has been advocacy for creating a hybrid model of teaching which combines both digital learning and face-to-face teaching. This seems to be the emerging trend so far as teaching-learning system in educational systems in the immediate future is concerned.

REFERENCES

IGNOU (2013). "Unit-1: Understanding Teaching and Learning", in *BES-002: Teaching-Learning and Assessment*, New Delhi: IGNOU.

Menon, S.B. (2020). "Limitations of Online Learning", in *The Hindu*, April 30.

4

Education in Quest of Identity

Role of Teacher Education

D.R. Goel

Since ages the universe has been concerned of Education. All were having access to Education for sharing their states. Educationists were universally respected. Now the scenario is changing. Why Education is losing its identity? All of us have largely failed in realizing identity of Education. Rather than other seeking guidance from Education, Education is being invited to receive dictations from State and Judiciary. Arbitrary policies and judicial over-activism are likely to damage Education. There is evident identity crisis of Education. It is high time for Education to realize its Identity. The question is why the identity crisis?

There is crisis of character. Soul of Education is being killed through ruthless expansion and privatization leading to marketing of Education. Market is being perceived as the arbiter of morality. Blind ultra-modernization has resulted into the corrosion of Eastern Values. We have lost our sensitivity to the basic values and SANSKARAS. The soul provides energy, whereas the SANSKARAS provide *modus operandi*, but, the unbridled marketing of Education has reduced Education to a commodity to be brought and sold mechanistically in the market. Expression without essence and laughter without resonance are worthless. Convocation without invocation is useless. Graduates and Post-Graduates, degrees of a degree are of little value. Degrees do not guarantee achievement. Achievement is a function of variety of factors in which Knowledge, not merely Degree, is one of the elements. What is the use of humanity degree which does not develop decency, decorum and discipline and fails to process us as human beings? What is the use of Science degree which does not reconstruct in us open minded scientific outlook? What is the use of law degrees if there is lawlessness. What is the use of Political Science Degrees if we fail to develop Statesmen? What is the use of Art which fails to manifest thematic creative expression? Mathematical formulas are empty and mechanistic if these fail to represent the reality. Social Science degrees which fail to produce Social and Civic Personalities and Citizens are of gross wastage. What is the use of the Doctor of Philosophy Degree if we fail to philosophize? What is the use of elections if we fail to find and elect RAJRISHIS?

Let us recall integral humanism of Sri Aurobindo and holistic Man of Vedic Period where the emphasis has been on holistic education for man-making: Physical, Mental, Social, Spiritual, Environmental and finally, universal being. Here we recall the efforts of Prof. T.N. Kapoor, Former Vice-Chancellor, Punjab University Chandigarh, who insisted that Principles and Philosophies of Education be taught even to the Commerce students.

Identity of Education

1. Education is not even considered an entity.
2. There is Public and Private Dichotomy in Indian Education.
3. Education has evidently failed to justify its nomenclature as Elementary, Middle and Higher.
4. Foundations of Education are becoming weak. There is degeneration of Educational Institutions rather than rejuvenation.

5. There are evident gaps amongst Input, Process and Output Norms.
6. There is more of Stereotyping and less of Innovation.
7. Mass Media in Education are either underutilized or not utilized.
8. There is more of a media crowd than media culture.
9. Present VIDYA lacks GUNVATTA.
10. Our Education is least functional.
11. Our emphasis is more on data, information and knowledge and less on wisdom.
12. There are more of unidirectional presentations and less of reflective dialogues.
13. There is little convergence amongst State, Society and Education.
14. TQM of Education is more of a slogan.
15. There are problems of Maintenance—Preventive, Corrective, Adaptive and Perfective.
16. There is adhocism in Education.
17. There is least focus on Value Education, Peace Education and Health Education.
18. There is no accountability of Return on Investment in Education.
19. There are problems in the entire Educational Management Information System Series.
20. Academic Performance Indicators need to be worked out more carefully.
21. Assessment and Accreditation Criteria need to be perfected.
22. Most of our Education Convocations are without Invocation.
23. Teacher Education has become the weakest link in Indian Education.
24. There is less focus on the Professional Development of Teachers.
25. Our Education is lacking in both the hard skills and soft skills.

26. There are wide gaps between developmental challenges and educational determinism.
27. We have failed grossly to sustain our Educational Heritage.
28. Our Education is impersonal rather than Personalized.
29. Our Education ceases to be holistic.
30. Research is scattered rather than interconnected.
31. Research is descriptive and evaluative rather than suggestive.
32. Action Research has almost disappeared.
33. We have grossly failed to retain our Pioneers in India.
34. We are more alienated than participatory.
35. Our creative faculties are not duly nurtured.
36. Constructivism is more talked of than practiced.
37. We have failed to promote our Small Scale Industry.
38. The State has started dictating Education.
39. Most of the Educational Administrators are Bureaucrats having little understanding of Education.
40. We have lost sight of our great Saints and Scriptures.
41. Our Education prepares us more for PRAVRTTI than NIVRATTI.
42. There is PAN card. There is AADHAR card. But there is no Education ID.
43. There is evident chaos in the society. Childhood is lost. Youth are wandering. Aged are bewildered.
44. We are indifferent towards Human Development Index and Universe Development Index.
45. There is rarely research for sustainable development.
46. We have more of imitation than original production.
47. Our Education is being governed by neo-liberalism, neo-capitalism and neo-colonialism.
48. Our Choice Base Credit System is for namesake.
49. There is rarely sharing of credits amongst various institutions.
50. We are poor in both internship and entrepreneurship.

Education in Quest of Digital Citizenship

There is a rapid evolution of Technology Pedagogy Content Knowledge. There is a move from dot to globe and point to morphology. But techno-pedagogic culture and quality are wanting. There is an ocean of OERs, MOOCs and all digital resources but, digital culture is wanting. We need to evolve and employ techno-pedagogic principles for e-communication. Rather than duplication and replication we need to enter into the realm of innovations and novel productions. Investing Pubic Exchequer in infinite volumes on digital technology may not have expected returns until we develop digital culture. Digital technology has its own ethos and culture which need to be developed. A large number of Educational Institutions are facing the problem of technology integration and maintenance. There are problems of management and maintenance—preventive, corrective, adaptive and perfective. Returns on investment are very rare.

There is an immediate need to observe techno-pedagogy, rather than producing the programmes arbitrarily. The scripter, director, producer, cameramen and the presenter ought to have a lot of understanding. The teleprompter ought to be used as a prompter, rather, than dictator. There ought to be compatible correspondence amongst sender, message, medium and receiver for healthy reach. There is a need to modernize technology in India. TPCK demands our Education System to be Techno-savvy, Pedagogy Expert and Content Master. Techno-Pedagogic Skills should find expression at the operational level.

A large number of the teachers feel alienated and alone in this digital age of networking and globalization. We, the 21st Century Teachers are lost in the realm of technology. We are neither techno-savvy nor info-savvy. We travel through the media crowd without being sensitive to it. We need to modernize temporally, spatially, logically, epistemologically, and technologically. Technology can facilitate our transition from dot to globe and point to morphology. Radio is extension of our voice, TV is extension of our views, computer is extension of our brains, motorbike is extension of our feet, clothes are extension of our skin, cell phones, i-phones, multimedia, i-Pads and e-Books and all other forms of technology are our extension. Technology can multiply the speed and life span. It can facilitate fast, full, meaningful life and living. At the same time, to overpower technological disease and discomfort we need to be sensitive to our basic values. If we fly high speed and high, then we need to learn cybernetically when to and how to exercise breaks.

Technology is well woven in almost all walks of life. But Education is relatively technologically backward. Every teacher should put in efforts to be techno-savvy, because it is Education and Education only which can deploy and integrate technology faithfully with a service motive. Indian teachers are highly adaptive and highly innovative. Very willingly, and passionately they are living the technological era of information explosion and media implosion.

How can life be a network of arrays of numerous skills, where ideas spring, feelings flow, motor creates, spirit reins, and the self-resonates with the sphere in this digital age? We teachers need to learn what to twit, whom to twit, how to twit, when to twit. How do I value face book? How should I construct my face book? Which messages should I yahoo *via* messenger? What should I SKYPE? What should I email? What should I Blog? Less Well's Model-Who, Says What, To Whom, Through Which Channel, and With What Effect needs to be employed in each communication. The communication has become very fast through e-mail and g-mail. We need to exercise instantaneous communication control, because, we cannot communicate and communication is circular and irreversible. Internet—the World Wide Web is a universal network. Innovators and Creators, Crackers and Hackers all reside here. The 21st Century Teacher has to be really perfectly fully complete, otherwise, how to teach the innocent, dedicated, cultured, but, bewildered challenging learners. More is so, because the present day globe is in the grip of self-invited problems. No evidence is required to the effects that the entire globe is facing cyber changes and challenges, Problems and Issues. All the Lockers, Prisons,

Viruses, Bio-meters, CCTVs, Tablets, Capsules and Problems are self-invited. We have more of digital crowd than digital culture. Too much of everything is bad. So the need of the hour is to bring about a healthy equilibrium between the conventional and the digital for the betterment of the society.

Education in Quest of Peace

Peace and Thinking Patterns

Mind has a tendency of wandering. Control on the mind demands inner control, not to be swayed away by any attraction or passion. Nothing can deviate a person with full inner control. We ought to be serene rather than turbulent, calm rather than stormy, expressive and booming rather than depressive and repressive, positive than negative, final and decisive rather than recursive and lurking, neutral rather than polar, modern rather than primitive, cultured rather than ultramodern, socio-centric and ethnocentric rather than self-centric and ego-centric, sharp and decisive rather than blunt and obsessive, wholistic rather than patristic, optimistic rather than pessimistic, happy rather than sad, simple rather than complex, considerate rather than rigid, social rather than unsocial, independent rather than dependent, broad minded rather than conservative, determined and active rather than idealistic and passive, logical rather than irrational, factual and theoretical rather than propositional and hypothetical, creative rather than stereotyped, pioneer than conservative and copier, confident rather than diffident, relaxed rather than stressful, focused rather than deviant, flexible rather than rigid, open rather than closed, resonating rather than stagnant and isolated, constructive and connective rather than destructive and disruptive, innovative rather than customary, resolved rather than engrossed, peaceful rather than disturbed, free rather than confined, striving rather than starving, resolved rather than recursive, final rather than obsessed, normal rather than psychoneurotic, lucid than ambiguous, fruitful than futile, innocent rather than cunning, intuitive rather than peripheral. But, how is to realize such a state? Thinking regulators demand healthy neurons and their interconnections, mental control, spiritual control, control on the motor muscles, simple living and high thinking. Thinking is the cause of both, peace and chaos. Thinking is trainable.

Peace: Real and Evident

Whatsoever is evident is not real, whereas, whatsoever is real is not evident. How to resolve the real and evident dichotomy to be in peace?

Peace: Cause-Effect and Reason

Reason between cause and effect is rarely perfect. Reasoning is never ever ultimate. So are the cause and effect gaps. It is a never ending quest in search of truth. How to reach the truth for the realization of peace?

Peace and Symbiosis

We ought to learn to live together. Rather that treating Mother Nature as a source we have started resourcing her. Rather than adoring nature, we have started exploiting her. Rather than being friendly with the nature we are becoming more and more hostile. We have moved away from naturalism to existentialism, from realism to idealism, from civilization to modernization. We have almost lost our cultural heritage and are becoming mad after modernization. Rather than being symbiotic we have become more and more alienated. Rather than being united we are becoming more and more fragmented. Rather than uniting into peaceful immersion we have shattered into chaos and fragmentation. The emerging question is how to revive peace?

Peace and Learning

Peace is the prerequisite for learning. Unless we are noise free we cannot receive. Without receiving there is no assimilation, reflection and learning. While receiving any stimulus there should be no noise—internal or external. Hence, peaceful state is a must for learning and learning outcome.

Peace and Sacrifice

Let us look at any entity in this universe and how much devotion, dedication and SAMARPAN these have. Be it silken cotton of the Silent Doctor SEMAL, KHAS KHAS and Nectar of POPPY, GULKAND of Rose, Essence and Fragrance of CHAMPA and CHAMELI, Medicine of AMALTASH, NIMBOLI of NEEM, Turpentine Oil of PINE, plight of honey bees, glow of glow worms, functions of insects and beetles. Secret of the universe lies in interrelation, interdependence, SAMARPAN and healthy coexistence.

Peace and Resilience

Variability and Central Tendency or deviation and regression are the realities. It is always desirable that we realize resilience and normal state at the earliest. Sooner it is realized less damaging it is. This is an age of stress and strain. But the state of peace demands instant resilience. There are numerous pressures these days, such as, high blood pressure, low blood pressure, compulsive obsessive neurosis, depression and hypertension, which could be both self-invited and environment offered. We ought to be strong enough not to deviate, if at all we deviate then there must be most efficient resilience.

Peace and Giving and Forgiving

Even in prayers we should make it a habit to report our achievement and contribution, rather than seeking grace. Peace rests in giving and forgiving. Nature is the best teacher who teaches us what to give, when to give, and how to give. We should realize the strength of giving and power of forgiving.

Peace and Unconditional Love and Affection

Peace lies in unconditional love and affection for all. Unconditional love and affection demand thorough knowledge of all. Knowledge base of all demands continuous quest for reality—search and research. Cause and effect relationship demands thorough reasoning. Reasoning is always limited. Even then we can realize unconditional love and affection which peace demands. Re-as-on is a continuous, infinite, never ending chain. We ought to transcend time, space and reason to realize our quest for vision.

Peace and De-becoming

Peace is a blissful journey through be, becoming, being and de-becoming. What we want to be? What are we becoming? What is our being? Even the highest level of knowledge base and wisdom reveal that our being howsoever rich and comprehensive is too wanting and limited. Functional feelings of our being help us identify and locate ourselves in this indeterminate and little known cosmos.

Peace and Justice

Peace demands truthfulness, compassion, forbearance, forgiveness, equity and equality. India is a sovereign, socialist, secular, and democratic republic. Constitution of India observes justice for all. No one has the right to be partial and unjust, irrespective of who we are, politicians or public, capitalists or below poverty line, doctors or patients, secretaries or open. No gap is permissible between democratic and republic, male and female, high and low.

Peace and Bi-polarity

Bipolarity is the open secret of the creation and sustenance of the universe. We need to understand the bipolar and their co-existence, such as, male and female, high and low, positive and negative, peace and chaos, hill and valley, heat and cold, Fire and Ice, Desire and Peace, Rich and Poor, Dare and Fear, Azad and Prisoner, Predator and Prey, Aggression and Depression, Repression and Expression, Laughter and Cry, Thief and Spy, Earth and Sky, Desert and Crowd, Hope and Despair, Abuse and Prayer, APRADHI and FARIYADI, GULAMI and AZADI, Devaluation and Neo-valuation, Saints and Scoundrels, Philanthropists and Dacoits, Producers and Takers, SMARPAN and DARPAN, Sordid Drama and Silent Spectators!

Peace and Happiness

We do not have sensitivity towards HDI, that is, Human Development Index what to talk of Universe Development Index. Human greed of manipulation, possession and hoarding has converted human beings from sources to resources. Return on investment should find expression in the form of peace and happiness.

Peace and Laughter

Laughter sustains and strengthens life by realizing peace. The two main chemicals that are used in when we laugh are Endorphins and Dopamine. Endorphins, the natural happy drugs are released from the pituitary glands into the blood, then into the brain and spine. Also Dopamine chemical is released in the brain and then are sent as signals to the other nerves of the body.

Peace and Tears

Shedding off the tears, sharing the sad state also relieves us of disease and discomfort and helps in realizing peace. We have basal tears, reflex tears and emotional tears. The cornea is continually kept wet and nourished by basal tears. Tear fluid contains water, mucin, lipids, lysozyme, lactoferrin, lipocalin, lacritin, immunoglobulin, glucose, urea, sodium and potassium. Lysozyme fights against bacterial infection. Reflex tears are released during irritation to the eyes say while cutting onion or pepper spray. Negative or positive emotions cause psychic tears. Emotional tears have more of protein based hormones.

Peace and Play

Arriving in the optimum state of energy keeps us calm and cool. Playing any game—Hockey, Cricket, Football, Bad Minton, Table Tennis, Lawn Tennis keeps us happy and gay. Athletics such as, Jump and Race, Disc Throw, Javelin Throw keeps us fit. Climbing up hill and coming down hill helps us sustain momentum. Peace and Play are perfectly interrelated.

Peace and Yoga

Peace begins when everything else ceases to be. Peace is complete *yoga* at the functional level. *Yoga* is that ultimate state of bliss when we are integrated unit self. Peace demands *Gyan Yoga, Bhakti Yoga, Karma Yoga* and *Raj Yoga*. Peace is by realizing which we can DARSHAN entire COSMOS. *Yoga* is the prerequisite for peace.

Peace and Health

Peace and Health are intimately related. Many a health issues, both, physical and mental are on the fore. How to observe sound health? Health, Happiness and Peace ought to be fully observed.

Education in Quest of Health

- Our food habits have changed. There is evident transition from home made food to fast food. It has come to the fore that these preserved foods are largely not hygienic. These usually contain excessive fats and spices and are acidic. Though the food is high calorie, but, it does not provide adequate energy. Also, the preservatives used, such as, nitrogen, chlorine, carbonic acid, vinegar and impure sugar (molasses) are harmful. Also, the refined wheat flour (*Maida*) consumes significantly more time for digestion. The fats overused for frying cause many a health problems. Consumers have changed their tastes as per the tastes of the producers, fair or foul. There is ocean of food stuff, but, non-compatible. What to choose? Where from?
- The entire environ is polluted. There are water pollution, air pollution, soil pollution and noise pollution. Which water to drink, which air to breathe, which vegetables and fruits to eat, and how to find noise free corner? There is environmental awareness but very rare environmental ethics. There is degeneration of environment. With the lust for luxury many a species are disappearing. Fully healthy people are no longer seen. Everyone suffers from one or the other disease. What is the resolve?

- The lifestyles have changed. We have moved from naturalism to existentialism. We have moved from simple living and high thinking to high living and simple thinking, from health is wealth to wealth is health. We are going far away from our heritage and culture. Truthfulness, compassion and forbearance seem to be mere slogans. We are in more of competitive societies than cooperative. The nuclear families have resulted into the alienation of children.
- We are using technology or technology is using us? We have media crowd, but, no media culture. There are many health hazards due to overuse of Technology. It is high time that we become techno-savvy, info-savvy, net-savvy and media-savvy.
- Our greatest disease is passion, possession, obsession. There are many a medical malpractices. There is a need to realize professional ethics.
- Malls are rising in India at a rapid pace, but, we do not have moll culture. Almost every hand has cell phone, A to Z phones, but, we do not have cell culture. Only God knows what we keep communicating round the clock. Health hazards are self-evident. Modernization and perfective maintenance ought to be there. Modernization and perfective maintenance demand precise regulatory mechanisms and controls.
- Each one of us should observe *Yoga* for sound health.
- We need to employ, both preventive and ameliorative measures for sustaining sound health.
- Health Education ought to be integrated with Educational Curricula at all levels, from pre-primary, through tertiary and continuing.
- We should observe healthy Heart and Brain entrainment Ratio.
- We should sustain our smiles and laughter under even the most adverse conditions.

- Human Development Index should be of prime importance for any nation.
- India should come up with Universe Development Index (UDI).
- Various States in India ought to learn from the development of each other.
- India should formulate National Health Policy at the earliest.

Current Educational Scenario

1. Attempts have been made to enrich the curriculum to provide for overall development of children through CCE. With all ifs and buts, with all Haves and Have Not, the CCE has its own Strength and Power. Continuous Comprehensive Evaluation is a Powerful Regulator. The voices of the Children in this context are—"Play Way Activities We Play, The Science We Experiment, The Mathematics We Speculate, Stories We Narrate, Games We Play, Musica/Notes We Generate, Keep Us Healthy and Gay. The continuous flow of the CCE has made our Studies full of life. The CCE has infused energy in all of us, the Teachers, Learners, Parents and the Society. We may be tired after days' work, but, we don't feel tired. CCE is not a burden. It is a band of Rhythm, Rhyme and Resonance. Along with the learners the innovativeness, creativity and efficiency of the teachers also increase significantly. The whole of Primary School System including Watchmen, Support Staff, Sweepers, Gardeners, Mess Staff, Office Staff, Teachers, Learners, Parents, Society, CBSE, the Primary Section Coordinator, School Management and the Principal Madam function synergistically. The entire Primary School System is fully lively and fruitfully functional due to CCE."
2. There is added focus on Multiple Intelligence and Life Skills.

3. Critical Pedagogy has been promoted in various dimensions of the School through. Cooperative Learning, Participatory Approach and Action Research.
4. Rarely attempts have been made to motivate children from marginalized sections of society for expression of their knowledge and skills related to work and to have cumulative human experience along with children from other sections.
5. Rare attempts have been made to develop Citizenship Skills. There is evident rejection of the old and acceptance of the new.
6. There are segregated schools on the bases of Public and Private, Medium of Instruction, Religion, Region, and School Boards. All this segregation has resulted into the fragmentation of the Society. There are marked differences between Municipal Corporation Schools and Private Schools, Native Schools and International Baccalaureates.
7. The private school students may have higher academic achievement, but, they may have ethos related limitations. Very often a non-native language is barrier in constructing knowledge.
8. Even now the children are deprived of the learning opportunities that occur in classroom with children from diverse Socio-Economic and Cultural Backgrounds.
9. A large number of Public Schools still suffer from shortage of facility of infrastructure. It affects adversely not only academic learning but also overall health of the children.
10. There are rare teachers who have both teaching competencies and teaching attitude.
11. Humane and Professional Teachers, both, in one are rarely found.
12. There is a need to redesign Teacher Education Curricula and modes of transaction, as well as, approaches to inculcate universal values, namely truthfulness, compassion and forbearance.

13. Our School Education has to be strong enough to appreciate the preamble of Constitution of India which demands determination and action to constitute, sustain and strengthen India into a Sovereign, Socialistic, Secular, Democratic, Republic State.
14. The sharp disparities between different Social and Economic Groups are everywhere in the perceptible range in India. Even now the children of the disadvantaged groups are educationally most vulnerable.
15. Though we have large number of multi-grade schools based on mechanical principle of Teacher-Pupil Ratio, within 1 kilometre of each habitation, yet, we have not been in a position to provide compatible pedagogy.
16. Child Centred Education is still in infancy.
17. Constructivist Learning Approach has been talked a lot, but, rarely implemented in the schools.
18. Many schools have initiated into Activity Based Approach, but, it needs to be strengthened.
19. Rarely teachers are competent to deal with Inclusive Classes.
20. Diagnosis and Remediation are done rarely.
21. School Stereotypes exist even now, such as, notion of uneducable children, marginalized groups, Gender Type Stereotypes, children with disabilities, first generation learners.
22. Problems of bridging the home language and school language.
23. A vast array of human vocations, such as, weaving, carpentry, farming and occupations, such as, shop keeping constitute a valuable form of knowledge. These forms of knowledge are of practical nature, tacit, but, often only partially articulated.
24. Neither the curricular nor the co-curricular activities are up to the mark.
    - Many a children in English Medium Schools are not at ease with English, worse is the scenario on vernacular.

- Mathematics Teaching-Learning is dull and dry.
- History and Civics are gone.
- No sensitivity to cultural heritage and religious heritage and eastern values.
- Social Sciences seize to have normative responsibility.
- Science is losing Scientific Outlook and In-look.
- Holism is a figment of imagination.

25. Health Education, Human Rights Education, Environmental Education, Art Education, Physical Education, Education for Peace and Harmony have become empty slogans.

Challenges and Reality

1. Manpower Planning is relatively absent in Education. There is remarkable increase in the number of Education Institutions.
2. There are mismatches between the Teaching Degrees and Levels Taught.
3. Some of the States filled new vacancies with Para-Teachers, while trained teachers remained unemployed.
4. In some of the States, such as, MP, Gujarat future teachers in the formal system will be "SHIKSHA KARMIS/ SHIKSHA SAHAYAK" on performance contract.
5. Indian Teachers have been teaching in the Schools in West Asia, particularly, the United Arab Emirates. Mathematics, Science and English Teachers are in maximum demand. Thousands of Secondary School Teachers are already employed in foreign schools.
6. There are problems of Education right from pre-natal stage to old age.
7. Children are losing their beauties of childhood.
8. Children are interested in fast and junk food than home-made food.
9. Children are going far away from nature, because, we have failed in sustaining the beauties of nature.

10. The eastern ethos and sensitivity to the basic values are fading.
11. The entire School Education—History, Civics, Language, Mathematics, Science are losing their essence.
12. The creativity of the children is killed by the schools.
13. There are problems of cell phones and face books.
14. Only God knows what the children Twit and Skype.
15. Adolescents are bewildered. It seems the Sociologists, Psychologists and Counsellors have largely gone defunct.
16. Educational Institutions have started disowning their own Product. What are the SET, NET, TET, TAT representatives of?
17. There is little convergence amongst State, Society, Education and Judiciary.
18. More than Solutions, there are Problems of all sorts of Education—School Education, Teacher Education, Medical Education, Engineering Education, Law Education, Art Education, Science Education.
19. Education, Research and Development are the least priority as is evident through the investment by the State.
20. Apex Institutions, such as, NCERT, NCTE, NUEPA, ICSSR, CIIL, UGC and NAAC have lot of potential but for expression.
21. Health Education and Environmental Education are the most neglected areas.
22. Public at large is indifferent towards Education.
23. Corporate Social responsibility finds rare expression.
24. Rather than holistic, what we have is fragmented Education.
25. There is now here dedicated Teacher Education in India.
26. The identity of Education as highest interdisciplinary is rarely recognized and respected.
27. Content-Pedagogy-Technology integrated Education is a big challenge.
28. Skill Training is lacking. Education is failing to appreciate innovative courses, such as, Taxonomy of Educational Skills.

29. Teacher Education on Life Skills, such as, lateral and critical thinking, innovativeness, problem solving needs to be strengthened.
30. With the implementation of SSA there is relatively better state of Education.
31. We need thorough preparation for Teacher Education at all levels, from Pre-Primary through Higher Education.

Capacity Building Courses in Teacher Education

Courses, such as, follows could be offered:

1. ICT in Education
2. Social Networking
3. Info-Savvy Skills
4. Techno-Pedagogic Skills
5. Teacher in the Digital age
6. Open Education Resources
7. Taxonomy of Educational Skills
8. Taxonomy of Educational Research
9. Educational Research Thrust in India
10. Collective Wisdom of India
11. Researching Pioneer Competency
12. Teacher Competency: Mapping and Management
13. Researcher Competency: Mapping and Management
14. Health Education in India
15. Corporate Social Responsibility and Education
16. Vocational and Occupational Skills
17. Management Skills
18. Life Skills and Attitude
19. Management Skills
20. Adjustment Skills
21. Special Education Skills
22. Human Development Skills
23. Accountability and Adaptability
24. Communication Skills
25. Self-Direction Skills

26. Social Responsibility Skills
27. Human Relations Skills
28. Emotional Skills
29. Spiritual Intelligence Skills
30. Innovation, Creation and Construction Skills
31. Hoilstic Education Skills
32. Interdisciplinary Skills
33. Value Integrated Education
34. Yoga Education Skills
35. Qualitative Research in Education
36. Employing Mixed Research Methodology
37. Development of Tools and Techniques for Educational Research
38. Shifting Paradigms of Teacher Education
39. Quality Indicators of Teacher Education
40. Ensuring Quality of Teacher Education
41. Identity of Education
42. Cultural, Moral and Religious Heritage of India
43. Developmental Challenges and Educational Determinism
44. Status of Educational Predicaments and Constitutional Right to Education
45. Status of Human Development Index in India
46. Universal Happiness Index
47. Status of Teacher Education in India
48. Establishing Equivalence of Teacher Education Modes
49. Formulating Teacher Education Policy
50. Establishing Norms for Teacher Education Parameters
51. Education for the Disadvantaged Groups
52. Inclusive Education
53. Continuous Professional Development of Teachers
54. Career Advancement in Teacher Education
55. Re-visiting Teacher Education Curricula
56. Re-Visiting Act, Norms and Regulations of Teacher Education

57. Establishment of Inter-University Consortiums in Teacher Education
58. Exploring the Possible Roles of State, Society, Education and Judiciary in Teacher Education
59. Research Agenda for Teacher Education
60. Developing Competencies of Teacher Educators for Enhancing Creative Writing Abilities of the Learners
61. ICT Aided Constructivist Approach for Professional Development of Teachers
62. Reflections on the Academic Performance Indicators
63. Indian Consortium of Research in Education and Strengthening Educational Research
64. Action Research as "My Research"
65. Research Synthesis and Meta Analysis
66. Educational Philosophy of India
67. Quality of Indian Teacher Education
68. Manpower Planning in Teacher Education
69. Digital Lesson Designing and Implementation
70. Developing Professional and Humane Teachers
71. School Curriculum Framework and Teacher Education Curriculum Framework
72. Teacher Education: Public and Private
73. Multiple Intelligence
74. Policies and Programmes
75. Assessment through Rubrics
76. Portfolio Assessment
77. Working with Community
78. Symbiosis
79. Participatory Approach of Problem Solving
80. Cooperative Learning
81. E-Learning Packages on various Methods
82. Specialized Teacher Education Programmes
83. Pedagogy: Critical, Reflective and Constructive
84. Teacher Education for Disadvantaged and Differently Abled Groups

85. Physical Education
86. Education for Skill Development
87. Education for Parenting
88. Development of Skills for Food Processing
89. Psychology of Infant, Child, Adolescent, Young, Adult and Ripe
90. Education of Eastern and Western Values.

Suggestions for Teacher Education Programmes

- There should be added focus on Learner Driven Pedagogy—Germination, Incubation, Creation, and Construction and Connection in Teacher Education.
- Identity of each and every Individual entity and Institution deserves recognition; otherwise, we seize to be. While being in greater power, it takes no time to delete, but, it takes life time to construct and connect. Any deletion has to be done more carefully, sensitively and sensibly. History has its own essence. It is not all gone.
- Any General Body of any agency of India, if seeks public opinion on any issue, then the public opinion ought to be duly respected. If public has faith in us, we should also have faith in public. Truthfulness, Compassion and Forbearance are the most beauteous attributes of India. This is how India is known since ages. Such issue based discussions be encouraged in Teacher.
- Courses, such as, Corporate Social Responsibility and Education, Health Education in India, Taxonomy of Educational Skills, Technology Integrated Education, and Inclusive Education ought to be introduced in Teacher Education.
- There should be added focus on *Yoga* Education, Health Education, Peace Education, and Humanity Education in Teacher Education Programmes.
- Digital Culture should be developed right through Elementary Education. Accordingly, the Teacher Education

should gear up for development of such culture among teachers.

- New Education Policy should ban Parallel Private Tuition Classes. The beauties of learning need to be respected. We cannot afford to mechanize learning.
- There should be due focus on both the hard skills and soft skills in our Professional Programmes.
- ICT ought to be fully utilized for sustainable development, that is, Socio-Economic-Environmental development. Teacher education should adopt ICT based education for sustainable development among students and teachers.
- Media culture should emerge out of the media crowd. Due measures have to be taken to control media addiction. There is a need to develop e-civilization.
- Education should develop liberation capabilities through reason, religion and rapport, where, reason is re-as-on knowledge, feelings and skills, because there is no ultimacy of knowledge, feeling and skills. Religion means to be one with the creator and Rapport is unconditional love for all. Such philosophy may be projected among students and teachers.
- The Inter-University Consortium in Teacher Education established at the BHU should be fully functional respecting the ethos of the recommendation of the JVC.
- The Mahamana Madan Mohan Malviya Chair for Cross Border Teacher Education at the BHU should find expression at the operational level. The constituent e-consortium of Cross Border Teacher Education for the Common Wealth Countries should be established at the earliest.
- NCTE—the regulatory body in Teacher Education should be revived without further loss of time.
- India should have immediate focus on Human Development Index and Nature Development Index.

- All the models like, BOOT, BOO, BOT have reasonably failed. There should be systematic efforts for integration of Technology in Education. Digital Culture should be developed more carefully. Teacher Education must promote such kinds of integrated model of teaching and learning.
- Elementary Education should be Elementary in the true sense. We should try our level best to revive and respect the beauties of childhood. We should not look children like programmed machines.
- Some vocations should be mandatory with choice at Secondary and not treat Senior Secondary levels as per National Education Policy, 2020.
- Higher Education has to justify its name as higher. Higher Education by virtue of its identity has to be Innovative. Higher Education should formulate and conduct Research on immediate problems. Teachers of higher education institutions must be professionally oriented on these functions.
- Digital Wave demands immediate Cyber Security. It is ideally desirable to be digital in all areas, but, such a wish and will demands immediate controls. Along with, constructors and connectors the world is full of hackers and crackers. The Teacher Education programmes be cautious about such phenomena.
- There should be immediate focus on Bipolarity in Indian Education. Along with Education our vigilance should be fully awakened, conscious and active.
  - ❖ Digital Testing.
  - ❖ Open Book Test.

Conclusion

The ultimate aim of Education is development of Universal beings. It deals in full, meaningful, happy, healthy, resonating and sustainable life of every organism and entity. There is need to move from Human Development Index to Universe Development

Index. There is a caution that progressively we are becoming market oriented than society oriented, profit oriented than service oriented, resource oriented than source oriented. Technology quotient is trying to superimpose intelligence quotient, emotional quotient, spiritual quotient, health quotient, and environment quotient. We are busy with the reviews than views. We are busy with deletion than construction and connection. It is high time that we revive our heritage and culture which is full of truth, compassion and forbearance. It is high time that we realize SHUBH LABH, that is, hard earned Profit through determination and action with full immersion seeking the beauties of life and living.

5

Teacher Development

A Constructivist Perspective

Biswajit Behera

There has been growing international consensus evidenced in research and in Organisation for Economic Co-operation and Development documents (OECD, 2005) that the quality of teachers matters in improving educational outcomes. This demands teachers are working with diversities. This requires more individualised approaches towards learning and teaching; dealing with computer supported collaborative learning that challenges teachers to think about its use to enhance learning and teaching. The International Education Advisory Board (2013) suggests that twenty first century learning is linked to information technology. 'How people learn' the way is also continuously developing (Bransford, Brown and Cocking, 2000) and has an impact on teachers for their education and development. The emphasis on preparing students as lifelong learners has led to changes in thinking about the ways teachers support learners and learning. OECD (2010) defines new qualities and competencies for 'new millennium learners'. These are identified as critical thinking, creativity, collaboration and Meta-cognition skills. Other affective skills include interpersonal (ranging from active listening to presentation skills to conflict resolution) and intrapersonal skills that helps the learner to equip for adaptability, self-management and self-development.

A quality teacher education in the 21st century needs to address the competence of 'constructive' and 'adaptive' among learners. This includes how learners actively construct their knowledge and skills; using self-regulated strategies to learn; situating in context and collaborative group task. The OECD's Programme for International Student Assessment (PISA) has identified the "need to assess problem solving abilities in order to equip young students with the skills they need for life" (Schleicher, 2011). This guides learning for understanding, that is particularly significant in the present teacher education climate.

These concerns are guiding and challenging teaching and learning through a dynamic combination of instruction and collaboration. For many teachers, these changes have meant re-defining their identity as a teacher. In recognising the importance of teachers in relation to learners it should follow the principle of 'learning how to teach'. This shapes different approaches of initial and continuing teacher education. A research relating to teacher educator's identity has focused on pre-service student-teachers with new teachers during induction periods (Murray, 2008).

Epistemological Consideration of Teacher Education

Teacher Education is unique context to infuse constructivist principles in school education. Teacher Education programme exposes teachers towards individualisation, discovery and open ended questioning. Teacher learning is viewed as opportunities to gain experience about their conceptual change of learning contents. The epistemological base towards preparing teachers includes:

(i) Human being constructs his/her knowledge.
(ii) Learning differs for individuals based on unique biological components.
(iii) Latent learning takes place when individual experiences a cognitive conflict.

(iv) Learning is in control of learning through the process of self-regulation.
(v) Learning is natural process of invention.

Rationale

An aim of teacher preparation should be the development of an ability to reflect on and learn from practical experiences. The integration of theoretical and practical knowledge and the eventual ability to be a reflective practitioner are realistic aims for teacher education programmes. In traditional approach of teacher education, the student-teachers are oriented towards rote knowledge, method of assessment tend to encourage scores. This discourages deep understanding of subjects.

Teaching requires integrating theoretical information with previous practical knowledge. Teachers will require training in high-quality content as well as pedagogy. Therefore, multidisciplinary contents are preferred in relation to the real-life situations of the learners (National Education Policy 2020). This is situated perspective of teaching. It views learning as change in an individual's participation in social activities as a result of acquisition of new knowledge (Lave and Wenger, 1991). Encouraging reflection on teaching practices help pre-service teachers to be innovative and critical of subsequent classroom teaching experiences; thus facilitates their professional experience. The integration of theoretical and practical knowledge can occur by engaging in activities that make implicit knowledge into explicit. Knowledge is generated in the shared context of teaching, learning, personal and social experiences through critical enquiry (NCFTE, 2009). Dewey (2001) once argued that if learning is to be meaningful, it must begin with what is already relevant. He supported qualitative evaluations to ensure students' growth. His proposed pedagogy makes use of student's current knowledge and builds considerate understanding of the domain of instruction. Revised Bloom's Taxonomy (Anderson & Krathwohl, 2001) also accounts for students' understanding, application, analysis, evaluation and creation of ideas.

Biggs (1979) model portrays three key categories of characteristics that must be aligned to create conducive learning environment. The first category consists of characteristics of the students, teacher, and classroom (prestage factors). Process factors are the interaction among students and teaching prestage factors and refer to the ways students' approach to learning. Product factors are the outcomes of student learning.

Social-Constructivist Pedagogy relies on social interaction and collaboration in meaning making. Course content presented through lectures should go along with assignments in which learners must reflect on and use new information. Knowledge is treated as external to the learner and something is to be acquired. Conceptual knowledge is generated based on experience, observations and theoretical engagement (NCFTE, 2009). In constructivist learning environments, assessment methods emphasize the learning process itself and encourage students to engage in reflective activities. Learning is conceived of as conceptual change. Learning is a search for meaning out of personal experience, and knowledge generation as a continuously evolving process of reflective learning (NCF, 2005). Theory as a "given" is to be applied in the classroom (NCFTE, 2009). So, integration of theory with practical knowledge helps in pre-service teachers' programme.

Teachers are responsible for providing opportunities for student interaction and for establishing a climate conducive to student participation. Teachers play as parent and community member to enable students to participate and flourish in the educational system throughout their lives (NCF-SE, 2023). In turn, students are responsible for actively engaging in interactive environments. All members of the teaching community must have a shared purpose and sense of responsibility in order to collectively engage in the learning process. Students' sense of responsibility for learning is not independent from their academic setting. Therefore, institutions should create learning communities that nurture student responsibility. Efforts should be made to increase alignment between student and context.

Constructivist Offerings

Teaching includes in the building of knowledge on systems of:

1. How children interpret the ideas in the subject?
2. What kinds of strategies students invent and use?
3. How to interpret the kinds of errors student make?

Constructivist offerings are structured with a focus to building knowledge on the following arguments:

1. *Complexity and Diversity of Professional Learning*

Professional learning needs with different knowledge, skills and expertise. It is recognised that teaching is becoming more complex and force on teachers' work style (OECD, 2005). Teachers work in local school contexts with diversified student population. They bring various knowledge, skills, values and dispositions to their teaching approaches in order to create learning environments. Quality of teaching is central to the needs of teacher's learning and professional development activity. So, the teachers need to be continuous learners and take greater responsibility for reflecting on the learning. OECD (2011) has suggested that "it is necessary to have both high quality initial teacher education and a coherent process of continuous professional development." Teachers should continuously revise, add to and enhance their knowledge and skills in their learning and teaching approaches. The continuum of teacher education engages teachers as lifelong learners. The teacher education is a process of continuous teacher learning in order to face the challenges of learning practice. It requires reflective practice through research and involvement in systematic professional development activities. Professional learning should meet peer-led and professional dialogue with others which support teacher's learning. It is also suggested that mentoring approaches and practical activities with authentic examples are effective approach for teacher development. This view is embedded with constructivist approach (Vygotsky, 1978) and theories of situated learning and communities of practice (Wenger, 1998). The emphasis is on teachers' engagement in enquiry, reflection, analysis and improve learning and teaching in relation to students' needs.

2. *Teacher Educators Working in Collaboration*

The diversity of learning needs call for a collaborative approach to teacher education. Teacher educators work in collaboration through integrating research and practice to promote innovation in learning and teaching. There is a need to apply collaborative skill to solve problems (Gonzales, Pickett & Hupert, 2002). A sustainable collaborative approach to teacher education requires a shift in system of ongoing teacher practice.

3. *Teacher's Learning and Change in Teacher's Belief*

Teacher's learning depends on their uptake of learning opportunities as well as power of its cognitive processing. The teacher's personal prerequisites such as cognitive skills, motivation and personality influence their uptake of learning opportunities which in turn facilitate the development of teacher (Kunter *et al.*, 2013). Role of emotion and cognition in predicting teachers' conceptual change processes are taken into consideration. Teachers' reflection on their instructional behaviour is considered as critical factor for helping teachers to change their beliefs and practices.

4. *Fostering Reflection during Teacher Education*

Constructivist teaching is embedded in a social context. In this context, groups of learners who share ways of thinking and communicating are called discourse communities (Putnam & Borko, 2000). Teacher discourse communities provide an opportunity to adopt a critical and reflective perspective on their teaching. This offers learning opportunities for novice teachers. One aim of teacher education programme is to develop reflective practitioners. As teachers are not able to reflect spontaneously, student-teachers must be introduced towards reflection during Teacher Education programme.

5. *Nurturing Teachers as Critical Learners*

The learners act on the input through their existing teaching framework. The teacher is viewed as the learner. The critical learning factors depend on teaching. These are as follows:

- Teachers have ideas about teaching before any method of instruction.
- Teacher's preconceptions about teaching are reinforced by early experiences in practicum courses and student teaching.
- Teacher's preconceptions about teaching and learning are not easily changed.

In order to gain meaningful knowledge about teaching, teachers need to recognise regularities, form propositions and restructure their conceptual frameworks (Hollingsworth, 1999). Regulation needs to deal with processes (methods) and contents in an integrated manner. Propositions relate specific student learning parameters, specific teaching strategies (like how to probe student ideas, how to challenge student understandings). Restructuring conceptual framework related to teaching requires that teachers consciously look for evidence of student learning, explore first hand implications for their own teaching and debate their ideas with other teachers.

The emphasis is on construction and transformation of knowledge about teaching. The teacher becomes researcher to study the source and progress of student ideas related to a particular topic. Research takes the pathways of data collection, data analysis and data development phases using student generated concept maps. In this stage, teachers take substantive ideas related to the topic.

Teacher Development on Constructivism

Constructivism approach assumes that there is no transmission from one pole to another. Rather it is personally constructed with scaffold learning environment. It has the perspective of self-monitoring, self-evaluation, cognitive flexibility and self-regulated approach. It emphasises on problem and considers multiple modes of learning. Nix, Fraser and Ledbetter (2003) considered that constructivist teaching models have the following dimensions: personal relevance, student uncertainty, critical voice, shared control and student negotiation. Personal relevance focuses on individual growth, autonomy and meaning to the concepts. Students create meaning through manipulative, asking questions and using relevant past experiences. Teachers who understand student uncertainty are encouraged to make questions in order to gain better understanding. Knowledge is acquired in a social context, that is evolving with human experience. Critical voice is developed by the teacher to foster classroom climate when students' involve in the dialogue (Freire, 1985). Students feel free to ask questions. The teacher's role in constructivist classroom changes from giving information to mediating activities in order to make conceptual understanding of the students. Shared control in the classroom facilitates students' engagement in contrast to teaching practices. It leads to student centred with an emphasis on student input. In such environment shared control is fostered when the teacher accelerates the work through collaboration. Vygotsky (1978) opined that student constructs meaning on an intrapersonal level through practical activity. It creates learning environment. Student negotiation occurs when teachers provide with the opportunity to describe and justify their new ideas about contents. Student negotiation is critical in the discourse of concepts so that students are able to create an understanding based on their current knowledge. Students' negotiation is considered as a key element in building classroom learning environment (Davis, 2006).

Building Constructivist Teaching

Teachers must have strong depth of content knowledge. Many teachers lack a strong belief in the effectiveness of constructivist teaching methods, profound knowledge and skills. It helps teachers to think, rethink and transform thinking towards teacher development programme of constructivist teaching practices. Teachers held beliefs in the area of learner and learning, teaching subjects, learning to teach, teacher's self and teaching role. These areas are interconnected (Voss, Kunter & Baumert, 2011). When teachers create their own questions and means for answering them, then they can construct their own understandings and can bring their classroom improvements. Constructivist paradigm views the 'context' in which learning is processed. Contextualising learner's existing knowledge in designing and developing e-learning programmes proves to be very useful (Vosniadou, 2001).

Constructivist teaching practices encompass the following steps: first, teachers pose problems of current, life-world and relevance. Its nature is multidisciplinary. The students work in-depth to search for answers. Posing problem in front of students' thinking creates classroom settings. Teachers engage students in interdisciplinary collaborative discourse and reality based problem solving. The teachers and students work jointly for the construction of new knowledge. Teachers structure lessons around important ideas and concepts but not facts. Learning occurs in the context. Constructivist teachers look for and value the students' points of view. By understanding students, the teachers develop an instructional strategy which facilitates learning (Table 6.1).

Table 6.1: Constructivist Strategies for Teachers

Strategies	**Constructivism Bases**
Provocation	• Develop curiosity • Ask questions • Identify situation where students lack
Investigation	• Brain-storming • Look for information • Experiment with materials • Observe specific phenomena • Collect and organise data • Employ problem solving strategies • Select appropriate resources • Discussion with others • Evaluate possible solutions • Engage in debate • Identify challenges
Justification	• Communicate ideas • Explain a model • Review the solutions • Utilise peer evaluation • Assemble multiple answers • Determine appropriate closure

(Contd.)

Strategies	Constructivism Bases
Realization	• Make decision • Apply knowledge and skills • Transfer knowledge and skills • Share information • Ask new questions • Use ideas for acceptance by others

The teachers adapt curriculum to challenge students' suppositions. Teachers assess student learning authentically and within the context of teaching. They set-up settings in which students can exhibit work and share ideas with classmates. The teacher's use of integrations overcomes the problem related to pedagogical. Teacher educators face those problems when students discard the theoretical principles stressed in the curriculum (Cook, Smagorinsky *et al.*, 2002). Thus, key component of constructivist teaching is to induce appropriate cognitive processing and to take student's prior knowledge into account.

Dimensions of Constructivist Teacher Development

Constructivism approach is the characteristics of teacher education transformation mandate. Teacher development approach must include consideration of constructivist practice. Teacher's knowledge to create constructivist learning environment is based on conceptual knowledge and pedagogical knowledge. Teachers attempt to understand the philosophical, psychological and epistemological foundation of constructivism it is conceptual knowledge. When they develop more complex approaches to designing instructional materials that constructivist learning require, it requires pedagogical knowledge. The teachers also try to understand the norms and values necessary to adapt the constructivism approach in multidimensional cultural realities of the classroom; this is their cultural knowledge.

1. *Humanistic Teacher Development*

Teacher's decision making is undoubtedly the crux of creative and critical thinking and is central to humanistic approach of teacher education. The impact of collective and individual learning on students has increased opportunities for teaching and decision making. The planning and preparation of lessons is not an easy task. Each learning community has its own dynamics. Teachers need to select strategies which are beneficial for group of students. The teachers facilitate a framework in which students actively engage, investigate, share and assess their own performance. By the way, students can integrate inquiry learning with skill development. A socially constructed curriculum is important for teachers to develop a supportive network among teachers who share a common interest in constructivist teaching and learning. The successful facilitation of student generated lessons requires teachers who are enough mature, experienced, resourceful and lifelong learners.

2. *Role of Content in Constructivist Teaching*

Constructivism is based on the three fundamental aspects: multiple forms of knowledge, role of past knowledge and social nature of knowledge. Multiple forms include declarative knowledge of content and concepts and procedural knowledge of actions and skills. Knowledge varies when different arrangements of facts, notations, reasoning, documentations, arguments, explanations are structured. These multiple forms of knowledge highlight the complexity of learning. Active, problem solving approach should be the content which includes interdisciplinary inquiry in teaching. Social nature of knowledge is created and transformed by each individual and by groups of people (Vygotsky, 1978). Learners should involve in talk, dialogue, public reasoning and shared problem solving. Classroom environment is counter-productive to learning. Therefore, teachers should illustrate collaboration between and among the teachers and the students.

Opportunities for discourse group facilitate pairing students for field experience. It fosters deeper understandings of classroom situations. Research has identified that linking of content with the process of teaching is the way of representing and formulating the subject that makes it comprehensive to others (Shulman, 1986). Pedagogy and culture make possible of teacher understanding about students and their environment. Understanding student includes students' abilities and learning strategies, developmental levels, attitudes, motivations and their prior conceptions. Context embraces teacher understandings of the social, political, cultural, and physical environment. Teacher education programme can help pre-service teachers in understanding of disciplinary content from a teaching perspective. The concepts which students learn, remains at the centre of constructivist teaching. Teacher education provides a multiplier effect. A constructivist approach shows us that content and process is not dichotomous (Brown & Adams, 2001).

3. *Constructivist Teaching and Instructional Design*

Instructional design is based on theory of learning and cognition. Constructivism values collaboration, individual autonomy, reflectivity, active engagement and personal relevance. Instructional focus has a shift from Teaching-For-Teaching-Sake to Teaching-For-Learning-Sake. Teacher education plans systematic approach to designing instruction. The shift from transmitting content to providing activity reflects the shift from a focus on teachers teaching to an emphasis on students learning. They must ensure students' need and motivation through needs assessment. They must retrieve prior knowledge for supporting task completion. The design must be based on the following principles:

- **Increased emphasis on the affective domain of learning:** The incorporation of this principle is made possible through personally relevant instruction, learners self-regulation by building skills, attitudes and beliefs and promoting individual autonomy.
- **Learning context that supports autonomy:** This can be done by embedding learning into learning activity itself, providing ill-structured problems in multiple representations through collaborative learning environment.

- **Constructivism Teaching and Technology:** Information, communication and collaboration are at the core of the constructivist learning process. Technology supported learning environments are created through case based learning. ICTs allow information through hypertexts and anchored instruction to be represented in cognitive task. This is effective when individualised learning is believed, peer learning and collaboration are facilitated, scaffolding is optimised and there is a diversity of teaching and learning strategies. ICTs have great potential in developing higher order thinking (HOT) tasks like defining problems, judging information, solving the problems, drawing appropriate conclusions. The computer can serve in the process of information gathering, inquiry and collaboration. Tools can benefit to obtain relevant information in the form of documents, photographs, transcripts, video and audio clips.

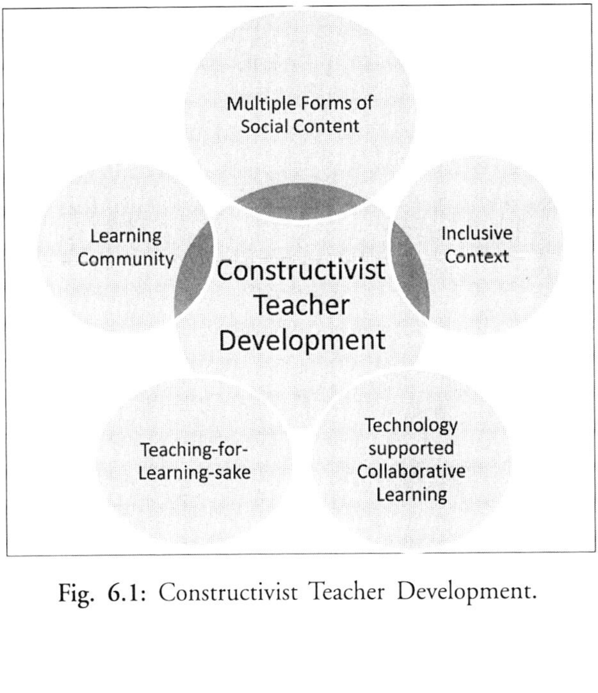

Fig. 6.1: Constructivist Teacher Development.

4. *Constructivist Teaching and Inclusive Setting*

Teaching is a talent. Teacher education programme should parallel the development of talents. The social context as well as the academic content is critical to the development of talent. An enriched environment is filled with opportunities in relation to the talent. Talents are complex and involve in an interconnected set of roles, behaviours and knowledge. The instructional approach will be based on these principles. In constructivist approach students are expected to engage in on-going reflection and meta-cognitive analysis in order to discover these principles. Inclusive environment is important for the growth of talent. The inclusive environment should address: (a) to apply collaborative skills to solve problems, (b) diversity with required knowledge, skills and behaviours needed for equitable and quality learning for all, and (c) instructional principles for the designing of constructivist learning environment.

Towards Constructivist Teacher Development Framework

Research on constructivist classroom practices provides evidences towards teacher learning and development. Facilitating effective teaching features constructivism perspectives in terms of the roles of teachers and learners in constructivism classrooms. To accomplish this, we must re-think schooling and reflect on how teacher development futures can be framed. The following questions are some of the guiding directions for development of framework for teacher development:

- What learners learn (diverse range of skills)?
- Where they learn (Social context)?
- How they learn (learning approaches such as problem based learning, self-regulated learning)?
- Who they learn with (peers, experts, and adults)?
- When they learn (collaboration)?

The framework is clearly defined way of implementing teacher development programme (Table 6.2). This engages appropriate planning, teaching and learning, collaboration and interaction among all members of the learning community.

Table 6.2: Constructivist Teacher Development Framework

Component I	Facilitating the learning process	• Teacher as a facilitator • Student engagement in activities • Student engagement in experiences
Component II	Pedagogy related to student understanding	• Higher order thinking skills • Integration of content and process skills • Linking concepts and evidence
Component III	Strategies based on interactions with students	• Resolution of misperceptions • Teacher-student relationships • Modification of teaching strategies to facilitate student understanding
Component IV	Teacher knowledge of subject matter	• Use of examples • Coherent lesson • Balance between depth and comprehensiveness • Valid content

Conclusion

To properly implement this idea, direct and explicit instruction is required. There is increasing evidence that quality of student work is demonstrated when teachers provide collaborative tasks. These principles bring together core elements for constructivist teaching-learning in the new millennium. This is the holistic vision towards lifelong learning.

REFERENCES

Anderson, L. and Krathwohl, D., *et al.* (Eds.) (2001). *A Taxonomy for Learning, Teaching, and Assessing: A Revision of Bloom's Taxonomy of Educational Objectives*. David Mckay Company: New York.

Biggs, J.B. (1979). "Individual differences in Study Processes and the Quality of Learning Outcomes", *Higher Education, 8*, 381-94.

Bransford, J., Brown, A. & Cocking, R. (Eds.) (2000). *How People Learn: Brain, Mind, Experience, and School.* Washington, DC: National Academy Press.

Brown, J. & Adams, A. (2001). *Constructivist Teaching Strategies.* Springfield, IL: Charles C. Thomas.

Cook, L., Smagorinsky, P. *et al.* (2002). "Problems in Developing a Constructivism Approach to Teaching: One Teacher's Transition from Teacher Preparation to Teaching." *The Elementary School Journal, 102*(5), 389-413.

Davis, B.M. (2006). *How to Teach Students Who Don't Look Like You: Culturally Relevant Teaching Strategies.* Thousand Oaks, CA: Corwin Press.

Dewey, J. (2001). "The Child and the Curriculum". In *The School and Society and the Child and the Curriculum* (ed.), Mineola: Dover Publications, pp. 103-23,

Freire, P. (1985). *The Politics of Education: Culture, Power, and Liberation.* Hadley, MA: Bergen & Garv.

Gonzales, C., Pickett, L., & Hupert, N. (2002). "The Regional Educational Technology Assistance Program: Its Effects on Teaching Practices". *Journal of Research on Technology in Education, 35*(1), 1-18.

Hollingsworth, S. (1999). "Prior beliefs and cognitive change in learning to teach." *American Educational Research Journal, 26*(2), 160-189.

IAEB International Education Advisory Board (2013). Learning in the 21st Century: Teaching Today's Students on their Terms, IEAB.

Kunter, M., Klusmann, U., Baumert, J. *et al.* (2013). "Professional Competence of Teachers: Effects on Instruction Quality and Student Development". *Journal of Educational Psychology, 105*(3), 805-20.

Lave, D. & Wenger, E. (1991). *Situated Learning: Legitimate Peripheral Participation.* New York: Cambridge University Press.

Murray, J. (2008). "Teacher Educators' Induction into Higher Education: Work Based Learning in the Micro Communities of Teacher Education", *European Journal of Teacher Education, 31*, 117-33.

NCERT (2005). *National Curriculum Framework 2005*, Author, New Delhi.

NCF-SE (2023). *National Curriculum Framework for School Education*, New Delhi: NCERT.

NCTE (2009). *National Curriculum Framework for Teacher Education*, Author, New Delhi.

NEP (2020). *National Education Policy 2020*, New Delhi: Ministry of Education.

Nix, R.K., Fraser, B.J. & Ledbetter, C.E. (2003). "Evaluating an integrated science learning environment (ISLE) using a new form of the constructivist learning environment survey (CLES)." A paper presented at the Annual Meeting of the American Educational Research Association, Chicago, IL.

OECD (2005). *Teachers Matter: Attracting, Developing and Retaining Effective Teachers*. Paris: OECD.

OECD (2010). Teaching and learning international survey (TALIS) Technical Report. Creating Effective Teaching and Learning Environments. Paris: OECD.

OECD (2011). *Building a High Quality Teaching Profession*. Paris: OECD.

Putnam, T. & Borko, H. (2000). "What Do New Views of Knowledge and Thinking have to Say About Research on Teacher Learning?" *Educational Researcher*, *29*(1), 4-15.

Schleicher, A. (2011). Pearson to Develop Frameworks for OECD's PISA Student Assessment for 2015.

Shulman, L. (1986). "Those Who Understand: Knowledge Growth in Teaching", *Educational Researcher*, *15*, 4-14.

Voss, T., Kunter, M. & Baurmert, J. (2011). "Assessing Teacher Candidates' General Pedagogical and Psychological Knowledge: Test Construction and Validation. *Journal of Educational Psychology*, *103*(4), 952-69.

Vosniadou, S. (2001). *How Children Learn*. Geneva, Switzerland: International Academy of Education (IAE)/International Bureau of Education (UNESCO)/IBE). (Educational Practices Series No. 7).

Vygotsky, L.S. (1978). *Mind in Society: The Development of Higher Psychological Processes*. Cambridge, MA: Harvard.

Wenger, E. (1998). *Communities of Practice: Learning, Meaning and Identity*. New York: Cambridge University Press.

6

Paradigm Shift in Teacher Education in Higher Education Institutions

Sunil Behari Mohanty

International Scenario of Teacher Education

Before going into the issue of paradigm change in teacher education and National Education Policy, 2020, a few situations have been witnessed in a few developed countries as received in reply to e-mail sent by the author. The international scenario of teacher education has been portrayed in the following nations:

United Kingdom

A professor working in a top-ranking higher education institution in the United Kingdom wrote:

> "Most of the large universities in the UK put on training courses for their own lecturers which are accredited by a national body; and many of those courses are open to academics from other universities. But I sense that you want to know how to become an academic in the UK. These days, that is achieved largely by developing a list

of one's own papers in academic journals. (I became an academic 30 years ago, after nearly 20 years as a non-academic administrator and I achieved that by working academically in the evenings, firstly, by taking several postgraduate qualifications and then having several papers published in academic journals and writing my first book ('*The Idea of Higher Education*', 1990). All that was done on top of a full-time job before I became an academic.

These days, people take a series of part-time junior academic roles as a research officer and part-time lecturing positions while writing their academic papers for the academic journals; and become established that way. It typically takes 8-12 years, if one is lucky, to get a full-time academic position. It is very hard work. Most don't make it. This will be disappointing to you, I fear, but it is the way the academic world is and has been for some time."

Norway and United Kingdom

A Norwegian, working as a consultant in a project of the European Union wrote:

> "Generally in the UK, university teachers are qualified through attaining membership of the higher education academy (https://www.advance-he.ac.uk) together with postgraduate qualifications in their subject.
>
> In Norway there is a rather *ad hoc* system of individual courses for tutors and so forth, but this varies from university to university. However, a post-graduate degree (Master or Ph.D.) is usually a prerequisite. For detailed information you would need to consult individual university websites. I hope this helps but let me know if it doesn't! Generally, the higher you go in the education system, the less your teaching abilities are tested or trained!"

An Indian, working as a principal lecturer, in a university in UK wrote:

> "Instead of doing the course some individuals can also write an essay which includes evidence of their teaching experience etc., and they can then apply for a Fellowship depending on level of experience to Advance HE directly."

(Please note that in UK, "Advance HE", is the earlier (HEA) Higher Education Academy.) Advance HE accredits initial and continuing professional development (CPD) programmes not only in UK, but also in other countries. It also awards four different categories of Fellowship, Associate Fellowship (AFHEA), Fellowship (FHEA), Senior Fellowship (SFHEA) and Principal Fellowship (PFHEA) to individuals throughout the world and as of May 2020, there were 1,30,000 fellows (Advance HE 2020). It has also brought out UK Professional Standards Framework (UKPSF) (Advance HE 2019). University of London has an Online Postgraduate Certificate in Learning and Teaching in Higher Education (1-5 years duration. The website says, "Study this programme anywhere in the world and receive a fully accredited University of London Degree."

United States

A professor in the United States wrote:

> "Generally, if a person has a Ed Dor PhD, they are not required to have any special teaching certificate to teach at the University. So much of a person being hired at a University, depends on their research interests and previous jobs. Also, they like to see if the candidate's interests fit with the needs of the department...
> I do not know what the advantage of the certificate at Harvard might be other than a refresher course."

(She referred about Harvard in relation to my query about 8 Weeks certificate course in Teaching in Higher Education).

An Indian settled in US and working as a Director, Curriculum and Assessment Design and Improvement in a College of Osteopathic Medicine, wrote:

> "Please find the attached 'Higher Education Teaching Certificate' information from Harvard University. I completed this course last year.
> I will be happy to help you develop a similar certificate course for Indian higher education faculty. If you prefer, we can have a short call to discuss it.
> There is no formal certificate course for higher education faculty, but usually in every university in the US they have 'Centre for Teaching and Learning'."

Another US Professor wrote:

> "The primary requirement for entrance into higher education teaching is the conferral of the doctoral degree. Higher education teachers are not 'trained' as you find with those from primary or high school teachers."

Harvard University, the third university in QS World University Rankings of 2020 (QS 2020) has an online Certificate course for teaching in higher education. Its duration is 8 weeks and instruction time 8-10 hours per week covering the topics: (1) Higher Education, (2) Teacher development, and (3) Teaching. The announcement states that during the course an aspirant to teach in higher education will be able to:

- "Tailor learning experiences to account for the backgrounds, abilities, and levels of students' knowledge.
- Use alternative teaching strategies, such as storytelling, as a method of teaching to engage students and deliver educational content effectively.
- Implement active learning techniques and effective classroom design to promote student learning and engagement.

- Incorporate active learning techniques within your disciplinary context to address identified learning objectives.
- Design a comprehensive curriculum or syllabus, specific to your disciplinary context."

Australia

An Indian, working as a faculty in Curtin University, Australia wrote:

> "In Australia there is no mandatory teaching qualification required to enter into a teaching job in Higher Education. Over the years most Universities have developed PD's focused on Pedagogy/Andragogy which are made compulsory for all academic staff new to university and/or profession.
> Curtin University's for teaching and learning four faculties are serviced by a central team. It delivers PD's for Curtin academic staff, check the link: https://clt.curtin.edu.au/. Curtin is aspiring to develop a fully online 100 credit programme for academic staff in higher education. I expect that we should be rolling it out some time in 2021."

Belgium

A faculty from University of Antwerp, Belgium wrote:

> "At our university, we have a specific training unit, situated at the Expertise Centre for Higher Education. A short description is found here: https://www.uantwerpen.be/en/about-uantwerp/faculties/antwerp-school-of-education/echo/
> The courses are quite obligatory in the trajectory for professorship, and very much accustomed to individual needs and questions."

Chile

A Professor from Chile, South America wrote:

> "We do not have Certificate/Diploma courses for Aspirants to Higher Education Teaching. We contract them on the basis of their academic stand (Master's or Doctorate holders). Young graduates may be contracted as assistants for specific university courses and that is also a way to enter into a formal academic position, but they must have or get a post-graduate degree."

Slovenia

Slovenia transits higher education teachers under the project "Innovative learning and teaching in higher education (INOVUP)" is co-financed by the Republic of Slovenia and the European Union from the European Social Fund. A Professor in his e-mail explained that Pedagogical and Andragogical Training Certificate is given after participation in four meetings and submission of two reports on the introduction of active learning methods in teaching in the pedagogical process.

Finland

A Professor wrote:

> "My short response is that every teacher working at a higher education institution has to go through a qualification course in Education. The length and credits will vary between the institutions and for instance at my university it is possible to continue from a basic to an advanced level."

Romania

A Lecturer wrote:

> "In Romania, the access in Higher Education is conditioned be a doctoral diploma in the field of the

job. The doctoral studies are different from a field to another, in my field it was a three years doctoral school in Educational Sciences."

Lithuania

A Professor wrote:

> "In our country, Lithuania, every university offers courses and in-service training for beginning teachers. In Vytautas Magnus University case, we have a course for first year doctoral students (for those who are going to be university teachers) on Didactics of Higher Education. It is of 6 credits course (equal to 180 academic hours) of contact hours with teacher and independent work. The course is a part of the study programmes of doctoral students." She clarified that "Didactics of Higher Education is free choice in some doctoral programmes and compulsory for Economics, Marketing, Management doctoral students."

The course document states that

"Upon completion of this module, doctoral students will be able to:

1. Interpret theoretical and political issues in education; participate in a scientific discussion with other researchers.
2. Identify students' study needs and objectives.
3. Interpret the process of university studies as a system.
4. Define the most important didactical parameters of higher education and their interdependence.
5. Select and apply proper study forms and methods.
6. Formulate evaluation criteria for study achievements.
7. Prepare a fragment of university study programme that is didactically substantiated, professional and methodologically supported.

8. Assess study process from perspectives of quality and achievement of objectives.
9. Evaluate and improve one's own didactics competencies."

Sri Lanka

A Senior Lecturer wrote:

> "In Sri Lanka, all the lecturers appointed to the university should follow certificate course in teaching at higher education institutions. This course is mandatory for confirming their post in the universities. Every university will call application based on the demand for the course."

Vietnam

A faculty from Vietnam National University wrote:

> "Please find attached a research paper about VN teacher competency framework. Also here is a link to a presentation about the topic: http://carla.umn.edu/conferences/past/LTE2015/docs/Dudzik.pdf. Teacher training programmes must meet this requirement.
> In general, in order to teach in Higher Education in Vietnam, teachers are required to have a Ph.D. in the field. Yet, in reality, most teachers are struggling to qualify. As a result, most lectures in Higher Education only have a Master Degree at this point.
> There is a Certificate for Aspirants for a teaching short course which participants can participate in to get qualified. At this point, such a programme is conducted mostly in Vietnamese, mainly in house, and lasts for about a week. There is no English description of the course available though."

Mongolia

A colleague, referring to my query about training courses in Mongolia for HE teachers, wrote:

> "We don't have such course ... unfortunately. Everyone who has a master degree comes for teaching job in higher education. It depends on some factors which is, maybe, our features."

European University Institute

Introduction to Teaching in Higher Education course provided by the European University Institute covers three areas: (1) Teaching and Learning, (2) Designing your course; and (3) Teaching Tactics.

In almost all advanced nations, programmes are available for training of would be teachers and training of existing teachers. Some of the programmes are to be selected and pursued by the candidate, whereas a few others are provided by the higher education institutions or national or regional bodies involved in improving quality of higher education teachers.

National Education Policy 2020 and International Experiences: In-service Education for Teachers of HEIs

In-service programmes fit the participants to new situations arising out of developments in instructional technology. For instance, Student-centred Learning and Teaching Practices (SLTP) is one of the important tactics. Klemenčič *et al.* (2020: 93), state that:

> "A shift to student-centred learning and teaching (SCLT) requires changes to institutional policies, as well as rules and regulations on learning and teaching, including those governing the hiring, promotion, remuneration, workload and professional development of academic and teaching staff. It also requires student involvement in institutional governance and quality assurance bodies."

This strategy can be effective in an inclusive curriculum that includes flexible learning pathways, technology-enhanced learning, learning, and teaching support, inclusive learning spaces and libraries, and community engagement and partnerships. These attributes have been mentioned in the current National Policy on Education, which in Art.11.5 at page 37 states that "Imaginative and flexible curricular structures will enable creative combinations of disciplines for study, and would offer multiple entry and exit points, thus, removing currently prevalent rigid boundaries and creating new possibilities for life-long learning."(Art.11.5, p. 37).

Training of Would-be Higher Education Teachers as Part of Course Work

This type of training is provided in a few countries of the Central Europe. In 2018, Staff and Educational Development Association (SEDA) at London brought out a publication containing *Early Career Academics' Reflections on Learning to Teach in Central Europe* (Pleschová & Simon, 2018). This document consists of case studies authored mostly by doctoral students, who were part of a new educational development programme that introduced them to student-centred approaches and innovative teaching methods and each study mentioned challenges and strategies applied to meet them.

NEP 2020 (Art 15.9, p. 43) postulates a new model of training of would be higher education teachers as part of Ph.D. Course work. It states that:

> "All fresh Ph.D. entrants, irrespective of discipline, will be required to take credit-based courses in teaching/education/pedagogy/writing related to their chosen Ph.D. subject during their doctoral training period. Exposure to pedagogical practices, designing curriculum, credible evaluation systems, communication, and so on will be ensured since many research scholars will go on to become faculty or public representatives/communicators of their chosen

> disciplines. Ph.D. students will also have a minimum number of hours of actual teaching experience gathered through teaching assistantships and other means. Ph.D. programmes at universities around the country will be re-oriented for this purpose."

If this plan is implemented, IUCTE must play vital role in developing appropriate subject specific support instructional materials including model lessons, without which higher education institutions cannot do this task. IUCTE may go for development of these materials in English language and Language in higher education of the Central Government for Hindi and Sanskrit and Tibetan may translate. State language universities may translate these into their state languages for use by their language Ph.D. students.

Our Training of Higher Education Teachers

The idea of training of higher education teachers was suggested by the Education Commission 1964-66 (Kothari, 1966: 154). In 1978, National Council for Teacher Education located in NCERT brought out its document "Teacher Education Curriculum—A Framework" which suggested one semester duration programme "to provide some pedagogical theory and general methods of teaching to college teachers in order that they may use more effective techniques than the traditional types of lectures and practical in teaching college students" (NCTE, 1978: 22).

In 1986, the National Policy on Education suggested teacher orientation on modern developments in teaching "at the beginning of the service as well as continuing education thereafter" (MHRD, 1986: 15). In pursuance of the direction given in the policy, in 1987-88, the University Grants Commission formulated Academic Staff Colleges Scheme. These colleges are now known as Human Resource Development Centres. In 2015, the Central Government brought out Pandit Madan Mohan Malaviya National Mission on Teachers and Teaching (PMMMNMTT) scheme. As per available records, in our situation, in-service programmes include orientation and refresher courses organized by 66 HRDCs (UGC, 2020) and through induction programmes for newly recruited faculty in HE in 70 institutions under PMMMNMTT scheme (MHRD, 2018). Cost of PMMMNMTT Induction programmes perhaps vary from 6 lakhs to 60 lakhs. High cost was due to non-availability of hostel facilities for participants and guest houses for resource persons and large hall for lecture for which hotels had to be booked. Refresher courses are subject-wise and have homogenous participant group, whereas orientation courses are not subject specific and have heterogeneous participant group. The face-to-face programmes become effective depending on the capacity of the resource person to keep the adult learners engaged in discussion and with peer involvement in answering question of another peer and raising various issues relevant for the participants.

NEP 2020 stated that:

> "In-service continuous professional development for college and university teachers will continue through the existing institutional arrangements and ongoing initiatives; these will be strengthened and substantially expanded to meet the needs of enriched teaching-learning processes for quality education. The use of technology platforms such as SWAYAM/DIKSHA for online training of teachers will be encouraged, so that standardized training programmes can be administered to large numbers of teachers within a short span of time" (Art. 15.10: 43).

Current pandemic and war cry from a neighbouring country may force cut in budget for higher education and the most affected may be in-service programmes. Hence, there is a need to have a relook at the ongoing practices for teacher preparation. A few instances of what goes wrong in the existing system of higher education teacher training may motivate appropriate authorities to take desired steps.

1. *Papers Submitted by Resource Persons in an Academic Staff College (Now HRDC)*

Many years ago, a Director of an academic staff college, located in a central university boasted about bringing out bound volumes of papers presented by resource persons at various orientation and refresher courses. There was a paper on teaching technique. When the Director was told that the said paper appeared like a chapter in an Encyclopaedia of Education of Pergamon Press, he took out the copy of the Encyclopaedia and found that the paper was exact copy, only name of the original author had been replaced by the name of the resource person. Resource persons get extra amount when they submit a written paper. That was the reason for such a step.

2. *Handbook Given to Participants in Induction Programme (Uncorrected documents from UGC platforms)*

Two years ago, in an induction programme, the participants had been given a handbook in which there was a paper on "Education Policies" that had been downloaded from one of the UGC platforms. The paper had many errors and its references were secondary sources. The material was written by a junior lecturer in sociology and had been reviewed by a Reader in sociology. When contacted about this drawback, the UGC officer in charge expressed helplessness stating that the author as well as the reviewer had been paid for the purpose. No independent agency has been involved in reviewing the materials available in online platforms. The haste in preparation of materials for online platforms is perhaps responsible for such lapses.

3. *Problems Faced by Participants of Teacher Development Programmes in the Field Situation*

Požarnik (2016: iii) in a foreword given to a European Union document, mentioned following problems faced by participants in applying their learning in professional development courses in the field:

> "Higher education teachers, even the most dedicated ones, often feel alone in their attempts to improve their work with students. This has been also highlighted by the evaluation study among the participants of in-service training courses. The vast majority of them mentioned that when trying to introduce different novelties and innovations, they do not face much opposition, but they are often ignored by their colleagues and superiors. The problems and proposed improvements of teaching are rarely discussed within the departments."

This problem may be universal and may also be applicable to our situation, questioning the necessity of investing huge amounts in in-service professional development programmes for higher education teachers. IUCTE may undertake impact studies for evaluating the need for continuation of induction and refresher courses and induction programmes. The professional development programmes when conducted in face to face mode have the advantage of peer to peer communication and development of awareness about functioning of higher education system at different places. However, the IUCTE may also consider making these programmes delivered online in morning and evening hours and having an evaluation for issue of certificate. In many developed nations, in-service programmes for higher education teachers is not compulsory. Many universities in advanced education systems, organize such programmes for their own teachers, even during lunch time or on holidays without making teachers remain absent from their classes.

The Higher Education Commission of India (HECI) may consider designating IUCTE as the National Centre for Teaching Excellence for HE (NCTEHE) and place existing HRDCs at the disposal of the IUCTE to make them function as Regional Centres for Teaching Excellence for HE (RCTEHE) with responsibility of promoting and supporting such centres in each higher education institution. IUCTE may distribute all university level institutions and their affiliated institutions among these RCTEHEs.

IUCTE may consider instituting an Online Excellence in Teaching in Higher Education course, to be made available for also aspirants from other countries. Participants from poor nations, who may not go for high fee charging courses in countries like UK and US may opt for this course. The RCTEHEs may also provide pre-job online certificate courses in local languages to be made available on payment basis.

NEP 2020, at page 43, mentions "A National Mission for Mentoring shall be established, with a large pool of outstanding senior/retired faculty—including those with the ability to teach in Indian languages—who would be willing to provide short and long-term mentoring/professional support to university/college teachers" (Art. 15.11). IUCTE may consider preparing support materials for the mentors who might have not been aware of recent developments in their subject areas. This task may be delegated to specific RCTEHE to develop support material in the concerned state language or translate nationally developed materials.

The HECI may consider entrusting to IUCTE the task of creating by 2021, "Bharat Professional Standards Framework for Teaching and Supporting Learning in Higher Education." It may consider to make it obligatory for each higher education institution, small or big, to have a Centre for Teaching Excellence, to take care of professional development of their own faculty, without making teachers remain absent from their routine work.

IUCTE may consider instituting Associate Fellowships and Fellowships for individual teachers, after considering their application submitted with supporting evidences as may be specified in the proposed professional standards framework. While charging individual applicants for fellowships, IUCTE may also consider instituting Honorary Fellowships on academicians based on their contribution to teaching and learning in higher education.

In case, IUCTE plans for short online teacher training courses for aspirants for a teaching job in higher education and another course for teachers on the job. Like University of London, IUCTE may consider giving in-service teachers to complete the course in 1-5 years. Of course, while Planning for such courses, it may take into consideration the circumstances that led to closure of Diploma in Higher Education run by the University of Madras, MS University of Baroda, Shivaji University, Kolhapur etc., and Master of Collegiate Teaching course by the University of Calicut.

As in the 2020 QS World Ranking of Universities, higher education institutions in the United States have occupied top 3 ranks; IUCTE may examine suitability of application of the approach to teacher training by these three US universities for our higher education system.

REFERENCES

Advance, H.E. (2019). *The UK Professional Standards Framework for Teaching and Supporting Learning in Higher Education.* Author, York. Retrieved September 3, 2020 from https://s3.eu-west-2.amazonaws.com/assets.creode.advancehe-document-manager/documents/advance-he/UKPSF%20large%20print_1570613686.pdf

Advance, H.E. (2020). *Fellowship.* Author, York. Retrieved September 3, 2020 from https://www.advance-he.ac.uk/fellowship

European University Institute (2020). *Introduction to Teaching in Higher Education,* Author, San Domenico di Fiesole (FI). Retrieved on August 28, 2020 from https://www.eui.eu/ServicesAndAdmin/AcademicService/Academic-and-Professional-Development/Introduction-to-Teaching-in-Higher-Education

Harvard University (2020). *Higher Education Teaching Certificate.* Author, Harvard, MA. Retrieved on August 28, 2020 from https://online-learning.harvard.edu/course/higher-education-teaching-certificate?delta=2Klemenčič, M., Pupinis, M., Kirdulyte, G. (2020). *Mapping and Analysis of Student-Centred Learning and Teaching Practices: Usable Knowledge to Support More Inclusive, High-Quality Higher Education -NESET Report*, Publications Office of the European Union, Luxembourg. doi: 10.2766/67668 https://op.europa.eu/en/publication-detail/-/publication/817b846d-6733-11ea-b735-01aa75ed71a1/language-en/format-PDF/source-search

Kothari, D.S. (1966). (Chairman) *Report of the Education Commission (1964-66).* Government of India, New Delhi.

MHRD (1986). *National Policy on Education 1986.* Government of India, New Delhi.

MHRD (2018). *Scheme of Pandit Madan Mohan Malaviya National Mission on Teachers and Teaching (PMMMNMTT) Guidelines.* Author, New Delhi. Retrieved on August 30, 2020 from http://nmtt.inflibnet.ac.in/Uploads/adminDoc/Revised%20Guidelines_20190429142023.pdf

NCTE (1978). *Teacher Education Curriculum—A Framework.* NCERT, New Delhi.

Pleschová, G. & Simon, A. (eds.) (2018). *Early Career Academics' Reflections on Learning to Teach in Central Europe.* SEDA, London. https://www.seda.ac.uk/resources/files/Early_career_academics_reflections_on_learning_to_teach_entire_book.pdf.

Požarnik, B.M. (2016). *Foreword.* In Aškerc, K., Cvetek, S., Florjanêiê, V., Klemenêiê, M., Požarnik, B.M. & Rutar, S. (Eds.) *Improving the Quality of Teaching and Learning in Higher Education from Theory to Practice, from Practice to Theory.* European Union, Ljubljana. Retrieved 2.9.20 from *https://www.cmepius.si/wp-content/uploads/2014/02/Monografija_splet.pdf.*

Quacquarelli Symonds (QS) (2020). *World University Rankings 2021.* Author, London.https://www.topuniversities.com/qs-world-university-rankings/methodology.

UGC (2020). *Human Resource Development Centres.* Author, New Delhi. As Retrieved on August 30, 2020 from https://www.ugc.ac.in/page/Human-Resource-Development-Centre(HRDC).aspx

University of London (2020). *Postgraduate Certificate in Learning and Teaching in Higher Education.* Author, London. Accessed September 3, 2020 from https://london.ac.uk/courses/learning-teaching https://london.ac.uk/sites/default/files/leaflets/leaflet-learning-teaching-he-2018-19.pdf.

Section II
CURRICULUM REFORMS IN TEACHER EDUCATION

7

NEP 2020: Gandhian Perspective

P.K. Sahoo

The National Education Policy (NEP), 2020 has made a breakthrough in Indian education system of the 21st century. The policy has intended to project holistic development of the country with global perspectives, of course, with due emphasis on Bharat centric or Indianness of education. The Indianness of Education is very well rooted and reflected in Gandhian thoughts in education and the experiment with truth of Gandhiji. The century old ideas and experiences guide the Indian vision of education in the era of globalization and its endeavour for sustainable development. The NEP 2020 has articulated educational perspectives and corresponding policy on school education with the need of the changing world and aspiration of India to be counted as a global power. Such perspectives of education is grounded in the social and political ideals of Gandhiji to a large extent. The basic tenets of national education as per Gandhiji were projected as:

- Education through mother tongue;
- Home environment and school environment nexus;
- Education to fulfil the needs of the masses;

- Teachers competency and good character;
- Free school education to all; and
- Education system to be controlled by people.

His vision of balanced development of cognitive, affective and psychomotor components of personality revolves around individuality with humanistic values and universal truth. The extent to which Gandhiji's perspectives on Indian life and education have been juxtaposed in the NEP 2020 shall reveal the presence of national spirit in the policy document. This chapter has focused on exploring basic ideals of Gandhiji on liberation and nationality; it examines the reflections of such thoughts in the NEP 2020 on school education. In this context, an attempt has been made to discuss in brief about Gandhian Philosophy of education subsequently the linkage of NEP 2020 with Gandhian thoughts on education has been explored through this write up.

Individual Enlightenment and Collective Self-reliance

Gandhi's focus on individual supremacy as self-regulating and self-governing being has been regarded as the basic tenet of freedom and progress of mankind. Individual freedom and self-initiated voluntary inquiry is linked with the motto of society's progress as well. This is very well integrated with individual's moral obligations towards others. Gandhiji's views on *'Swaraj'* or self-rule is understood in the form of voluntary internalization of one's obligation towards the society. Hence, individual freedom is utilized with conscience and ethics for betterment of others as well as the nation. Moreover, individual's understanding of inner strength and potentials is geared towards holistic development of mankind through willing submission to social restraint. In this respect, Gandhiji considered 'self-rule' as a positive concept. He emphasized on the role of education to make an individual self-reliant' and bold enough to contribute his/her best for collective progress of the society. Gandhiji's concept of self-reliant education is to be interpreted in the preview of internal emancipation of individual. An educated and internally self-reliant person can participate fearlessly in external spheres of economic and political life with voluntary spirit.

Autonomous Individual

The concept of autonomous individual is the basic tenet of Gandhain ideology. He de-emphasized control of power in the hands of larger state and capitalist forces. Individual dignity and freedom to take charge of self are rooted in his inner sense as well as in the grassroots experiences. Any kind of suppression inherent in social structure is to be overcome through individual's collective participation, so that the inequities and discriminatory practices in social, economic and political life can be overcome through non-violent social action. In this respect, education's role is more contextual and meaningful as per Gandhiji's perception. Social inclusion can be achieved through integration of ethical and humane approach by recognizing autonomy of every individual. According to Gandhiji, individuals are autonomous in the sense of making their own life as per own choices and action. Education's role in recognizing child's autonomy in making choice in learning process and learning activities is very much significant in this context. Learners' participation in various learning experiences and realizing the worth of various activities internally provides opportunity for strengthening cognitive and skill based moral practices in education. Hence, encouragement of children's educational decisions and participation at grassroot level must be integrated with the socio-cultural milieu of the school. The learning environment must be free from outer domination and violence. Voluntary involvement in learning practices shall provide opportunities for strengthening internal experiences with the contextual environment. Gandhiji perceived life to be morally meaningful for all people; and students' participation in group activities will develop a sense of common interest or good. Hence, community living practices leading to peace in inner and outer sphere of life are considered valuable in the school culture.

SATYA and AHIMSA

As a basic Gandhian principle every individual endeavours to follow the path of *Satya* and *Ahimsa*. The evils of social and political system need to be countered by *Ahimsa*. Building foundation for love for truth and non-violent action is the mission of the school system. In this context, Gandhiji emphasized on *Purity of Means*. The process is considered more meaningful than the product. Non-violence is not just an ideal, but considered as the most essential principal for Social Action. Hence, at school level, the learning practices and its relevance to life is considered move valuable proposition for quality education. According to Gandhian principle, purity in action will certainly lead to purity in products. Instead of product orientation (in terms of examination results), the teaching-learning system must emphasize on learner friendly practices in a conducive school environment. Mutual trusts, co-operative and collaborative learning based projects, constructive duty orientation must be focused with non-violent curricular practices of the school system.

Besides school education, Gandhiji emphasized on the common masses to be trained in the acts of non-violence and harmony. *Ahinsa* is the power of the stronger and not the week. This incorporates purity of process involving head, heart and hand. The action of a good citizen is appreciated if he challenges the might of bureaucratic state on the basis of *Dharma*, *Satya* and *Ahimsa*. Such ideas act the foundation of a broad based holistic education system meant for the school and society.

Complete Freedom in Individual Life and Society

According to Gandhiji, self-rule is rendered as disciplined rule from within. *Purna swaraj* (complete freedom) is inclusive in nature. It leads to the sum total of the self-rule of the individuals. Hence, education must lead to complete freedom of individuals with possession of virtues like Truth and Non-violence. He said that individual *swaraj* was logically and conceptually prior to the notion of collective or national *swaraj*. "Self-government means continuous effort to be independent of government control whether it is foreign government or whether it is National. It will be a sorry affair if people look up to the government for regulation of every detail of life"(Gandhi, 1962).

Swaraj of Gandhiji means acquiring inner freedom. It means Indians gain sovereignty over themselves and over their nation. It also applies to economic as well as political aspects of life. In this context, the development orientation projected by the Nobel laureate A.K. Sen is more relevant where he emphasized on development as, real human 'freedom', such as political freedoms economic facilities, social opportunities, transparency guarantees and protective security. Such human freedom is the key parameter of development (Sen, 1999). Gandhiji was of the opinion that children must learn and think independently and to live and behave independently. The holistic education must encourage the initiative for complete freedom. The orientation towards *swaraj* must be initiated from the school life itself.

NEP 2020: Cognitive Development Oriented School Curriculum

The above stated principles of Gandhiji regarding individual, state and freedom have direct linkage with Gandhiji's ideals of education. Such ideals appear to be relevant to the Indian education system, since Gandhian ideals are inseparable from the contemporary movement for inner freedom, peace and sustainable development of the global society.

Gandhiji was critical about the bias of modern education towards intellectual activity oriented curriculum delinked from development of cognitive and affective dimensions of personality dissipation. To him, "unless the development of the mind and body goes hand in hand with a corresponding awakening of the soul, the former alone would be a poor lopsided affair. By spiritual training I mean education of the heart. A proper and all-round development of the mind, therefore, can take place only when it proceeds *pari passu* with the education of the physical and spiritual faculties of the child. They constitute an indivisible whole. According to this theory, therefore, it would be a gross fallacy to suppose that they can be developed piecemeal or independently of one another" (Gandhi,1962). Gandhiji focused on experiential learning to develop knowledge, skills and spiritually it while being engaged in craft centred vocational education as an integral component of school curriculum. Gandhiji said, "Supposing he (Learner) is set to some useful occupation like spinning, carpentry, agriculture etc. for his education and in that connection is given a thorough comprehensive knowledge relating to the theory of the various operations that he is to perform and the use and construction of tools that he would be wielding. He would not only develop a fine healthy body but also a sound, vigorous intellect that is not merely academic but is firmly rooted in and is tested from day to day experience" (Gandhi, 1962). He emphasized on integration of subject curriculum with intellect, body and heart by means of practical hands on experiences of manual work, problem solving activities,recreation and creative expressions. Liberal education will give the learner, a perfect well balanced, all-round education in which the intellect, the body and the spirit have full play and develop together into a natural harmonious whole. A proper and harmonious combination of all the three is required for the making of whole man and constitutes the true economics of education (Harjan, 8.5, 1937, in Gandhi,1962).

Gandhiji listed down different curricular areas of school education like arithmetic, science, health, agriculture, weaving, music, military science and home management (for women) as well as physical training. Such curricular experiences will lead to character formation of individuals. Rationality must be linked with morality through learners' engagement in practical activities. The value of labour and self-reliance are interrelated with each other. The inner self-reliance is gained through learners' exposure to local specific need based education like agriculture and weaving. Experiential learning will lead to cultural awakening of children as well as their critical reflections on social, economic and political affairs of the society. In this regard, Gandhiji emphasized on proper co-ordination between home, community and school environment.

A cursory view of NEP 2020 on school education reveals that the NEP 2020 in its spirit talks about holistic education with learners' exposure to different areas of development of personality. It emphasizes on holistic development of learners with global orientation. "The goal will be to create holistic and well rounded individuals equipped with key 21st century skills" (NEP, 2020). On curriculum structure NEP insists on discipline orientation, reduced in content, from late preparatory stage onwards. Except, foundational stage which will consist of play activity based learning with focus on mannerism, health, and hygiene, rest of the stages of schooling focus on discipline based knowledge. Of course, there is enough scope for cognitive oriented learning practices like discovery approach, group based activities and analysis based learning. The course contents in different disciplines like science, mathemathics, arts and social sciences will cover, key concepts, ideas, applications and problem solving. In other words, the rote learning practices will be overcome by the development of abilities of students in understanding, application, analysis and critical thinking. The policy document claims that different stages of school education viz., foundational, preparatory, middle and high school (first and second) are designed to optimize "learning for students based on cognitive development of children" (NEP 4.2). The above highlights concentrate on intellectual development of learners, with a bias towards structural knowledge areas. Of course, there is some scope for interdisciplinary it on dealing with certain concepts and problems as highlighted in the school curriculum. The policy document has not discerned the scope of development of rest of the components of personality, viz. development of vocational skills incorporating psychomotor areas, and development of morals, ethics and values concerning human life and sustainable development.

To the utter surprise, these components have been clubbed together under the heading of skills, such as scientific temper, evidence based thinking, creativity and innovativeness, sense of aesthetics and art, oral and written communication; health and nutrition, physical education, wellness fitness and sports; collaboration and teamwork; problem solving and logical reasoning; vocational exposure and skills; digital literacy, coding and computational thinking; ethical and moral reasoning; including knowledge and practice of human and constitutional values (such as patriotism, sacrifice, non-violence, truth, honesty, peace, righteous conduct, forgiveness, tolerance, mercy, sympathy, helpfulness, cleanliness, courtesy, integrity, pluralism, responsibility, justice, liberty, equality and fraternity; gender sensitization; fundamental duties, citizenship skills and values; knowledge of India (including Indian knowledge systems); environmental awareness, water and resource conservation; current affairs and knowledge of critical issues, facing local communities, states, the country and the world (NEP 4.23). The list may be extended further. The curricular experts may find it cumbersome to understand whether such points are really categorized as skills? Or they cover ethical, moral and value dimensions concerning personality development. While, the policy document narrates the learning process prone to cognitive, subject centric areas of curriculum, much is anticipated to deal with the process involved in value components as well as psychomotor skills, particularly in the context of occupational and vocational skills. In this respect, Gandhian concept of integration of curricular experiences needs to be reflected distinctly in the new curriculum framework. More specifically, the position of vocational crafts in the context of other curricular components appears to be placed in isolated position. The futuristic vision with multiple preferred areas of learning with reality at grassroots level need to be worked out to do justice to different stages of development focusing on cognitive, affective and psychomotor domain of personality. The balanced personality with appropriate integration of thought (intellect), feelings (ethics) and deed (skills) must be visible in the curricular practices with a view to reach "Truth" and lead non-violent and peaceful life.

Medium of Instruction and Language Studies

The issue of medium of instruction in the Indian school system has been a crucial point of debate since the colonial period. Gandhiji advocated for mother tongue/local languages to be the medium of instruction at school stage. In fact, this was the main prank of agenda for National Education System propounded by him during the 1930s. Gandhiji had said that "the enrichment of mother tongue what is needed is not knowledge of English but love and respect for one's own language." To him, language serves dual purpose in individual and national life. As a medium of instruction, it serves the purpose of development of personality. Simultaneously "language shapes itself-according to the qualities and actions of those who speak that particular language" (Gandhiji, 1962). Since education is imparted through alien language, the gap increases between home and school. At large education becomes an instrument of social exclusion. The gulf becomes wider between the educated classes and the masses. Besides ethnic identity Gandhi was more concerned about the linguistic and cognitive issues related to development of child taught through alien language. From the initial stage of his participation in national movement and leadership in establishment of National Education Institutions he insisted on mother tongue to be the *lingua franca* of school education. Mother tongue plays a significant role in development of thinking process, proper communication of thoughts and feelings, creation of ideas, creative expressions, communicating with the masses, establishing proper co-ordination between intellect, emotion and action, and carriage of cultural and ethnic richness. Gandhiji was vocal against English as a medium of instruction for the Indian kids. In his educational agenda, mother tongue was the first and foremost principle for promotion of the Indian education and individual freedom.

Besides mother tongue, Gandhiji was vocal about learning of other vernacular languages of the country. As a dictum of *Satyagrahashram*, he propagated for Indians to learn as many Indian languages as possible. However, he was not averse to education of

English language, particularly, from the point of view of learning science and technology, learning Western literature, thoughts and philosophy and for employment purpose. To him "there was nothing wrong in our people learning English and using it for earning money, especially as it did help in the growth of some of our countrymen. But the suggestion cannot be advanced to support the use of English as the medium of instruction in imparting education" (Gandhi, 1962). He emphasized on, "… the progress of our country will largely depend on the right decision on the question of medium of education. I am sure that when the mother tongue is thus respected and restored to the rightful status of an official language, it will reveal powers and capacities of which we are unaware at present" (Gandhi, 1962). This is a matter of great concern that the mother tongue and medium of instruction still remains as an inconclusive decision in the context of public perception towards English medium schools and the state's role to promote English medium schools in merely spoken population by encouraging privatization in school education in every nook and corner of the country. Moreover, even though in all, 22 regional languages have been declared as scheduled languages of the country, a large number of Indian languages considered as mother tongue of children are not covered so far in the 8th Schedule of the Constitution of India. Hence, the complexities arise for education through mother tongue amongst children of different ethnic groups of the country. Hindi and English languages are official languages of the country. Study of those languages must get along with regions languages got prominence in different regions of the country.

In this regard, the NEP 2020 has taken a clear cut stand on mother tongue as medium of instruction, study of regional languages, official language and foreign languages at different stages of schooling. The policy statement states "wherever possible, the medium of instruction until at least Grade 5, but preferable Grade 8 and beyond, will be home language/mother tongue/local language. Therefore, the home/local language shall continue to be taught as a language wherever possible"(NEP, 2020).

This means, even though, in spirit the policy appreciates the mother tongue/local language as medium of instruction, the universalization of policy implementation on this matter will have constraints, may be because of ethnicity as well as urbanization and migrant population. The policy has not taken a obligatory stand on this matter. As a result of this, we will witness with regard to mushroom growth of private English medium schools all-over the country, time to come.

The policy statement insists on the three language formulae as per first National Policy on Education, 1968. On the matters concerning bilingualism with special reference to science and mathematics from Grade 6 onwards this is expected that the students will be well-versed about spoken English language on science and other subjects. The policy statement emphasises on development of quality learning texts in mother tongue/local language and/or second Indian language. The policy highlights the learning processes related to language development of learners on the basis of linguistic analysis of Indian Sanskrit and other classical languages of the country. However, the provision for teachers' education on these issues is very much crucial. Especially, teaching-learning practices concerning English language as alien to linguistic background of the Indian languages, pose a major concern for teacher development as well as children's learning at school stage.

Decentralization of Curriculum and Management of Schools

Decentralisation, was the motto of Gandhian concept of *swaraj* or self-rule: Gandhian concept of '*Gram Swarajya*' emphasized on indigenous culture, knowledge system, economy and polity. Decentralization and autonomy of individual at grassroots level promotes self-reliance from the point of views of internal as well as external area of development of personality. State is considered as a centralist force for imposition of ideals through coercive measures? On the other end, decentralized efforts at grassroots level encourages self-determination, voluntary participation in co-operative practices for development at village level. Gandhiji's concept of free school education for all was to be considered as insistence on local community participation with the support of the nation state. To Gandhiji national education "should be free. Education should not be made to depend on money. Just as the sun gives light to all equally and rain pours down for all, even so learning must be made available to all. Lastly, the people themselves must have control over the planning and carrying out the education" (Gandhiji, 1962). Hence, people's participation in educational management at grassroot level is considered as their own responsibility.

The NEP 2020, touches the issue of community involvement in the context of efficient resourcing in the establishment of school complex as per recommendation of the Education Commission Report, 1964-66. The policy highlights the need for provision of "School complex management committees (rather than simply school management committees) for more robust and improved governance, monitoring, oversight, innovations and initiatives by local stakeholders. Building such larger communities of schools, school leader, teachers, students, supporting staff, parents and local citizens would energize and enable the schooling system and in a resource-efficient manner (NEP 2020). "Such provision appears to be encouraging one for the public education system. The doubt prevails on the private management schools which flourish in the localities all-over the country by availing direct and indirect subsidies from the state. Of course, there may be accountability of such institutions to the centralized regulatory bodies. The community say over such kind of managements have been restricted to a large extent. The policy highlights formal requirements at state level, such as also "transparent public disclosure all regulatory information, as laid down by the State Schools Standards Authority (SSSA) will be used extensively for public oversight and accountability" (NEP 2020). In other words, such school accountability will be demonstration towards the centralized statutory bodies at state level, instead of the local public and the parents.

Equitable and Inclusive Education

Gandhiji focused on social inclusion and equity as foundation of true democracy. The philosophy was highlighted in Part IV of the Constitution of India. Learning for all have been well addressed by NEP 2020. It strongly emphasizes on "the education system must aim to benefit all of India children so that no child loses any opportunity to learn and excel because of the circumstances of birth or background." The policy document has incorporated laudable provisions for education of the socially and economically disadvantaged groups (SEDGs) in terms of gender identities, socio-cultural identities, geographical identities, disabilities and socio-economic conditions while efforts will be made strengthen existing provisions of special education, girl students' education and geographically remote area children's education. The NEP highlights the commitment to endorse the recommendations of the Rights of People with Disabilities Act, 2016, declaring certain regions of the country with large populations from SEDGs as special education zones (SEI) and constituting a (NEP 2020) Gender Inclusion fund for equitable education of all girls as well as transgender children.

The major issue is concerned with making provision for decentralized school curriculum with focus on socio-cultural identity, economic needs, and indigenous knowledge base of the SEDG children. Need based decentralized curriculum integrated with experiential learning process can break the gulf between the advantageous sections of society and the SEDG children in terms of educational outcomes. This will lead to self-reliance of SEDG children with exposure to the democratic life at individual level as well as at societal spheres. There is enough scope for provision of inclusive learning environment with proper value orientation as mentioned in NEP, viz. "respect for all persons, empathy, tolerance, human rights, gender equality, non-violence, global citizenship"(NEP 2020). The policy statement proposes to develop curricular materials, relevant and related to all communities.

Inclusiveness will be possible through humanistic approaches adopted by the school system facilitated by the civil society and the state. Such practices will enlarge the scope for attainment of sustainable development goals.

Teacher Development

There have been systematic interventions for quality teacher education corroborating curricular requirements of the school system. While major focus of teacher education has remained on competency development with pedagogic orientation and practices, there has been a great doubt about the proficiency of teachers to tackle school related problems with full commitment. Teachers lagging in demonstrating professional ethics in their day-to-day functions has been a matter of concern for teacher education system. "Gandhiji was more concerned about competent teachers with good character"(NCTE, 1999). The NEP places teachers in the centre of the school. There is an urgency to ensure professional ethics oriented teacher preparation through quality teacher education inputs.

The scope of teachers' functions has been perceived to be much wider as per NEP 2020. Besides delivery of teaching-learning and evaluation responsibilities, their role is more significant in building positive learning environment in the school set up. The NEP 2020 highlights that "the role expectations of principals and school teachers will explicitly include developing a caring and inclusive culture at their schools, for more effective learning for all, and for the benefit of all in their communities" (NEP 5.13). There has been special emphasis on continuous professional development (CPD) of working teachers. The policy statement focuses on teachers having, "flexibility to optimize their own development as teachers" (NEP 2020). Much has been talked about CPD for professional competencies of teachers. However, the missing part on this venture is teachers' self-initiative in bringing transformation in own knowledge, values and practices suiting to development of learners, professional community and the school system. There is a lot of scope for exploring the opportunities of participatory approach in professional development of teachers on continuous basis in own school situation. In this regard, the professional bodies of teachers will have to play a major role in building constructive environment for teacher learning, participatory projects, collaborative ventures at local, regional and national level. Autonomous practices for self-development and teachers' leadership in decision-making must be encouraged at grassroots level. On the contrary, the standardized formal, centralized statutory bodies on teacher education system have paid little attention to facilitate and ensure ethics oriented professional development practices in teacher development. The situation has been more alarming because of promotion of commercialism and privatization in teacher education system. This has created a blockage in autonomous initiative of teachers and teacher educators in self-transformation. Exploring the opportunities for transformation of teachers with humanistic and democratic values for social inclusion is a great challenge for teacher development programmes in the liberal and privatized system. In this regard, the NEP 2020 highlights on professional orientation in Teacher Education need to be implemented with great care at institutional level.

Conclusion

No doubt the NEP 2020 is of utmost relevance to the expectations from school system in the globalised society. National system of education draws its spirit from Gandhian thoughts of individual enlightenment, holistic development of head, hand and heart with exposure to grassroots level experiences and global vision. The Gandhian ideals of school education are reflected in many respects in the NEP 2020 to fulfil the dreams of an inclusive society. This is a continuous process to explore more and more to be nearer to the Truth and Non-violence in the pluralistic society of India since education is a natural right of individual, its quality must be ensured and protected by the nation state for every Indian child. Of course, the futures challenges lie resolving conflicts related to obtaining peace in the materialistic world through education.

REFERENCES

Gandhi, M.K. (1962). *True Education,* Ahmedabad, Navajivan Publishing House.

MHRD, Government of India, New Delhi (2020), *National Education Policy.*

NCTE, New Delhi (1999). *Gandhi ke Saikshik Vichar.*

Sen, A. (1999). *Development as Freedom*, New York: Alfred A. Knopf.

8

Policy Conscious Teachers and their Perception Towards TEP

Akha Kaihrii Mao

This chapter is an attempt to understand and raise certain questions with regard to the perception of politically conscious teachers and their everyday engagement with their practice and also *vis-à-vis* with that of the relearning through the Teacher Education Programme (TEP). Here, the term 'politically conscious' is meant to indicate a group of teachers who have come together as an organisation for engaging with the system and raising other issues of concern to their field. The group began about 3 years back with the coming together of like-minded individual teachers working in public schools at different levels (primary to senior secondary level in government schools in Delhi) and research scholars in the field of education. It started as a small, informal group of friends and has not been registered till date. The group is located in Delhi but nevertheless engages now and then with various other organisations across the country. Some of the examples of their engagements include: reaching out to the community to discuss their concerns in education and generate an understanding of the vision of a common school system, bringing out a short research based booklet on and against corporal punishment and a similarly produced report on and against the interventions of private players in government school system in Delhi, producing and distributing leaflets on an alternative conception of teachers' day, organising protest meeting against the government's decision to extend the post-retirement re-employment of teachers in schools, extending support to and participating in nation-wide movements against privatisation, commercialisation and communalisation of education etc. The author has been associated with the said group through his and their common association with the university.

Methods of Inquiry

A questionnaire was provided to the teachers individually and after a gap of a couple of days informal group discussions with pairs were held with them centring on the themes of the questionnaire. Afterwards, the recordings of the discussions were listened to and transcribed to look at the dominant concerns and perspectives shared by them. (This exercise is not an attempt to compare the orientation towards teacher education programmes between our select group of politically conscious teachers and those other teachers not considered so inclined.)

The chapter tries to find answers to some of the lead questions pertaining to the inquiry: How do teachers look at their own practice *vis-à-vis* their teacher education experience? Have they observed any discernible development in their practice over time since they joined teaching, till date? Are they satisfied with those changes or not? If 'yes', What contributed to those changes? Can the teacher education programme be said to have contributed to those changes? Whether they see that the collective they have formed has only a political role or it influences their pedagogy and does this have any impact on their commitment to teaching? What was it in the teacher education programme which they feel has helped, influenced and shaped them as teachers? What are some of the areas, issues, which they feel, in the light of their practice, should have been part of the teacher education programmes they went through?

How do they see the phenomenon of teaching in public schools by non-qualified persons coming from the voluntary sector?

For the purpose of the chapter the information gathered from the informal discussions is arranged under the following sub-headings.

Teachers Own Practice *vis-à-vis* their Teacher Education Experience

There is a general agreement that their teacher education programme has definitely contributed to their practice. While it proved difficult for them to pinpoint the exact components which have directly benefited their teaching, they were more confident about identifying the academic elements which were focused on socio-political sensitization on pedagogic issues concerned with caste, class and gender. Some of them credited their teacher education programme in which they were introduced to activities such as clay modelling, drawing, theatre/performing arts and child psychology for equipping them to understand and engage more meaningfully with their students.

Discernible Development in their Practice Over Time since they Joined Teaching till Date

It was possible for the teachers to identify broad shifts in their temperament over time, along with a growing understanding of students' contexts. Though, at least one teacher was forthright to say that she had not been teaching for sufficient span of time to discern any marked change in her practice. Some of the changes they could clarify were an increase in patience, growing understanding of students' varied learning curves, better ability to address the contexts of their schools etc. For example one of the teacher said, "I can at least say for myself, that the experience of having taught for some years have made me to be more patient as compared to my initial phase as a teacher. Because having taught 2-3 cycles of students, I know that different students have their own learning curve. So even if some students are not fast at learning say in class-II, I have seen that some of them are able to pick it up in the next class or a later state and one can see the flowering happened suddenly. At times a student may not be regular at all in the class due to various reasons and if we expect the same level of learning from that particular student like the other students it is not fair. So, experiences have helped me as teacher to be patient."

Factors Contributing to those Changes

What is worth underlining is that they pointed to their teaching experience, fellow colleagues' work, academic pursuits and organisational associations too for enabling them to grapple with pedagogic challenges in classrooms. One of the teachers pointed out that, "teaching is praxis and practice based", therefore, for him experience of teaching for many years help and shape a teacher to become a 'teacher'. The teachers also give credit to their fellow-teachers in contributing some of the changes. For example, a teacher pointed out how in his own school he could see some difference with the kind of attitude and approach some new teachers joined the school from different teacher education programme such as the B.El.Ed. He says that though he did not observe their classroom pedagogy he could see a difference in these young and new teachers interacting more freely with students and engaging with them and also do not seem to believe in the textbook as the source of all knowledge in the class. He also says that he learned from one of his colleagues of implementing in practice what was in his mind. He cited the example of using television as a medium of teaching-aid with small children. He says that the knowledge of using it as an idea was there but the real usage of the TV as teaching-learning tool affectively was learned from his colleague.

Role of Teacher Education Programme in Contributing to Those Changes

As mentioned above, they were emphatic in attributing their professional education for making them better equipped teachers than they would have been otherwise. Nevertheless, they also opined that it was not possible to talk in terms of a cause and effect relationship between their professional course and teaching; rather, it was more sensible to speak in terms of being strengthened with a humanistic and progressive vision of not only teaching as a profession but the discipline of education itself.

Perception of the Collective They have Formed and its Political Role and its Influences on their Pedagogy and Impact on their Commitment to Teaching

There was an unanimity among the teachers regarding the positive feedback of their work as teachers have received from their organisational association. Since, they do not see themselves as part of a traditional union but as a collective committed to the ideals of equality, fraternity, liberation and justice, they shared a sense of increased and internalised commitment to the defence and advance of those ideals not only in their particular classrooms and schools but in terms of the policy-level and systemic interventions and 'assaults'. Moreover, they articulated that this effect must not be seen as limited to issues bracketed as political as it extends to discussing and sharing pedagogic strategies with each other. These involve exchanging notes, seeking professional advice from each other and gaining understanding of the wider happenings in the field of education from members working at different levels, in different bodies. One of the teacher shared how the 'collective' and its initiative in reading together and also in bringing out booklet for example on an against corporal punishment in schools by the group members has help to be more self-reflective on his own handling and dealing with students in the class and the school. He said that working on the booklet has created more awareness and now he realised that how many of the teachers' behaviour towards students were wrong. He also shared that now-a-days the school environment is not conducive for meaningful teaching-learning due to various non-academic workload pressure on the teachers. In this situation, it is the collective which gives a platform to share one's own frustration and also try to help in finding means and ways of negotiating the pressure collectively. Most importantly he said that group collective helps him be self-aware of him as a teacher.

Their Understanding of the Teacher Education Programme and its Influence in Shaping them as Teachers

What is worth underlining is that they pointed to their teaching experience, fellow colleagues' work, academic pursuits and organisational associations too for enabling them to grapple with pedagogic challenges in classrooms. One of the teachers elaborated by saying "as a teacher it was difficult to clearly point out how much of his activities are influenced by the teacher education programme (he did B.Ed.)." However, he said that, "the B.Ed. programme's liberal part of philosophy, sociology and politics has had its influence on me as a teacher." He said, "it is difficult to quantify its influence because for someone who has done B.Ed., M.Ed. or other courses does not mean they/those other degrees/learning, exposures and experiences does not have its influence."

Areas, Issues, which they Feel, in the Light of their Practice, should have been part of the Teacher Education Programmes they went through

They felt that there was the need for greater sensitization to various issues, legal aspects concerning various Acts, child rights, sexual violence, issues related to minorities, *dalits* and their rights, and exposure to various non-academic tasks. They felt that unless these issues are oriented to the student-teachers during their teacher education programme it will be very difficult for them to work as teachers when they join schools. It was also felt that the duration of the practice-teaching in teacher education programme, such as the B.Ed. was too short to make sense of the relationship between theory and practice. One of the teachers who had done his teacher education programme through the DIET pointed out that there is an urgent need to update the curriculum too. One of the teachers pointed (sarcastically) that due to numerous non-academic work on government school teachers, it will be good if DIET students are taught how to maintain registers during their teacher education programme. He cited that even if you do not engage in teaching-learning, if your registers are maintained properly and up-to-date you feel 'quite safe'.

Their Understanding on the Phenomenon of Teaching in Public Schools by Non-qualified Persons coming from the Voluntary Sector

The teachers were not just sceptical but also critical of the increasing phenomenon of non-qualified persons coming/allowed to 'teach' in public schools. Their concerns were largely centred on a decrease in the professional and academic inputs required for teaching, a reduction in the standards set for and expectations from public schools in comparison to the private schools catering to the children of the elite classes and the harmful effects of trying to rest what should be a national, public-funded, common and robust concern on the bases of an uncertain charitable or profiteering sectors. So they are opposed to the permission given to people with no professional qualification coming to teach in government schools on three things. First, as stated above it sends a message that teaching is a profession which does not need any prior qualification or training, therefore, it is a threat to the teaching profession. Secondly, it creates inequality between the government schools and the private low fee charging schools with that of the so-called elite private schools. Because it is seen that in the government and the private low fee charging schools, the government permits teachers with no professional Teacher Education to teach but one does not find those people teaching in the elite schools. So they say that it is also a threat to how the government policy will be framed. Thirdly, these teachers who come to teach as teachers in government schools through many of the NGOs are not qualified enough and they come with very narrow and limited expectations from the students. One of the teachers says, "These teachers' expectations from the students is only making them clear the class-X or class-XII only and then getting into some kind of employment. They do not expect anything beyond this from the students so it limits the horizons of the students when taught with such narrow expectations." Another teacher says that "even if one someone comes to the school to teach with a good intention if one is not trained or have a teacher education degree they will not be able to make good students. He gave an example of a sweet maker (halwai wala). He says, "even if the best of ingredients is used to make sweets, if the person does not know how to make the sweet it will not make a good and tasty sweet." For him teaching involves values and ethics which those coming for short period of interventions in schools are only interested in learning outcomes in a short span of time. They do not engage with students for long duration engaging with them in the understanding and development of students in areas of values and ethics which takes a lot of efforts and time from the teachers.

Conclusion

Teacher education institutions should be embedded in universities as they provide a more conducive and democratic environment for academics, scholars and practitioners to not only engage with their parent disciplines but also carry a continuous intellectual dialogue across disciplines. It is also noticeable that many members of the said organisation are either still pursuing higher education formally or keeping themselves even personally engaged with the university. One way to understand their coming together and carrying forward a politicised intellectual intervention with the system is to see the central and enabling role of the institutional space of a university in this process. Their story till date tells us that teacher preparation institutions must not remain cocooned from the hustle-bustle of an autonomous academia. Another lesson we can take away from their collective is to reinvigorate the academic content of our teacher education institutions. As the example of the teachers' collective presented here suggest, the urgency of both these arguments is particularly enhanced under the politico-economic circumstances being created by an accelerating neo-liberalism. We can also read another message in the work of the group. The possibility of a professional identity developing among teachers is directly related to at least two factors. One is that of the academic, disciplinarian strength of their institutions. The other is to do with the kind and extent of activism they are able to engage in as collectives. Both these bear a unique relationship with the autonomous setting and republican-responsibility of a university.

9

Reshaping Teacher Education Curriculum

B.C. Das and *Namita Sahoo*

Reshaping teacher education curriculum has been imperative for two genres of teacher role: (i) encouraging, supportive and humane facilitator in teaching-learning situations who enables learners to discover their talents, to realize their physical and intellectual potentialities to the fullest, to develop character and desirable social and human values to function as responsible citizens; and (ii) an active member of the group of persons who make conscious efforts to contribute to the process of renewal of school curriculum, to maintain its relevance to the changing societal and personal needs of learners, keeping in view the experiences gained in the past and the concerns and imperatives that have emerged in the light of changing national development goals and educational priorities. These expectations suggest that the teachers have to be responsive and sensitive to the social context of education, learner diversities, as well as in the macro national and global contexts, the national concerns for achieving the goals of equity, parity, social justice and also excellence (NCERT, 2005).

The preparation of teachers contributes a great extent to the quality of school education. Since, the term quality has been redefined as fitness for the purpose, teacher education has to consider two distinct basic premises: one is the emerging demands of present day school education and other is the evolvement of relevant vision for the most needful teacher preparation. This chapter zeroes in on need for empowerment of teachers, teacher education vision as evolved by international and national agencies, teacher education curriculum with reference to its vision guides and vision driven parameters for quality improvement in teacher preparation. Further, a shifting teacher role in emerging teaching-leaning scenario has been examined with reference to learners' need and technological advancement.

Global Vision of Teacher Education

The expectations from the teacher are manifold and multifaceted. As the International Commission on Education (*Learning: The Treasure Within*, UNESCO, 1996) suggests the importance of the role of the teacher as an agent of change, promoting understanding and tolerance, has never been more critical in the Twenty-first century. The need for change from narrow nationalism to universalism, from ethnic and cultural prejudice to tolerance, understanding and pluralism, from autocracy to democracy in its various manifestations, and from a technologically divided world where high technology is the privilege of the few to a technologically united world, places enormous responsibilities on teachers who participate in the moulding of the minds and characters of the new generation. The stakes are high and the moral values formed in childhood and throughout life become of particular importance. UNICEF's overarching goal for Teacher Education (TE) is to strengthen government systems that enhance the capacity of teachers to deliver quality education—with equity. Specifically, the following changes are planned:

1. Professionalization of the teaching profession by establishing stronger linkages with the higher education sector and promoting longer duration (four-or five-year) pre-service courses for teachers, along with continuous in-service

professional development opportunities that nurture teachers through a process of personal transformation and growth.

2. A strong cadre of teacher educators who have a clear vision and understanding of practical experience in applying these in classrooms, and strong facilitation and mentoring skills.
3. Training programmes that use constructivist methodologies that enable teachers to reflect on their beliefs, attitudes and classroom experience, and to discuss together to plan the innovations they want to bring into their own classrooms.
4. A culture of continuous collaboration with Teacher Resource Centres having a variety of reading materials and resources regularly used by Trainers and Teachers, and Teacher Mentors who offer regular on-site support to teachers.
5. Teachers that are empowered to become reflective practitioners, equipped with the vision, attitudes, knowledge and skills required to design effective classroom strategies to meet diverse learners' needs, along with the freedom and support needed to implement these.

Goals-to-reach

The Global Thematic Consultation on Education in the Post-2015 Development Agenda proposed "*Equitable, Quality Education and Lifelong Learning for All*" as the overarching goal for education. It also recommended developing specific goals, indicators and targets around a number of priority areas.[1] It has been one of the priority areas of the post-2015 education agenda of UNESCO. UNESCO, as lead agency for education for sustainable development (ESD), has been actively promoting the role of education in the follow-up to the United Nations Conference on Sustainable Development (Rio+20) and the current process for setting the Sustainable Development Goals (SDGs) and is working with partners to generate recommendations and define next steps to inform the post-2015 development agenda.[2] While much has yet to be decided, the overarching framework of the post-2015 development agenda is likely to be defined by one set of global goals to eradicate poverty in the context of sustainable development.[3] Since its launch in 2000, the existing EFA agenda has helped to drive remarkable progress, but some critical areas remain unaddressed and progress has slowed in recent years and EFA will remain an unfinished agenda.[4] Insufficient opportunities to access higher levels of learning, including for the acquisition of knowledge and skills in ICT ("e-literacy"), especially in the developing/low-income countries, is resulting in a knowledge divide with serious consequences on the chances of employment in today's technology-driven worldwide.[5] In addition to being a stand-alone goal in the post-2015 development agenda, education should also be integrated into other development goals as an important means for their implementation, thereby highlighting the interaction of education with other goals.[6] The post-2015 education agenda must clearly recognize the importance of education for individual empowerment, national socio-economic development and human development. In addition to the acquisition of basic knowledge and skills, the content of learning must promote understanding and respect for human rights; inclusion and equity; cultural diversity; and foster a desire and capacity for lifelong learning and learning to live together, all of which are essential to the realization of peace, responsible citizenship, and sustainable development.[7]

The following principles may be applied to guide the future education agenda[8]:

(1) Education is a fundamental human right[9] and inextricably linked to the realization of other rights.

(2) Education is a public good. The state is the custodian of the principle of education as a public good. At the same time, the role of civil society, communities, parents and other stakeholders is crucial in the provision of quality education.

(3) Education is a foundation for human fulfilment, peace, sustainable development, gender equality and responsible global citizenship.

(4) Education is a key contributor to reducing inequalities and reducing poverty by bequeathing conditions and generating opportunities for better, sustainable lives.

Growing evidence of poor quality education contributing to low learning levels and learning deficits (or inequalities) has led policy-makers and the international community to a renewed focus on improving the provision of quality education.

Several key aspects contribute to improving the quality of education:

(a) Recruiting and retaining well trained and motivated teachers, who use inclusive, gender-responsive and participatory pedagogical approaches to ensure effective learning outcomes,
(b) Providing content that is relevant to all learners and to the context in which they live,
(c) Establishing learning environments that are safe, gender-responsive inclusive and conducive to learning, and encompass mother tongue-based multilingual education,
(d) Ensuring that learners reach sufficient levels of knowledge and competencies according to national standards at each level,
(e) Strengthening capacities for learners to be innovative and creative, and to assimilate change in their society and the workplace and over their life spans, and
(f) Strengthening the ways education contributes to peace, responsible citizenship, and sustainable development and inter-cultural dialogue.

Shifting Roles of Teachers

A UNESCO publication, *The Changing Role of the Teacher*, states: 'There was a time when the teacher's role was to pass down to the younger generation the knowledge, experiences and mythology of a slowly evolving society. The pace of change in contemporary society has made this role redundant. The modern teacher must be, among other things, a change-agent. It does not matter whether one is addressing the situation in a developing country or an industrialized nation, the problem remains the same. What are the new dimensions of his/her role, and how is the teacher to be trained to fulfil that role. In examining the changing role of the teacher we need to see the changes as being a response to, and an attempt to confront, pressures of a society undergoing constant transition—that is, from one of transmitter of culture to one of transformer of culture. *Transmission* of culture refers to culture as relatively static and sees mankind's role as being a relatively passive one in which culture shapes the individual, while *transformation* of culture connotes that mankind is a creator of culture. It is of course quite difficult to take just one of the two views, because man is both a creator and a creature of his culture. This has clear implications for what is expected of teacher-educators and teachers. This particular section[10], which deals with the changing status and roles in the Asia-Pacific region, begins with the quotation from the UNESCO publication for three reasons. First, it illustrates the fact that the impact of economic, social and cultural changes on the role of the teacher is an area that has been of long-standing interest to UNESCO. Second, it highlights the issue as being a persistent one which requires the development of long-term rather than short-term strategies and solutions. Third, it shows an area of concern that transcends national boundaries, because all countries, both developed and developing, seek more effective ways to better equip their teachers to more adequately cope with their roles in the classroom, school and local community. What is stressed is that education is a dynamic not a static phenomenon. Changes in society are always reflected in educational structures and reforms, such changes often being the result of a continuous process of scientific and technological development. These processes of change have also been accelerating exponentially. Changes have tremendous implications for educational development. For teachers, this also means change *via* in-service education/training and, more importantly, through self-education to update knowledge and skills—which is not easy to effect. The countries in the region are culturally diverse, they also face certain common categories of problems, and so it is anticipated that they can perhaps do more (through mutual co-operation) to devise some common solutions to those problems. In view of this and to help ensure that limited human and financial resources are used most effectively and efficiently in the interest of developing high-quality programmes, there is a greater need and possibility for sharing resources in the region through the development of a multi-state or an intra-regional approach to teacher education than is currently being explored.

Teacher Education in India

The National Education Policy, 2020 vision statement for rejuvenation of teacher education highlights:

- By 2030, only educationally sound, multidisciplinary, and integrated teacher education programmes shall be in force.
- As teacher education requires multidisciplinary inputs, and education in high-quality content as well as pedagogy, all teacher education programmes must be conducted within composite multidisciplinary institutions. To this end, all multidisciplinary universities and colleges—will aim to establish, education departments which, besides carrying out cutting-edge research in various aspects of education, will also run B.Ed. programmes, in collaboration with other departments such as psychology, philosophy, sociology, neuroscience, Indian languages, arts, music, history, literature, physical education, science and mathematics.
- Moreover, all stand-alone TEIs will be required to convert to multidisciplinary institutions by 2030, since they will have to offer the 4-year integrated teacher preparation programme.
- The 4-year integrated B.Ed. offered by such multidisciplinary HEIs will, by 2030, become the minimal degree qualification for school teachers. The 4-year

integrated B.Ed. will be a dual-major holistic Bachelor's degree, in Education as well as a specialized subject such as a language, history, music, mathematics, computer science, chemistry, economics, art, physical education etc.

- Beyond the teaching of cutting-edge pedagogy, the teacher education will include grounding in sociology, history, science, psychology, early childhood care and education, foundational literacy and numeracy, knowledge of India and its values/ethos/art/traditions, and more.
- The HEI offering the 4-year integrated B.Ed. may also run a 2-year B.Ed., for students who have already received a Bachelor's degree in a specialized subject. A 1-year B.Ed. may also be offered for candidates who have received a 4-year undergraduate degree in a specialized subject. Scholarships for meritorious students will be established for the purpose of attracting outstanding candidates to the 4-year, 2-year, and 1-year B.Ed. programmes.
- Each higher education institution will have a network of government and private schools to work closely with, where potential teachers will student-teach along with participating in other activities such as community service, adult and vocational education etc.
- In order to maintain uniform standards for teacher education, the admission to pre-service teacher preparation programmes shall be through suitable subject and aptitude tests conducted by the National Testing Agency.
- The use of technology platforms such as SWAYAM/ DIKSHA for online training of teachers will be encouraged, so that standardized training programmes can be administered to large numbers of teachers within a short span of time.

The National Council for Teacher Education (NCTE) in its National Curriculum Framework for Teacher Education, 2009 states the broader vision of teacher education programme in India.

- Teacher education is integrative and elective and cannot be prescriptive. It should be open and flexible suiting to the changing contexts, as the aim is to empower the teachers to relate themselves to those changing contexts.
- Modern teacher education functions under a global canvas created by the concepts of 'learning society', 'learning to learn' and 'inclusive education'. The concern is to make teacher education liberal, humanistic and responsive to the demands of inclusive education.
- Modern pedagogy drives its inspiration more from sociological and anthropological insights on education. There is increasing recognition of social context as a source for rejuvenating teaching and learning. Multi-cultural education and teaching for diversity are the needs of contemporary times.
- The existence of diversity of learning spaces and curriculum sites (farms, workplaces, home, community and media) apart from classroom is universally acknowledged. The diversity of learning styles that children exhibit and learning contexts in which teachers have to function—oversized classrooms, language, ethnic and social diversities, children suffering from disadvantages of different kinds—are also getting wider attention.
- The tentative and fluid nature of the knowledge base of teacher education is now increasingly realized which makes reflective practice of the central aim of teacher education. Pedagogical knowledge has to constantly undergo adaptation to meet the needs of diverse contexts through critical reflection by the teachers on their own practices.

Goals-to-reach

- To offer hands-on support to help states develop and successfully implement comprehensive roadmaps for Teacher Education reform under the new TE Scheme/ Mission in the light of National Education Policy 2020.

- To work towards strengthening of District Institute of Education and Training (DIETs) and capacity-building of DIET Teacher Educators in states, through partnerships with other Resource Organizations.
- To generate resources to strengthen TE programmes and methodologies, to translate the vision of NCF 2005/ NCFTE 2009/or the subsequent NCF 2023 and NCFTE based on NEP 2020 into a reality in classrooms.
- To explore quality options for Training Untrained Teachers, and help states implement these solutions for meeting RTE-Samagra Siksha goals without compromising quality.
- To partner with states and selected universities to develop Schools of Education to become Centres of Excellence in Teacher Education, conducting innovative TE programmes (B.El.Ed, Integrated B.A/B.Sc-B.Ed Programmes, M.A/M.Sc-B.Ed Programme, and Integrated B.Ed-M.Ed Programme etc.) as well as interdisciplinary research on elementary/secondary education.

Incompatible with the current pedagogical emphasis on teacher education needs to build teacher capacities to construct knowledge, to deal with diverse contexts and to develop abilities to discern and judge in moments of uncertainty and fluidity, the characteristics of teaching-learning environments (NCERT, 2009).

The teacher education programmes have to comprise such features as would enable the teachers or student-teachers to care for children/learners who love to be with them; understand children within social, cultural and political contexts; view learning as a search for meaning out of personal experience; understand the way learning occurs, possible ways of creating conducive conditions for learning, differences among students in respect of the kind, pace and styles of learning; view knowledge generation as a continuously evolving process of reflective learning; view knowledge not necessarily as an external reality embedded in textbooks but as constructed in the shared context of teaching-learning and personal experiences; be sensitive to the social, professional and administrative contexts in which they have to operate; be receptive and constantly learning, own responsibility towards society and work to build a better world; develop appropriate competencies to be able to not only seek the above understandings in actual situations but also be able to create them; have a sound knowledge base and basic proficiency in language; identify their own personal expectations, perceptions of self, capacities and inclinations; and consciously attempt to formulate one's own professional orientation to determine his/her role as a teacher in situation specific contexts (NCERT, 2006).

The NCF 2005, NCFTE 2009 and NCF 2023 have focused on the major shifts in teacher education programme, which needs to be a quick look while planning any teacher education programme for teachers. Accordingly, the policy recommendations of NEP 2020 talks about reforms in teacher education reads as, "the high respect for teachers and the high status of the teaching profession must be revived and restored for the very best to be inspired to enter the profession, for teachers to be well-motivated and empowered to innovate and for education to, therefore, reach the heights and levels that are truly required to ensure the best possible future for our children and our nation." The following highlights are linked with the spirit of NEP 2020:

- The learner and learning process constitute the certainty of all endeavours of school education. The learner is seen as active participant rather than passive recipient of school learning; and his/her capabilities and potentials are seen as dynamic and capable of development through direct self-experience. Teachers need to develop empathetic understanding of the learners and insights into their thinking and learning.
- Learning should be appreciated as a participatory process that takes place in the shared social context of the learner's immediate environment consisting of peers, family members and social community. The social climate of the

school and classroom exert a deep influence on the process of learning and education as a whole.

- Different contexts lead to difference in learning. Learning in school is influenced and enhanced by the social contexts outside the school. Therefore, the programme should help teachers to develop social sensitivity and consciousness of their human sensibilities.
- Teacher assumes a position of centre stage as a source of knowledge, as custodian and manager of all teaching-learning process and executor of all educational and administrative mandates. In this context, the teacher's role needs to be shifted from being a source of knowledge to being a facilitator of learner's efforts to transform information/experiences into knowledge/wisdom.
- Knowledge in teacher education programme needs to be multidisciplinary and integrated in nature within the context of education. Knowledge is not to be viewed as external to the learners but as something that is actively constructed during learning. Teacher education should integrate academic knowledge and professional learning meaningfully.
- Teacher education programme needs to provide the space for engagement with issues and concerns of contemporary Indian society, its pluralistic nature, and issues of identity, gender, equity, livelihood and poverty. It should help the teachers to reconceptualise citizenship education in terms of human rights and approaches of critical pedagogy; emphasize environment and its protection, living in harmony within oneself and social environment; promote peace, democratic way of life, constitutional values of equality, justice, liberty, fraternity and secularism, and caring values.
- In view of multiple facets of objectives of teacher education, the evaluation/assessment protocol needs to be comprehensive and continuous using various modes like self-assessment, peer assessment, teacher's feedback and formal formative and summative assessments.

- All appraisals aim at improvement, understanding what the strengths are, what are to be improved and what are the next goals in the learning process.
- In brief, the new vision of teacher education will be more responsive to changes in the school system as it envisages a significant paradigm shift. The major shifts are given in Table 9.1.

Table 9.1: Major Shift in Teacher Education

From	To
• Teacher centric, stable design • Teacher directions and decisions • Teacher guidance and monitoring • Passive reception in learning • Learning within the four walls of the classroom • Knowledge as given and fixed • Disciplinary focus • Linear exposure • Appraisal, short, few	• Learner centric flexible process • Learner autonomy • Facilitates, supports and encourages learning • Active participation in learning • Learning in the wider social context • Knowledge as it evolves and is created • Multidisciplinary educational focus • Multiple and divergent exposure • Multifarious and continuous

Quality Improvement in Teacher Education

The NAAC and NCTE have entered into a MoU for quality assurance in Teacher Education (NCTE Act 12k). The following parameters and related criteria have been prescribed for quality improvement in Teacher Education (Table 9.2).

The parameters and the related criteria as shown in Table 9.2 have indicated the way to quality improvement in Teacher Education. The NAAC and NCTE have been encouraging for quality assessment of Teacher Education Institutions in India. The NAAC has enumerated the benefits of quality assessment of Teacher Education Institutions in the following manner:

Table 9.2: Parameters and Criteria of Assessment of Teacher Education Institutions

Parameters	Criteria of Assessment
P-I. Curriculum Designing and Planning	1. Admission procedure 2. Details of working and teaching days 3. Student ability level 4. Features of current syllabi and mechanisms for its monitoring and mid-course correction 5. Developing new courses; gestation time and running new courses 6. Curriculum design (Institutions' mission and goals, Feedback mechanism, Institution-school communication, Inter/multidisciplinary components)
P-II. Curriculum Transaction and Evaluation	1. Curriculum transaction aspects, components and details 2. Faculty professional development and seminars, conferences etc. for others 3. Faculty appraisal techniques 4. Focus on specific aspects: value education, civic responsibilities, personality development, community orientation, learn-to-learn etc. 5. Evaluation scheme: Theory-assignments and project work, Practice teaching, curricular activities, work experience, SUPW, tutorial, seminar etc. 6. Other teaching-learning innovations
P-III. Research Development and Extension	1. Research related activities: research by faculty, research by scholars (M.Ed., M.Phil., Ph.D.), financial inputs for research and research projects (completed, in progress and outlay) 2. Extension: Types of extension activities, support to Government Organizations and NGOs, NSS and NCC 3. Development: various material development activities

(*Contd.*)

Parameters	Criteria of Assessment
P-IV. Infrastructure and Learning Resources	1. Infrastructure existing and projected expansions (Financial inputs for future development especially Academic Growth, Maintenance, Utilization, Upkeep of campus) 2. Learning resources (Library and its facilities, Library annual budgets: books and periodicals, Reprographic, audio-visual material and internet related facilities, Library stock, Computers' availability and use, Laboratories' availability, maintenance and utilization
P-V. Student Support and Progression	1. System efficiency: results, NET and SLET related, annual examaminations 2. Alumni association 3. Feedback mechanism (from trainees) 4. Financial help and types 5. Guide and consultancy services and personal and academic counselling 6. Placement services and its use 7. Admission related facilities and their publicity 8. Recreational/leisure time facilities especially indoor 9. Activity clubs: cultural and literary
P-VI. Organization and Management	1. Internal coordination and monitoring mechanism 2. Steps for improvement of organization and management 3. Academic calendar 4. Faculty recruitment 5. Professional development of non-teaching staff 6. Fee structure 7. Heads of expenditure and excess/deficit budget 8. Internal audit

(Contd.)

Parameters	Criteria of Assessment
	9. Welfare programmes and grievance redressal system 10. Endowment and Reserve Funds 11. Internal Quality check and TQM 12. Modern managerial concepts and practices 13. Twinning programmes, student exchange programmes and collaboration with SCERT, NCERT and NUEPA

- Helps institutions to know their strength, weaknesses and opportunities through an informed peer review process;
- Gives institutions a new sense of direction and identity;
- Initiates institutions into innovative and modern method of pedagogy;
- Enhances collegiality on campus; it helps institutions to identify internal areas of planning and resource allocation;
- Provides society in general and employers in particular with reliable information on quality of education offered;
- Promotes inter- and intra-institutional interactions; and
- Provides funding agencies with objective data for performance based funding.

Paradigm Shift in Teaching-Learning

The paradigm shift in teaching-learning at school education stage and teacher role has been witnessed in the context of:

- Industrial age model of education *versus* Digital age model of education;
- Broadcast model of learning *versus* Enquiry based learning;
- Individual learning *versus* Collaborative learning;
- Teacher relevance is at threat;
- Mere mastery of knowledge is not sufficient;
- Discussion, debate and collaboration; and

- Instant adjustment/conceptualization of context and content.

Table 9.3: Traditional classroom *versus* Flipped classroom

Traditional classroom	Flipped classroom
• Information is delivered in classroom • Information processing takes place at home • Knowledge consumers • Has a physical space • Physical space/architecture of classroom shapes the communication flow • Communication and knowledge is based on top-down flow of information • Does not encourage communication and cooperation between the students • Teacher is the only source of information	• At home • In the classroom (exercises and group work) • Knowledge Producers • Physical space is not essential • Communication flows in multiple channels • Teachers and students are co-producers of information/ knowledge • Encourages intensive involvement and participation of students • Multiple sources of information

Preparing Teachers with Digital Pedagogy

1. *Spatio-Temporal Dimension: Ubiquitous Learning*

- Learning in digital era can happen anywhere and anytime.
- No space or time boundaries.
- Beyond the walls of classroom and cells of time table.
- Lifelong learning is possible in all contexts.

2. *Epistemic Dimension: Active Knowledge Production*

- Learners become active knowledge producers (Ex: project based learning, experiential learning and apprenticeships -using multiple knowledge sources).
- Learners' need to be activity engaged.

- Horizontal (peer to peer) learning/relationships are encouraged.
- Shift from Cognition/memory to knowledge presentation/ representation.

3. *Discursive Dimension: Multi-model Learning*

- Use of new media resources.
- Use of digital media to link text, diagrams, tables, datasets, video documentation, audio recordings etc.

4. *Evaluative Dimension: Recursive Feedback*

- New assessment systems.
- Continuous machine-mediated assessment.
- Just-in time feedback.
- Quantitative assessment and Qualitative assessment go together.

5. *Social Dimension: Collaborative Intelligence*

- Learning as social activity rather than individual memory.
- Secrecy of learning replaced by open learning and sharing.

6. *Cognitive Dimension: Meta-cognition*

- Extensive giving and receiving feedback.
- Learners are both self and peer assessors.

7. *Comparative Dimension: Differentiated Learning*

- The experience *'to be on the same page'* relevant for traditional teaching.
- In digital era: learning takes different patterns (time, types of content, tools) to be on the same page. Technology makes it possible!

  The age old idea that spells, "I am a teacher and I have knowledge;

  Get ready; here it comes!

Your goal is to take data into your memory, so you can recall it to me when I test you."

Is no longer appropriate for the digital age as there has been continuous and faster—

- Information explosion.
- Multiple sources of information.
- Digital orientation of students.
- Students' growing desire to converse and share.
- Students as partners in the learning process.
- Current generation views learning place should be fun and play.
- Learning process should open up minds throwing up challenges.

Key Action Areas Suggested

- Disruptive Technologies—Disruptive Instruction Models.
- Linear Thinking to Exponential Thinking.
- Physical identity to Digital identity.
- Different strokes to different people.

Hence, a 4D Framework to digitize, disrupt, dematerialize and democratize is suggested.

Conclusions

It can be concluded that teacher education institutions must take enough care in adapting shifting vision and guidelines of international and national agencies of education while preparing next generation teachers. Education is so much more than mere transfer of information. Teachers are the knowledge leaders. They are not supposed to pass the 'information only' to students. Information has to be assimilated. Teachers have to take the role of a leader, a manager, a facilitator of knowledge. Students have to connect the information to what they already know developmental models, learn how to apply the new knowledge and how to adapt this knowledge to new and unfamiliar situation.

NOTES

1. UNESCO and UNICEF (2013), "Envisioning Education in the Post-2015 Development Agenda". Executive Summary. Global Thematic Consultation on Education in the Post-2015 Development Agenda, en.unesco.org/post2015/sites/post2015/files/Post-2015_EN_web.pdf.
2. For UNESCO's position on Rio+20, see UNESCO (2012), *From Green Economies to Green Societies*, pp. 13-22 for education, http://unesdoc.unesco.org/images/0021/002133/213311e.pdf.
3. The importance of education has also been recognized under other themes of the global MDG consultation, including in the Post-2015 Thematic Consultation on Environmental Sustainability. A "good education" was voted as the top priority, before better health care and good governance in MY WORLD, a United Nations global survey aiming to capture priorities for the next set of global goals to end poverty. See: http://data.myworld2015.org/
4. This draws on analysis in the forthcoming 2013/4 *EFA Global Monitoring Report*, along with the 2012 *EFA Global Monitoring Report*, based on data from the UNESCO Institute for Statistics database as well as other sources including from internationally-comparable household surveys presented in the World Inequality Database on Education (WIDE).
5. UNESCO 2012. Education and skills for inclusive and sustainable development beyond 2015. Thematic Think Piece prepared for the United Nations Task Team on the Post-2015 United Nations Development Agenda.
6. This can be undertaken through the development of education related indicators for health, employment etc. UNESCO (2012).
7. UNESCO Principles on Education for Development beyond 2015.
8. For further details on each of these principles please refer to the UNESCO education sector websites.
9. See Article 26 of the Universal Declaration of Human Rights which states: (1) everyone has the right to education. Education shall be free, at least in the elementary and fundamental stages. Elementary education shall be compulsory. Technical and professional education shall be made generally available and higher education shall be equally accessible to all on the basis of merit.
10. Based on the paper prepared by Dr. Leonardo de la Cruz and Dr. H.K Paik, entitled *Changing Status and Roles of Teachers in Asia and the Pacific: Implications for Educational Developments, 1988.*

REFERENCES

NAAC (2010). *Quality Enhancement in Teacher Education*, Bangalore.

NCERT (2005). *National Curriculum Framework for School Education*, New Delhi.

NCF (2005). *National Curriculum Framework*, New Delhi: NCERT.

NCF-SE (2023). *National Curriculum Framework for School Education*, New Delhi: NCERT.

NCTE (2009). *National Curriculum Framework for Teacher Education*, New Delhi.

NEP (2020). *National Education Policy, Government of India*, MHRD/ Ministry of Education.

UNESCO (1996). *Learning: The Treasure Within, Report of International Commission on Education*, Paris.

UNICEF.in/Whatwedo/15/Teacher-Education#sthash.JLxBued0. Nfs6auMm.dpuf.

10

Student-Teachers' Perception towards Integrated Teacher Education Curriculum

P.K. Sahoo and *Priyanka Sharma*

The teacher education curriculum plays an important role in the present education system. The various teacher education programmes have been restructured to strengthen the base of school system. The NCTE has emphasized the process dimension of curriculum with longer duration of different programmes to develop professionalism among student-teachers of different stages. It insisted on a holistic perspective of teacher education programme. NCTE regulation (2014) has incorporated various forms of integrated approaches in teacher preparation at elementary level and secondary level. The NCTE has prepared the guidelines for implementation of Integrated B.El.Ed. programme, BA.B.Ed/B.Sc.B.Ed. Programme in composite institutions. The NEP 2020 highlights "Teacher education for all levels Foundation Preparatory Middle and Secondary will take place within... Four- year Integrated Teacher Education Programme, combining content, pedagogy, and practical training." The curricular reforms in teacher education have emphasized on prolonged internship activities in real school situation. While process aspects have been given priority in teacher preparation, continuous evaluation of learners as an inbuilt component have been focused in stage specific teacher education programmes. The semester programme, credit based assessment and choice based credit system have been implemented as per UGC norm at university level. It is pertinent to explore perception of student-teachers enrolled in School Education of different central universities to know the extent of benefits earned through learning integrated programme of teacher preparation.

Rationale of the Study

There have been studies which in reveal meaningful findings about structural reform in teacher education curriculum. Saleha (2012) found that student-teachers viewed internship programme as a real opportunity to refine and improve their teaching skills in actual school setting. The results of the interviews with the principals revealed that internship programme was of crucial importance and it had positive impact on the performance of student-teachers. Sarangi (2015) conducted a study of four-year integrated teacher education programme in India. The objectives of the study were to investigate the reason that led to the opening of four-year integrated teacher education courses. Historical method is used for collecting data and information. The study revealed the history of pre-service programmes of teacher education. Pervasive problem of teacher education in the country was the tendency to resist change and maintain *status quo* while the tempo of social, scientific and technological changes had accelerated. It is high time for the educational thinkers, planners and administrators to free the teacher education from the chains of this *status-quoism*.

Chakrabarty (2016) stated that work based learning through Internship has to be implemented. The study revealed that the permission from the Inspector of School be sought for conduct of Internship in schools; respective schools must express willingness in such type of arrangement and student-teachers should be well adjusted in respective schools. Adhikary (2017) reported about teacher trainees' mixed perception towards the two-year B.Ed.

programme in Assam. Dhull and Sharma (2017) conducted "*A Study on Curricular Reforms in Teacher Education*". The first draft of teacher education curriculum was published in 1978 and since then almost after every ten years, a new framework having modifications in accordance with contemporary needs was made available by NCTE. Mahato and Behera (2018) focused on "*Attitude of B.Ed. Student-Teachers towards Practicum*". The study revealed that student-teachers' attitude towards Practicum did not differ significantly. Prajapati (2018) revealed that the integrated programmes are of innovative nature in teacher education. They enhance student engagement through interdisciplinary experiential and dynamic learning. The practice teaching, school administration and management bring the reality of a professional environment in the learning process. Students enrolled in such programmes get two degrees by investing three years in the place of four years. Students not only invest one year less but also learn a deep pedagogical content knowledge in these programmes. Universities and institutions having appropriate faculties can run these programmes. Sahoo and Sharma (2018) found student-teachers appreciation of teacher education programme, in RIE, Bhubaneswar and IASE, Cuttak, Odisha. Of course, some Arts stream students had expressed dissent notes about the duration of programme. These studies have focused on general issues concerning teacher education. Sahoo and Sharma (2018) had conducted study on "*Teacher Educators' and Student-Teachers' Perception of Evaluation Process of Teacher Education Programmes at University level in U.P*". The study intended to explore student-teachers' and teacher-educators' perception towards evaluation process in the context of programme background. It was found that the students and teachers of university education departments having exposures to evaluation reform, provided meaningful feedback about evaluation of learners and evaluation of institutions. Yibeltal (2019) conducted study on "*Perceived Pedagogical-Content Knowledge of Teachers: Classroom Practices of as Correlates of College of Teachers Education Students' Academic Result*". The study revealed that teachers perceived their Pedagogical knowledge with higher weightage than the expected mean. It was much higher than the satisfactory level. There are very few studies conducted on integrated programmes of teacher education. Many changes are needed to improve the present curriculum. It was thought appropriate to explore student-teachers perception towards curriculum reform in the B.A.B.Ed. and B.Sc.B.Ed. programmes offered by the school of Education of Central Universities of the country. It is presumed that the students of university education departments having exposures to reform, will provide meaningful feedback about such process. Hence, the present study has been conducted to explore their views of student-teachers about different aspects of perspectives in education, practicum and school internship. The present study is restricted to four year integrated B.A.B.Ed. and B.Sc.B.Ed. programmes offered in the Central Universities.

Objectives of the Study

1. To study the perception of Integrated B.Ed. students towards different areas of B.A.B.Ed./B.Sc.B.Ed. Curriculum.
2. To study the association between the discipline background of students and their perception towards different aspects of B.A.B.Ed/B.Sc.B.Ed. Curriculum.

Hypothesis of the Study

The discipline background of students and their perception towards different components of B.A.B.Ed and B.Sc.B.Ed are associated with each other.

Methods and Procedures

The four year integrated B.Ed. students of all the central universities were the population of this study. Universities, viz. Indira Gandhi National tribal University, Amarkantak, Madhya Pradesh and Central University of Tibetan studies, Varanasi, UP have been included in the Sample institutions of the study. Descriptive survey method was used to conduct the study. One questionnaire for student-teachers was used for data collection purpose. As stated above study was delimited to the Arts and Science student-teachers enrolled in four year B.A.B.Ed and B.Sc.B.Ed. programmes of the Central Universities. Since, the sample respondents were selected purposively, descriptive statistics and χ^2-test of independence was used for analysis of data.

Analysis and Interpretation of Data

The analysis and interpretation of the study have been presented in Table 10.1 .

Table 10.1: χ^2-test of independence between student-teachers discipline background and their perception towards the foundation courses on education theory, aims of education etc. help student-teachers to understand theoretical background of education.

Discipline	Agree	Disagree	Not Decided	Total	χ^2-value
Arts	88(88%)	11(11%)	1(1%)	100	16.2*
Science	65(65%)	25(25%)	10(10%)	100	NS
Total	**153**	**36**	**11**	**200**	

Note: *— Significant at .05 level.
NS— Not Significant.
Figures in Parentheses indicate percentages.

It can be noticed from Table 10.1 that the calculated χ^2-value of independence between response is found 16.2. The obtained value is more than the table value (5.99) at .05 level of significance with df: 2. Thus, the observed value is found significant. Hence, the perception of Arts and Science students are significantly associated with each other. A large majority of Arts students (88%) agreed about the foundation courses on education theory, aims of education etc. help student-teachers to understand theoretical background of education in comparison to their Science stream counterparts (65%).

Table 10.2: χ^2-test of independence between student-teachers discipline background and their perception towards division of basic and advanced level foundation courses are relevant to the integrated programme

Discipline	Agree	Disagree	Not Decided	Total	χ^2-value
Arts	75(75%)	22(22%)	3(3%)	100	4.03*
Science	70(70%)	20(20%)	10(10%)	100	NS
Total	**145**	**42**	**13**	**200**	

Note: *— Significant at .05 level.
NS— Not Significant.
Figures in Parentheses indicate percentages.

It can be noticed from Table 10.2 that the calculated χ^2-value of independence between response towards students is found 4.03. The obtained value is lesser than the table value (5.99) at .05 level of significance with df: 2. Thus, the observed value is not found significant. Hence, the perception of Arts and Science students are not significantly associated with each other. A majority of Arts and Science students (70-75%) agreed about division of basic and advanced level foundation courses are relevant to the integrated programme.

Table 10.3: χ^2-test of independence between student-teachers discipline background and their perception towards foundation courses provide in-depth study of processes of child development and learning concepts and perspectives in education

Discipline	Agree	Disagree	Not Decided	Total	χ^2-value
Arts	67(67%)	28(28%)	5(5%)	100	5.09*
Science	78(78%)	15(15%)	7(7%)	100	NS
Total	**145**	**43**	**12**	**200**	

Note: *— Significant at .05 level.
NS— Not Significant.
Figures in Parentheses indicate percentages.

It can be noticed from Table 10.3 that the calculated χ^2-value of independence between response towards students is found 5.09. The obtained value is lesser than the table value (5.99) at .05 level of significance with df: 2. Thus, the observed value is not found significant. Hence, the perception of Arts and Science students are not significantly associated with each other. A majority of Arts and Science students (67-78%) agreed that foundation courses provide in-depth study of processes of child development and learning concepts and perspectives in education.

Table 10.4: χ^2-test of independence between student-teachers discipline background and their perception towards the theory courses engage students in autobiographical notes and give opportunities for reflection on educational problems

Discipline	Agree	Disagree	Not Decided	Total	χ^2-value
Arts	78(78%)	15(15%)	7(7%)	100	12.7*
Science	55(55%)	25(25%)	20(20%)	100	NS
Total	**133**	**40**	**27**	**200**	

Note: *— Significant at .05 level.
NS— Not Significant.
Figures in Parentheses indicate percentages.

It can be noticed from Table 10.4 that the calculated χ^2-value of independence between response towards student is found 12.7. The obtained value is more than the table value (5.99) at .05 level of significance with df: 2. Thus, the observed value is found significant. Hence, the perception of Arts and Science students are not significantly associated with each other. A large majority of Arts students (78%) agreed about the theory courses engage students in autobiographical notes and give opportunities for reflection on educational problems in comparison to their Science stream counterparts (55%).

Table 10.5: χ^2-test of independence between student-teachers discipline background and their perception towards the courses on language and communication, critical and creative thinking are useful for better performance in teaching activities

Discipline	Agree	Disagree	Not Decided	Total	χ^2-value
Arts	85(85%)	10(10%)	5(5%)	100	19.2*
Science	57(57%)	25(25%)	18(18%)	100	NS
Total	**142**	**35**	**23**	**200**	

Note: *— Significant at .05 level.
NS— Not Significant.
Figures in Parentheses indicate percentages.

It can be noticed from Table 10.5 that the calculated χ^2-value of independence between response towards student is found 19.2. The obtained value is more than the table value (5.99) at .05 level of significance with df: 2. Thus, the observed value is found significant. Hence, the perception of Arts and Science students are significantly associated with each other. A large majority of Arts students (85%) agreed about the courses on language and communication, critical and creative thinking are useful for better performance in teaching activities in comparison to their Science stream counterparts (57%).

Table 10.6: χ^2-test of independence between student-teachers discipline background and their perception towards Constitution of India and human rights and environment education develop sociological understanding of student-teachers

Discipline	Agree	Disagree	Not Decided	Total	χ^2-value
Arts	78(78%)	20(20%)	2(2%)	100	20.1*
Science	50(50%)	35(35%)	15(15%)	100	NS
Total	**128**	**55**	**17**	**200**	

Note: *— Significant at .05 level.
NS— Not Significant.
Figures in Parentheses indicate percentages.

It can be noticed from Table 10.6 that the calculated χ^2-value of independence between response towards B.Ed. students and teachers is found 20.1. The obtained value is more than the table value (5.99) at .05 level of significance with df: 2. Thus, the observed value is found significant. Hence, the perception of Arts and Science students are significantly associated with each other. A large majority of Arts students (78%) agreed about Indian constitution and human rights and environment education develop sociological understanding of student-teachers in comparison to their Science stream counterparts (50%).

Table 10.7: χ^2-test of independence between student-teachers discipline background and their perception towards skills pertaining to ICT and Educational technology are integrated properly with various courses

Discipline	**Agree**	**Disagree**	**Not Decided**	**Total**	**χ^2-value**
Arts	85(85%)	10(10%)	5(5%)	100	3.2*
Science	75(75%)	15(15%)	10(10%)	100	NS
Total	**160**	**25**	**15**	**200**	

Note: *— Significant at .05 level.
NS— Not Significant.
Figures in Parentheses indicate percentages.

It can be noticed from Table 10.7 that the calculated χ^2-value of independence between response teachers and Arts is found 3.2. The obtained value is lesser than the table value (5.99) at .05 level of significance with df: 2. Thus, the observed value is not found significant. Hence, the perception of Science and Arts students are not significantly associated with each other. A majority of Arts and Science students (75-85%) agreed that pertaining to ICT and Educational technology are integrated properly with various courses.

Table 10.8: χ^2-test of independence between student-teachers discipline background and their perception towards skills pertaining to ICT and Educational technology contributed to develop teaching competency of student-teachers

Discipline	Agree	Disagree	Not Decided	Total	χ^2-value
Arts	68(68%)	30(30%)	2(2%)	100	20.2*
Science	52(52%)	25(25%)	23(23%)	100	NS
Total	**120**	**55**	**25**	**200**	

Note: *— Significant at .05 level.
NS— Not Significant.
Figures in Parentheses indicate percentages.

It can be noticed from Table 10.8 that the calculated χ^2-value of independence between response teachers and Arts is found 20.2. The obtained value is more than the table value (5.99) at .05 level of significance with df: 2. Thus, the observed value is found significant. Hence, the perception of Science and Arts students are significantly associated with each other. A large majority of Arts students (68%) agreed that skills pertaining to ICT and Educational technology contributed to develop teaching competency of student-teachers. in comparison to their Science stream counterparts (52%).

Table 10.9: χ^2-test of independence between student-teachers discipline background and their perception towards reflections on short field studies in a variety of contexts does not encourage linkage of ground reality with theoretical understanding

Discipline	Agree	Disagree	Not Decided	Total	χ^2-value
Arts	65(65%)	23(23%)	12(12%)	100	13.0*
Science	40(40%)	35(35%)	25(25%)	50	NS
Total	**105**	**58**	**37**	**150**	

Note: *— Significant at .05 level.
NS— Not Significant.
Figures in Parentheses indicate percentages.

It can be noticed from Table 10.9 that the calculated χ^2-value of independence between response towards teachers and B.Ed. student is found 13.0. The obtained value is more than the table value (5.99) at .05 level of significance with df: 2. Thus, the observed value is found significant. Hence, the perception of Science and Arts students are not significantly associated with each other. A large majority of Arts students (65%) agreed that reflections on short field studies in a variety of contexts does not encourage linkage of ground reality with theoretical understanding in comparison to their Science stream counterparts (40%).

Table 10.10: χ^2-test of independence between student-teachers discipline background and their perception towards observation and interaction with children and teachers in a range of settings help student-teachers to clarify the educational needs and problems of children

Discipline	Agree	Disagree	Not Decided	Total	χ^2-value
Arts	88(88%)	9(9%)	3(3%)	100	3.7*
Science	78(78%)	15(15%)	7(7%)	100	NS
Total	**166**	**24**	**10**	**200**	

Note: *— Significant at .05 level.
NS— Not Significant.
Figures in Parentheses indicate percentages.

It can be noticed from Table 10.10 that the calculated χ^2-value of independence between response towards student is found 3.7. The obtained value is lesser than the table value (5.99) at .05 level of significance with df: 2. Thus, the observed value is not found significant. Hence, the perception of Arts and Science students are not significantly associated with each other. A majority of Arts and Science students (78-88%) agreed that observation and interaction with children and teachers in a range of settings help student-teachers to clarify the educational needs and problems of children.

Table 10.11: χ^2-test of independence between student-teachers discipline background and their perception towards teaching foundation courses develop understanding of education as a discipline

Discipline	Agree	Disagree	Not Decided	Total	χ^2-value
Arts	83(83%)	14(14%)	3(3%)	100	11.2*
Science	63(63%)	25(25%)	12(12%)	100	NS
Total	**146**	**39**	**15**	**200**	

Note: *— Significant at .05 level.
NS— Not Significant.
Figures in Parentheses indicate percentages.

It can be noticed from Table 10.11 that the calculated χ^2-value of independence between response towards student is found 11.2. The obtained value is more than the table value (5.99) at .05 level of significance with df: 2. Thus, the observed value is found significant. Hence, the perception of Arts and Science students are significantly associated with each other. A large majority of Arts students (83%) agreed that teaching foundation courses develop understanding of education as a discipline in comparison to their Science stream counterparts (63%).

Table 10.12: χ^2-test of independence between student-teachers discipline background and their perception towards educational studies facilitate student-teachers to learn key concepts and principles related to Secondary school teaching

Discipline	Agree	Disagree	Not Decided	Total	χ^2-value
Arts	80(80%)	17(17%)	3(3%)	100	1.44*
Science	78(78%)	21(21%)	1(1%)	100	NS
Total	**158**	**38**	**4**	**200**	

Note: *— Significant at .05 level.
NS— Not Significant.
Figures in Parentheses indicate percentages.

It can be noticed from Table 10.12 that the calculated χ^2-value of independence between response students is found 1.44. The obtained value is lesser than the table value (5.99) at .05 level of significance with df: 2. Thus, the observed value is not found significant. Hence, the perception of Arts and Science students are not significantly associated with each other. A majority of Arts and Science students (78-80%) agreed that educational studies facilitate student-teachers to learn key concepts and principles related to Secondary school teaching.

Table 10.13: χ^2-test of independence between student-teachers discipline background and their perception towards study of pedagogic studies on own B.Sc/B.A. level subjects is useful to link subject knowledge with pedagogic principles and experience of teaching in schools

Discipline	Agree	Disagree	Not Decided	Total	χ^2-value
Arts	76(76%)	21(21%)	3(3%)	100	6.9*
Science	63(63%)	25(25%)	12(12%)	100	NS
Total	**139**	**46**	**15**	**200**	

Note: *— Significant at .05 level.
NS— Not Significant.
Figures in Parentheses indicate percentages.

It can be noticed from Table 10.13 that the calculated χ^2-value of independence between response towards students is found 6.9. The obtained value is more than the table value (5.99) at .05 level of significance with df: 2. Thus, the observed value is found significant. Hence, the perception of Science and Arts students are significantly associated with each other. A large majority of Arts students (76%) agreed that study of pedagogic studies on own B.Sc/B.A. level subjects is useful to link subject knowledge with pedagogic principles and experience of teaching in schools in comparison to their Science stream counterparts (63%).

Table 10.14: χ^2-test of independence between student-teachers discipline background and their perception towards study of pedagogic studies on own B.Sc/B.A. level subjects is useful to link subject knowledge with pedagogic principles and experience of teaching in schools

Discipline	Agree	Disagree	Not Decided	Total	χ^2-value
Arts	89(89%)	10(10%)	1(1%)	100	20.1*
Science	63(63%)	25(25%)	12(12%)	100	NS
Total	**152**	**35**	**13**	**200**	

Note: *— Significant at .05 level.
NS— Not Significant.
Figures in Parentheses indicate percentages.

It can be noticed from Table 10.14 that the calculated χ^2-value of independence between response towards students is found 20.1. The obtained value is more than the table value (5.99) at .05 level of significance with df: 2. Thus, the observed value is found significant. Hence, the perception of Science and Arts students are significantly associated with each other. A large majority of Arts students (89%) agreed that the Pedagogic courses provide opportunities to integrate subject knowledge with experiences of teaching in schools in comparison to their Science stream counterparts (63%).

Table 10.15: χ^2-test of independence between student-teachers discipline background and their perception towards curriculum and studies provide the basic knowledge about school subjects

Discipline	Agree	Disagree	Not Decided	Total	χ^2-value
Arts	76(76%)	14(14%)	10(10%)	100	3.9*
Science	65(65%)	25(25%)	10(10%)	100	NS
Total	**141**	**39**	**20**	**200**	

Note: *— Significant at .05 level.
NS— Not Significant.
Figures in Parentheses indicate percentages.

It can be noticed from Table 10.15 that the calculated χ^2-value of independence between response towards students is found 3.9. The obtained value is lesser than the table value (5.99) at .05 level of significance with df: 2. Thus, the observed value is not found significant. Hence, the perception of Science and Arts students are not significantly associated with each other. A majority of Arts and Science students (76-65%) agreed that curriculum and studies provide the basic knowledge about school subjects.

Table 10.16: χ^2-test of independence between student-teachers discipline background and their perception towards student-teacher specializing in teaching different school subjects give major emphasis on in-depth study of own branch of study in science or arts simultaneously

Discipline	**Agree**	**Disagree**	**Not Decided**	**Total**	**χ^2-value**
Arts	86(86%)	12(12%)	2(2%)	100	3.8* NS
Science	75(75%)	22(22%)	3(3%)	100	
Total	**146**	**39**	**15**	**200**	

Note: *— Significant at .05 level.
NS— Not Significant.
Figures in Parentheses indicate percentages.

It can be noticed from Table 10.16 that the calculated χ^2-value of independence between response towards students is found 3.8. The obtained value is lesser than the table value (5.99) at .05 level of significance with df: 2. Thus, the observed value is not found significant. Hence, the perception of Science and Arts students are not significantly associated with each other. A majority of Arts and Science students (86-75%) agreed that student-teacher specializing in teaching different school subjects give major emphasis on in-depth study of own branch of study in Science or Arts simultaneously.

Table 10.17: χ^2-test of independence between student-teachers discipline background and their perception towards language courses are not able to develop communicative capabilities among the student-teachers of the language in which they teach

Discipline	Agree	Disagree	Not Decided	Total	χ^2-value
Arts	80(80%)	14(14%)	6(6%)	100	5.4* NS
Science	73(73%)	25(25%)	2(2%)	100	
Total	**153**	**39**	**8**	**200**	

Note: *— Significant at .05 level.
NS— Not Significant.
Figures in Parentheses indicate percentages.

It can be noticed from Table 10.17 that the calculated χ^2-value of independence between response towards students is found 5.4. The obtained value is lesser than the table value (5.99) at .05 level of significance with df: 2. Thus, the observed value is not found significant. Hence, the perception of Science and Arts students are not significantly associated with each other. A majority of Arts and Science students (80-73%) agreed that language courses are not able to develop communicative capabilities among the student-teachers of the language in which they teach.

Table 10.18: χ^2-test of independence between student-teachers discipline background and their perception towards ICT courses provide opportunities for development of expressive and receptive capacities including listening, speaking, reading and writing

Discipline	Agree	Disagree	Not Decided	Total	χ^2-value
Arts	78(78%)	12(12%)	10(10%)	100	4.5* NS
Science	65(65%)	22(22%)	13(13%)	100	
Total	**143**	**34**	**23**	**200**	

Note: *— Significant at .05 level.
NS— Not Significant.
Figures in Parentheses indicate percentages.

It can be noticed from Table 10.18 that the calculated χ^2-value of independence between response towards students is found 4.5. The obtained value is lesser than the table value (5.99) at .05 level of significance with df: 2. Thus, the observed value is not found significant. Hence, the perception of Science and Arts students are not significantly associated with each other. A majority of Arts and Science students (78-65%) agreed that ICT courses provide opportunities for development of expressive and receptive capacities including listening, speaking, reading and writing.

Table 10.19: χ^2-test of independence between student-teachers discipline background and their perception towards self-development, performing arts and languages are useful in development of personality

Discipline	**Agree**	**Disagree**	**Not Decided**	**Total**	**χ^2-value**
Arts	79(79%)	13(13%)	8(8%)	100	4.5*
Science	68(68%)	22(22%)	10(10%)	100	NS
Total	**146**	**39**	**15**	**200**	

Note: *— Significant at .05 level.
NS— Not Significant.
Figures in Parentheses indicate percentages.

It can be noticed from Table 10.19 that the calculated χ^2-value of independence between response towards students is found 3.3. The obtained value is lesser than the table value (5.99) at .05 level of significance with df: 2. Thus, the observed value is not found significant. Hence, the perception of Science and Arts students are not significantly associated with each other. A majority of Arts and Science students (79-68%) agreed that self-development, performing Arts and languages are useful in development of personality.

It can be noticed from Table 10.20 that the calculated χ^2-value of independence between response towards students is found 12.5. The obtained value is more than the table value (5.99) at .05 level of significance with df: 2. Thus, the observed value is found significant. Hence, the perception of Science and Arts students are significantly associated with each other. A large majority of Arts students (85%) agreed school internship in teaching help student-teachers learn and enhance their professional role in real school situation in comparison to their Science stream counterparts (63%).

Table 10.20: χ^2-test of independence between student-teachers discipline background and their perception towards school internship in teaching help student-teachers learn and enhance their professional role in real school situation

Discipline	**Agree**	**Disagree**	**Not Decided**	**Total**	**χ^2-value**
Arts	85(85%)	10(10%)	5(5%)	100	12.5*
Science	63(63%)	24(24%)	13(13%)	100	NS
Total	**148**	**34**	**18**	**200**	

Note: *— Significant at .05 level.
NS— Not Significant.
Figures in Parentheses indicate percentages.

Table 10.21: χ^2-test of independence between student-teachers discipline background and their perception towards integrated course students should get opportunity for practicum in the third year and fourth year of the programme

Discipline	**Agree**	**Disagree**	**Not Decided**	**Total**	**χ^2-value**
Arts	75(75%)	16(16%)	9(9%)	100	2.38*
Science	65(65%)	22(22%)	13(13%)	100	NS
Total	**140**	**38**	**22**	**200**	

Note: *— Significant at .05 level.
NS— Not Significant.
Figures in Parentheses indicate percentages.

It can be noticed from Table 10.21 that the calculated χ^2-value of independence between response towards students is found 2.38. The obtained value is lesser than the table value (5.99) at .05 level of significance with df: 2. Thus, the observed value is not found significant. Hence, the perception of Science and Arts students are not significantly associated with each other. A majority of Arts and

Science students (75-65%) agreed that integrated course students should get opportunity for practicum in the third year and fourth year of the programme.

Table 10.22: χ^2-test of independence between student-teachers discipline background and their perception towards a minimum of 20 weeks of internship in school during the course enables student-teachers to reflect on school practices

Discipline	**Agree**	**Disagree**	**Not Decided**	**Total**	**χ^2-value**
Arts	78(78%)	16(16%)	6(6%)	100	2.8*
Science	69(69%)	19(19%)	12(12%)	100	NS
Total	**147**	**35**	**18**	**200**	

Note: *— Significant at .05 level.
NS— Not Significant.
Figures in Parentheses indicate percentages.

It can be noticed from Table 10.22 that the calculated χ^2-value of independence between response towards students is found 2.8. The obtained value is lesser than the table value (5.99) at .05 level of significance with df: 2. Thus, the observed value is not found significant. Hence, the perception of Science and Arts students are not significantly associated with each other. A majority of Arts and Science students (78-69%) agreed that a minimum of 20 weeks of internship in school during the course enables student-teachers to reflect on school practices.

Table 10.23: χ^2-test of independence between student teachers discipline background and their perception towards student-teachers are engaged at two levels—upper primary and secondary to deal with both levels of teaching

Discipline	**Agree**	**Disagree**	**Not Decided**	**Total**	**χ^2-value**
Arts	88(88%)	11(11%)	1(1%)	100	15.7*
Science	67(67%)	20(20%)	13(13%)	100	NS
Total	**155**	**31**	**14**	**200**	

Note: *— Significant at .05 level.
NS— Not Significant.
Figures in Parentheses indicate percentages.

It can be noticed from Table 10.23 that the calculated χ^2-value of independence between response towards students is found 15.7. The obtained value is more than the table value (5.99) at .05 level of significance with df: 2. Thus, the observed value is found significant. Hence, the perception of Science and Arts students are significantly associated with each other. A large majority of Arts students (88%) agreed that student-teachers are engaged at two levels—upper primary and secondary—to deal with both levels of teaching in comparison to their Science stream counterparts (67%).

Table 10.24: χ^2-test of independence between student-teachers discipline background and their perception towards visits to innovative centres of pedagogy and learning, innovative school, educational centres, teaching-learning centres develop acquaintances of student-teachers with ideal institutional system

Discipline	**Agree**	**Disagree**	**Not Decided**	**Total**	**χ^2-value**
Arts	85(85%)	5(5%)	10(10%)	100	3.18*
Science	78(78%)	12(12%)	10(10%)	100	NS
Total	**163**	**17**	**20**	**200**	

Note: *— Significant at .05 level.
NS— Not Significant.
Figures in Parentheses indicate percentages.

It can be noticed from Table 10.24 that the calculated χ^2-value of independence between response towards students is found 3.1. The obtained value is lesser than the table value (5.99) at .05 level of significance with df: 2. Thus, the observed value is not found significant. Hence, the perception of Science and Arts students are not significantly associated with each other. A majority of Arts and Science students (85-78%) agreed that visits to innovative centres of pedagogy and learning, innovative school, educational centres, teaching-learning centres develop acquaintances of student-teachers with ideal institutional system.

Table 10.25: χ^2-test of independence between student-teachers discipline background and their perception towards the schools provide full co-operation for practice teaching activities

Discipline	Agree	Disagree	Not Decided	Total	χ^2-value
Arts	75(75%)	14(14%)	11(11%)	100	4.02* NS
Science	67(67%)	25(25%)	8(8%)	100	
Total	**142**	**39**	**19**	**200**	

Note: *— Significant at .05 level.
NS— Not Significant.
Figures in Parentheses indicate percentages.

It can be noticed from Table 10.25 that the calculated χ^2-value of independence between response towards students is found 4.02. The obtained value is lesser than the table value (5.99) at .05 level of significance with df: 2. Thus, the observed value is not found significant. Hence, the perception of Science and Arts students are not significantly associated with each other. A majority of Arts and Science students (75-67%) agreed that the schools provide full co-operation for practice teaching activities.

Conclusion

The study revealed that student-teachers had positive appreciation towards integrated programme. The majority of Arts student-teachers (88%) were of high opinion on the student-teachers engaged at two levels—upper primary and secondary—to deal with both levels of Teaching and Skills pertaining to ICT and Educational Technology are integrated properly with various courses than that of science student-teachers counterparts. The Arts student-teachers expressed more favourable opinion on different areas of Indian constitution and human rights and environment education develop sociological understanding of student-teachers etc. Majority of student-teachers of Arts and Science discipline highly agreed that division of basic and advanced level foundation courses are relevant to the integrated programme, that educational studies facilitate student-teachers to learn key concepts and principles related to Secondary school teaching and educational studies facilitate student-teachers to learn key concepts and principles related to Secondary school teaching. However, a large majority of student-teachers showed agreement that teaching foundation courses develop understanding of education as a discipline. As a whole, Arts and Science student-teachers had expressed positive opinion about the three components of that is perspectives in education, curriculum and pedagogic studies and practicum and school internship introduced as per NCTE regulation, 2014. Moreover, the perception of student-teachers need to be explored through further studies on Integrated Teacher Education Programmes for different levels of school education.

REFERENCES

Adhikary A. (2017). "A study on the Perception of the Teacher Trainees Towards Two-Year B.Ed. Programme Implemented in the Teacher Education Institutions in Assam". *International Journal of Scientific and Research Publications*, Volume 7, Issue 9, September 2017, 385 ISSN 2250-3153.

Chakrabarty, D. (2016). "Implementation of Internship in 2 Year B.Ed. Course—A Challenge or Routine Task". *IRA International Journal of Education and Multidisciplinary Studies (ISSN 2455–2526)*, *3*(3).

https://shodhganga.inflibnet.ac.in/handle/10603/58749

Kumar, P. (2018). "Innovative and Integrated Programmes in Teacher Education: A Suggested Model". *International Journal of Research and Analytical Reviews* (*IJRAR*). August 2018, Volume 5, Issue 3, E-ISSN 2348-1269.

MHRD, Government of India, New Delhi (2019). *Draft National Education Policy, 2019.*

Namita & Sharma (2018). "Teacher Educators and Student-Teachers' Perception of Evaluation Process of Teacher Education Programmes at University Level in U.P. Examination Reform for Quality Education in India—Challenges and Opportunities". *Educational Quest: An International Journal of Education and Applied Social Science*, pp. 258-268, December 2018, ISBN 97893-88879-10-1.

Nataraja, R. (2016). "Attitude of Teacher Trainees towards Two Year B.Ed. Programme and their Future", *Scholarly Research Journal for Humanity Science and English Language.* April-May 2016, Vol. 3/15, pp. 3646-3649.

Sahoo, P.K & Sharma, P. (2018). "Student Teachers' Perception Towards Curriculum Reforms in Teacher Education Programme in Odisha". *Educational Quest: An International Jornal of Education and Applied Social Science*, Vol. 9, No.1, pp. 1-11, April 2018, New Delhi Publishers.

Saleha, P. (2012). "Internship Program in Education: Effectiveness, Problems and Prospects". *International Journal of Learning & Development.* ISSN 2164-4063 2012, Vol. 2, No. 1.

Sharma, S. & Dhull, I. (2017). "Curricular Reforms in Teacher Education", *An International Peer Reviewed & Referred Scholarly Research Journal for Interdisciplinary Studies*, May-June 2017, Vol. 4/31, ISSN No. 2278-8808.

Yibeltal, Y. (2019). "Perceived Pedagogical-Content Knowledge of Teachers: Classroom Practices of as Correlates of College of Teachers Education Students' Academic Result". *International Journal of Research in Teacher Education, 10*(2), 34-53.

11

School Internship Practices in Teacher Education Programmes

P. K. Sahoo and *Ashok Kumar*

School internship is a practical approach to holistic development of professional qualities of student-teachers enrolled in pre-service teacher education programme (TEP). It promotes learning of would-be teachers in a school environment through a continuum of sustained engagement with students and the school. It incorporates their exposure of student-teachers to different functions of a school involving teachers' role therein, while understanding the intricacies of functioning of classroom teaching and other activities of school through participant observation and reflections. Moreover, student-teachers planned interventions to tackle several classroom based teaching-learning problems not only develop their knowledge, rather it enables them to act upon real situation with practical knowledge and skills. It provides opportunities to develop insight into new perspectives and motivates the pupil-teachers to learn through experiences of teaching and performing different tasks related to functioning of a school. It means, internship is not just linked with practice teaching of a stipulated number of lessons in a school. Rather it builds a comprehensive base to develop inclusive understanding of professional skills and its application in real school situation with sustained involvement. Scaffolding practices are considered integral part of school internship under dynamic supervisory role of teacher educators and mentor teachers in organising experience based pupil-teacher practices. Continuous interaction among peers and supervisors on pupil-teachers' problems and learning points create conducive environment for planning different activities, creating better classroom environment and conducting instruction. The learning points are focused through reflective practices among pupil-teachers under close guidance of supervisors and mentors.

School Internship in Teacher Education Programmes: International Perspectives

The International status of teacher education hints at the practice situation, which spread over 6 to 8 weeks' duration. Towards the end of the 20th century, the teacher development activities with school development programme schools were nurtured through Teacher Education Institution (TEI) and school level collaboration. It is the responsibility of TEIs to provide "a school population with a cadre of perspective teachers, several higher education faculties and curriculum assistance over a period of several years" (Ducharme and Ducharme, 2020). Through this practice teacher education students got better field exposure in the schools. The schools were benefited by interaction with faculty members of TEIs. The major focus was on curricular improvement of schools as well as of teacher education programmes.

The experience of Finland reveals that (Kansanen, 2003) school internships are organised at different levels of teacher education. The local level experiences are interlinked with teacher education practices at different levels. They are classified as Basic practice and field school practice. Basic practice experiences are gained by the pupil-teachers in the university training schools. The pupil-teachers do observations and portfolio analysis. Field school practice is organised in the neighbouring schools. The pupil-teachers' work in collaboration combined field trips and visits to educational institutions. The third level practice involve subject teaching practice by pupil-teachers as per school timetable for a considerable duration. The pupil-teachers prepare teaching plans in discussion with peers. They use research based teaching skills. The practices involve reflective learning of teacher trainees through real situation based teaching experiences. The student portfolios are prepared during practice teaching. Peer assessment is encouraged with fairness and expectations for quality enhancement in teaching practice.

The Canadian experience (Nuland, S.V., 2011) on initial teacher education reveals that irrespective of the nature of TEP all the programmes include a field experience. The teacher candidates get engaged in supervised evaluated teaching in classrooms under the guidance and supervision of qualified host teachers of practising schools. The host teachers play a significant role in preparation of teachers through practicum organised in respective schools. They are assigned the duty of observing practice teaching, sharing observations, giving suggestions on teaching, supporting resources and motivate the teacher trainees to work through problems of practice. The host teachers also function as evaluators. The faculty supervisors and the host teachers work in collaboration with the pupil-teachers on planning, execution and evaluation of teaching practices of pupil-teachers. Regular feedback session include discussion with pupil-teachers. The theory practice relationship is strengthened through school internship programme.

School Internship in Indian Teacher Education System

In Indian context, NCTE Curriculum Framework for Teacher Education (2009) focused on school Internship as an integral component of teacher education. Accordingly, NCTE Regulations (2014) made it mandatory for teacher education curriculum of every pre-service TEP.

D.El.Ed. Programme

The norms and standards for curriculum of D.El.Ed programme, as per NCTE (2014), highlights school internship as one of the key components of teacher development practices. There must be a synergy of teacher education institution (TEI) and neighbouring elementary schools for sustained engagement of learners in school activities throughout the D.El.Ed. programme duration. This should be minimum of 2 weeks activities including following components: (a) 4 weeks for classroom observation during the first year, and (b) minimum period 16 weeks to be devoted for activities concerning elementary classes consisting of primary (I to V) and upper primary (VI to VIII) level. Besides teaching-learning activities in neighbouring schools, the teacher trainees are supposed to visit innovative centres of pedagogy and learning innovative schools and educational resource centres as a part of school internship. The management must ensure proper co-ordination between teacher education institution and sufficient number of recognised elementary schools for school internship. It also states attachment of primary/elementary institution with the teacher education institution as desirable criteria. With regard to programme implementation it is stated that a partnership between the TEI and the school must be fostered through both curriculum and the running of TEI. The TEIs and the participating schools shall ensure mutually agreed mechanism for mentoring, supervising, tracking and assessing the student-teachers.

B.El.Ed. Programme

Similar norms and standards were also highlighted for B.El.Ed. programme by NCTE (2014) by making it more specific with regard to internship practices. It covered "Planning for teaching, teaching-learning, observation of classrooms, engaging in continuous and comprehensive assessment for learning, writing reflective journals developing resources and designing activities and undertaking classroom-based research project." The students can be engaged in the teaching practices in the government and private schools with sustained engagement.

B.Ed. Programme

The NCTE norm and standards (2014) envisaged for B.Ed. (2 year as well as 4 year Integrated Teacher Education Programme) School internship. It highlights this component to "lead to development of broad repertoire of perspectives, professional capacities, teacher responsibilities and skills." The programme structure remains same as of elementary teacher education programme, of course, with special provision of teaching in elementary (Classes VI-VIII), secondary (classes IX-X) or senior secondary (Clases XI-XII) schools. The programme implementation covers different activities including practice teaching. The practices should incorporate peer observations, teacher observations and faculty observations during school internship.

School Internship as the Link Between Theory and Practice

Teaching has three phases, such as: preparatory phase, interaction phase and evaluation phase. Teacher learning preparation phase during school internship includes various activities, like observation of teaching in real classroom situation, maintaining teacher diary, learning-teaching skills, timetable preparation, preparation of lesson plans and development of lesson plans. The preparatory activities lead to teaching practices in concerned subject areas of pupil-teachers, called interaction phase. The last phase of teaching practices is assessment and evaluation phase. The formative evaluation is done at every stage of practice teaching. Moreover, summative evaluation takes place towards the end of teaching practice by the mentor teachers and supervisors. Besides teaching practices, other school based experiences are organised, like preparation of school records, library work, psychological tests, school level cultural meets, personality development practices covering physical *yoga* and sports and community development works and projects. The pupil-teachers take part in assisting school students to organise various programmes. They also participate in various school activities as internal members of the school system. The curriculum of concerned teacher education institutions earmark the objectives and procedural details of school internship at elementary teacher education and secondary teacher education programme (Chennat, 2014).

Empirical Studies on School Internship

Research evidences on these programmes have a wide coverage of practice teaching programmes of traditional teacher education programme. A few studies focus on the role of school internship in teacher learning in the Indian context. Sahoo and Sharma (2018) conducted study on student-teachers' perception of reform in teacher education curriculum and noticed positive response of student-teachers towards school internship based practice teaching. A significant pedagogy oriented teacher learning study concerning school internship was conducted by Kushwaha (2018). The study focused on teacher learning processes at pre-internship phase of B.El.Ed. programmes of University of Delhi. Qualitative research method was employed to answer different research questions, viz. how do interns learn during internship on a TEP?; what kind of support and challenge is necessary for learning to occur during internship?; and what constitutes teacher learning during internship? The study revealed following findings: The pre-internship learning covered apprehensions about school based programmes and learners preparedness to face different challenges during internship. The diversity in progress of practice teaching was noticed during internship in different contexts. The post-internship threw light on reflections on overall functioning of internship and their own performances. Supervision played a significant role in school internship. Student-teachers' self-involvement along with cooperative learning with peers contributed to understand teaching-learning, its goal and priorities in their context. The class students' participation in teaching-learning activities initiated by interns helped them to understand learners, learning environmental and their own performances in teaching. The researcher concluded that a student-teacher need understanding of own topic and get well prepared to teach; flexibility in lesson plan must be adopted in planning process; teachers' autonomy on the spot decision making during teaching need encouragement; school environment and curricular programme schedule must be taken into consideration in practice teaching by the interns. Practice teaching linkage with ground reality and theoretical principles need to be focused in school internship. It must encourage collaborative efforts of the TEIs and school system with due focus on teacher learning issues in the TEIs.

Study on School Internship in B.Ed. Programme

A descriptive data based analysis of school internship in B.Ed. programme in TEIs of UP state has been conducted by the authors. The study covered questionnaire survey of 1000 pupil-teachers' experiences on school Internship. It also included selective interviews and observation of school internship practices in 40 Teacher Education Institutions of UP. The highlights of the study are stated in the following with special references to teacher learning related to practice teaching in different phases, as per B.Ed. curriculum. The findings of the study have been presented in three sections:

- Status of operation of school Internship,
- Student-teachers' reaction on practice teaching and school experiences, and
- Qualitative observation.

Status of Operation of School Internship

Observation Sessions

It covered observation of school activities, classroom teaching by school teachers, activities of class teacher and teaching practices of peers as preliminary activity of school internship. This was revealed in the study that in the case of government and aided TEIs, 72 per cent of B.Ed. students participated in observation practices very often, whereas only 60 per cent non-government institution students did so during school internship. As a whole, a moderate strength number of students (44 to 51%) made use of checklist in observation of prescribed teaching activities and school observation practices has not gone well programmed to some extent.

Teachers' Skill Development Practices

Prior to school based practice teaching, skill development practices are promoted by the teacher educators in respective subject areas. In many cases traditional microteaching practices are adopted to train pupil-teachers on basic skills like Introduction of lesson and Blackboard writing, Questioning, Explanation, Reinforcement, Illustration with examples and communication skills. This was noticed that a large majority of government and aided institution students get exposure (80 to 85%) to skill development training on above areas through microteaching sessions than that of their non-government TEI counterparts (60 to 72%). Observation of model skill lessons and peer teaching in classroom condition as well as video/U tube lessons were in moderate practice among student-teachers in the TEIs (51-53%). Peer feedback and supervisor feedback are also used in moderate cases (53%). Such kind of activities enabled student-teachers to link their skills in real room teaching practices during school internship. In this respect, technical approach of preparation for practice teaching prevailed in the B.Ed. programmes of the TEIs of the UP state.

Timetable Preparation

This element of school internship aims at initial preparation for teaching practices. Student-teachers' acquaintance with subject timetable and the procedures adopted in development of suitable timetable in a class as well as in a school act as the foundation of teaching practices. Large majority of student-teachers (74%) expressed that major priority is given on how to prepare class timetable and school timetable keeping in view curricular weightage and teacher workload. Student-teachers also learnt (55%) developing teacher timetable. Such learning takes place mainly in group interaction basis among peers (55%) to some extent the supervisors and mentor teachers assist them in this respect (46 to 53%).

Teaching Learning Material (TLM) Development

The School internship promotes TLM preparation as an integral component of planning the units and lessons for practice teaching and identifying appropriate resources for teaching-learning in their own subject areas. Different kinds of TLMs are developed by the student-teachers in the forms of traditional materials like chart (67%), poster (71%), model (61%) and pictures (63%). To some extent, the student-teachers got experience of using PPT lessons (47%) with the help of LCD projectors and CD and U-Tube materials (34%). Such materials were developed through peer cooperation, assistance of mentor and the supervisor (52 to 54%). It needs more support by TEI resources in collaboration with practising schools.

Development of Plans and Delivery of Lessons

The student-teachers got experience of developing unit plans and lesson plans mostly under the guidance of supervisor (54%) and to some extent with the help of mentor (42%). As a matter of concern, the stipulated norm of delivery of around 20 teaching lesson plans in each subject was not followed during school internship. The problem was much of worry in private TEIs where only 50 per cent students delivered 16 to 20 lessons in the first subject and second subject of teaching. Of course, in the case of government and aided TEIs, 54 to 80 per cent of student-teachers abided by the curricular norm. It shows the weak management of teaching practices, particularly among private TEIs. Peer interaction contributed moderately on delivery of lessons of student-teachers (42%). Most of the pupil-teachers expressed that (54%) their lessons were frequently supervised by the supervisors. To some extent, the mentor of the student-teachers observed the lesson delivery (54%). They made use of lesson plans keeping in view the objectives, course content nature, students' background and classroom environment (55%). The classroom management was done mostly through interaction with students. Discipline was maintained through group work in class to some extent (74%) and through motivation (49%). It requires co-ordination between class teachers and the pupil-teachers.

Assignment and Evaluation Practices

The student-teachers got exposures to develop appropriate questions on different difficulty level of learners (53%) on subject areas. Assignments were also prepared for different subjects in relation to their teaching lessons. Majority of student-teachers (54%) stated about the guidance of supervisors, mentors and own group members in this process. They did evaluation of students' performance on the tests and assignments. They maintained students' performance records under the supervision of mentor and supervisor.

Student-Teachers' Reaction towards School Internship

Observation Sessions

It was noticed that majority of student-teachers (53 to 63%) expressed positive reaction towards observation sessions in the initial stage of school internship. They stated that such experience contributed towards understanding teaching competencies, understanding school activities and preparing road map for further course of action during school internship. The student-teachers (56%) did not appreciate supervisors' negative feedback at initial stage of internship since it was not motivating for them.

Writing Teachers' Diary

Majority of student-teachers (60-63%) gave positive opinion on the role of writing teachers' diary on practice of teaching skills, understanding and classifying classroom teaching activities, time management and achievement of practice teaching competencies. Of course, a sizable number of student-teachers (44%) were critical about the role of teachers' diary in making teaching practices effective. It indicated about the formal status of diary writing by the teacher trainees during school internship.

Timetable Development Practice

This was noticed that a large majority of (88%) student-teachers stated about understanding of class timetable enable them to systematise their activities. Their job classification became easy (88%). They got exposure for understanding timetable preparation in the context of classroom teaching of teachers.

Preparation of Lesson Plans

Barring a few student-teachers, 86 to 88 per cent of student-teachers recognised the significance of developing lesson plans in achievement of objectives of practice teaching, systematic teaching-learning activities in classroom, getting proper direction to organise teaching practices and proper preparation and making teaching practices. Since lesson planning was the major focus of school Internship, this was taken seriously, by the teacher trainees, of course with traditional orientation.

TLM Development

Around 81 per cent student-teachers gave favourable opinion about their participation in development of TLM. They appreciated that use of TLM made their teaching effective.

Use of Teaching Skills

It was revealed that majority of student-teachers (57%) stated about adequacy of teaching skill development practices enabled them to teach well during practice teaching. Around 38 per cent of student-teachers stated about teaching skill development practices are not sufficient enough to make teaching practices effective. They were also critical about ineffective role of teaching skill development practice to deal with real classroom teaching. Of course, majority of them (56%) appreciated positive impact of learning basic teaching skills prior to practice teaching.

Practice Teaching Activities

A vast majority of (90%) around a few student-teachers appreciated the provisions made for practice teaching. Around 90 per cent student-teachers talked about positive effect of orientation teaching, development and use of TLM, making optimum use of supervisors' and mentors' feedback, co-operation of peers in discussion on critical issues of practice teaching and gradual development of teaching competencies through peer interaction during school internship.

Evaluation Practices

A large majority of student-teachers (80% and above) expressed positive opinion about their involvement in various kinds of student evaluation related activities in real school situation and the role of supervisors and mentors in such practices. They were satisfied with their involvement in development of achievement tests, assessing students' performance in class test and giving feedbacks and understanding students' academic progress continuously.

School Activities and Management of School Internship

Majority of student-teachers (56%) were critical about their involvement in library activities during school internship. Barring this experience, the student-teachers were having positive views about other experience related to management of school activities. They (81%) appreciated the practices of maintaining school records. A large majority of student-teachers (82%) appreciated their co-operative involvement in various kinds of welfare activities like cleanliness activities, community development activities and social awareness practices. However, majority of them (51%) were not favourable to health oriented practices in the schools. A large majority of student-teachers (81%) appreciated their involvement in games and sports activities and cultural meets during school internship. Different project works undertaken during school internship had also positive impact on them (82%).They developed skills for conducting projects. Their interest on projects was also nurtured during school internship. Almost 90 per cent of the respondents appreciated the management aspects of school internship particularly with regard to planning, co-ordination, monitoring, supervision and evaluation of concerned activities.

Overall Development of Professional Qualities of Student-Teachers

A large member of student-teacher participants (76 to 88%) appreciated the role of school internship in different areas of professional development, like involvement of pupil-teachers, development of self-confidence in handling practice teaching, being fair in dealing with students during practice teaching and development of sense towards respect for peers, mentor and the supervisors. They got exposure to evaluate students' performance during class teaching and after teaching judiciously, development of logical thinking related to course content, pedagogic principles and its application, own conceptual clarity and helping students in concept formation practices. They were motivated to bring development of own self, got inspiration on solving critical problems, taking lead on various kinds of school activities, being flexible in dealing with different situations during internship, learning to take responsibility on own activities and its outcome and trying best to assist students in their learning. These findings revealed positive impact of school internship on student-teachers as per their own perception.

Qualitative Observation: As a Regulatory Obligation

School internship has made an entry in TEP in structural form. The pedagogical process perspectives of TEP need reorientation. A structural change of TEP accommodating various kinds of structured activities in real school situation may project certain changes in student-teachers' learning. However, certain basic issues concerning curricular orientation for establishing suitable linkage between theory and practice on the one hand and practice and theoretical understanding on the other hand have been reflected in prevailing school internship programme. The management factor has also played a significant role in it. For instance, this was observed that basic components of maintaining student-teachers' diary, observation of class teaching, skill development practices, lesson planning, practice teaching and supervision facilities have not been taken seriously in the private TEIs. The government and aided institutions fared better than that of private institution counterparts on these areas. For instance, the private TEI student did not pay proper attention to maintaining student-teachers' diary. Their attendance was very thin in teaching skill practice sessions. There was lack of proper co-ordination between school timetable and practice teaching timetable. Moreover, the private TEI students did not deliver stipulated number of practice teaching lessons during school internship. They were found mostly indisciplined and apathetic on such programme. Proper monitoring and co-ordination was absent in private institutions and concerned teaching schools. Even though, the government institutions stick to curricular norms to a large extent, supervision programme followed centralised approach giving less autonomy to student-teachers for student-teacher interaction. Mentors' participation was also of restricted nature. Co-ordination between TEI and practice teaching school was not very much co-cordial and proactive towards teacher development practices. Above all, the structural change in accommodating school internship could not promote major transformation in teacher learning practices. The TEPs were found support from those schools having commitment towards quality of schooling as well as cooperative venture in teacher learning. The culture of school initiative in teacher development programme has not been visible so far. Local level school support to internship programme is dependent on the initiative of TEIs and its collaborative approach for promoting school quality and teacher development. It requires comprehensive approach of planning TEPs through involvement of TEIs and the school management. Such scenario is not yet visible in the current school internship programmes in general.

Conclusion

School internship plays a significant role in making teacher learning practices more realistic by integrating theoretical understanding of teaching with practical understanding of teaching through practical experiences of student-teachers. It can promote reflective learning of student-teachers through own initiative for transformation, human interaction and feedbacks of peers, mentor and supervisor. Such practices must have scope for promoting student-teacher autonomy in experimenting innovative teaching practice in context specific situations. The TEIs must focus on quality management of school internship in collaboration with local level schools as a partner for promoting teaching-learning in the schools. Experiences on linkage of theory and practice in internship must have great value for strengthening professional base of teacher development programme.

REFERENCES

Chennat, S. (2014). "Internship in Pre-service Teacher Education Programme: A Global Perspective", *Impact Journals*, Vol. 2, No. 11.

Edward and Ducharme, M. (2020). Ref.httpts://education state university. com 21, May.

Kansanen, P.J. (2003). *Teacher Education in Finland.* https://www. researchgate.net/publication 242259693

Kumar, A. (2019). *Adhyapak Shikhan Sansthaon main B.Ed. Internship ke Kriyanwayan ka Adhyayan.* Unpublished Ph.D. Thesis, University of Allahabad.

Kushwaha, A. (2018). *Understanding Teacher Learning During Internship on a Teacher Education Programme in India*, Unpublished Ph.D. Thesis, University of Delhi.

NCTE (2009). *National Curriculum Framework of Teacher Education*, New Delhi: NCTE.

NCTE (2014). *Regulations for Teacher Education Programmes*, New Delhi: NCTE.

Sahoo, P.K. and Sharma, P. (2018). "Student-teachers' Perception towards Curriculum Reform in Teacher Education Programme in Odisha", *Educational Quest: An International Jounal of Education and Applied Social Science*, *9*(1):1-11.

Shirlrey Van Nuland (2011). *Teacher Education in Canadian Journal of Education and Training : International Research Pedagogy*, Vol. 37, No. 4.

12

Perception of Students and Teacher Educators about M.Ed. Curriculum

P. K. Sahoo and *Priyanka Sharma*

Teacher Educators' education is an integral component of teacher education system. Teacher educators prepare teachers and contribute significantly to professional development of teachers engaged in different stages of education. Since teacher education cover wide range of professional activities concerning stages of schooling and curricular diversities, teacher educators' role become more dynamic and complex in nature. Teacher educators' backgrounds are heterogeneous in nature. They are engaged in different kinds of pre-service and in-service teacher education programmes offered in teacher education institutions at higher education and school education levels. Teacher educators' roles are of diversified nature. Accordingly, their educational backgrounds are of heterogeneous nature. Of late, there has been momentum to focus professionalism in teacher education programmes as well as in education of teacher educators. The sense of identity as teacher educators inside the framework of teacher education has been a matter of discussion at national and international fora.

Basically teacher educators are considered as competent professionals engaged in carrying out curricular practices of pre-service and in-service teacher education programmes at elementary and secondary stages. This is argued that the quality of teacher educators shall contribute to academic, pedagogic and research proficiencies of teachers engaged in schools.

The European Trade Union Committee for Education (2008) highlighted the significance of qualities of teacher educators involved in the education of futures school teachers. McGee and Lawrence (2009) insisted on professional preparation of teacher educators on the ground that "teacher educators work with teachers to promote and support professional learning..."

While defining teacher educators, Even (2012) stated that the term "teacher educators" commonly refers to both those who educate prospective teachers and those who educate practicing teachers, that is to those "who initiate, guide and support teacher learning across the life span." In general, this is understood that the teacher educators are formally engaged in educating the prospective teachers in teacher education institution as per norms and guidelines set by statutory body of teacher education or other competent authorities. Education for teacher educators is associated with discipline based theoretical understanding on education, pedagogic principle based competency development practices and research competencies in the field of education. Since teacher education curriculum deals with subject domain knowledge and teaching-learning evaluation practices teacher educators' mastery over subject domain knowledge have been considered as an essential requirement for subject training programme. Of late, there have been discussions over bringing different components of professional education of teachers into the fold of education of teacher educators, viz. discipline orientation pedagogic principles and competencies relevant to subject teaching and research competencies in the field of education. Teacher educators' education programme may not be restricted to one basic degree depending on multiplicity in curricular provisions of stage-specific teacher education programmes. However, the concern for teacher educators' education has remained on Masters Degree in education programme.

Even though there have been provisions to promote interdisciplinary background of teacher educators including liberal study of education discipline as qualification of teacher educators.

Curriculum Reform in Teacher Educators' Education

For the first time, in India, the National Curriculum Framework for Teacher Education (NCFTE) prepared professional development of teacher educators. The document discussed in detail about the perspectives of education for preparing teacher educators and meeting the requirements for stage-specific teacher education at elementary and secondary level. The document was very much critical about the liberal nature of M.Ed. programme and was inadequate to have deeper discourse in education and an opportunity for interdisciplinary inquiry." There were also limited perspectives for research projects in teacher education programmes with "little scope for professional development and research in the key areas of school education..." The document criticised the dominance of positivistic approach of study of educational phenomena having little connection with innovative experiments conducted in the country over four decades.

The NCFTE suggested creation of multilateral entry points for the study of educational studies, development of knowledge based studies related to teacher education and encouragement of studies in cognate disciplines outside education. Teacher educators must be exposed to professional experience based interventions in teacher preparation activities in teacher education institutions as well as during school based activities. The NCFTE also insisted on developing teacher educators for teacher education in early childhood education, elementary education and secondary teacher education.

Taking a clue from NCFTE, 2009, Justice Verma Commission (2012) emphasised on strengthening quality of teacher educators' education by means of making it stage-specific, specialised and dynamic in nature. It emphasised on M.Ed. programme in the areas of elementary education and secondary education respectively. Varieties of foundational and school subject discipline courses. The structure of M.Ed. programme was spread over two year duration with more scope to accommodate theoretical and practical experiences in teacher preparation with specialisations in curriculum studies, pedagogic studies, policy, finance and foundational studies. It looked for encouraging entry of talented faculty with disciplinary specialisations in social science education, language education and mathematics education. It also suggested for entry of basic discipline based experts to enter to the job of teacher educators. Moreover, multidisciplinary background people must be encouraged to join research degree programme in education without necessarily requiring a degree in teacher education as an entry qualification. It was an optimistic proposal to ensure a wider pool of talent towards posts of teacher educators. Such recommendation hinted at making liberal requirement for teacher educators without insisting on Masters degree in education as an essential qualification. Such recommendations were perceived to be controversial in nature by the professionals in teacher education forums of the country.

Status of M.Ed. Programme at University Level up to 2014

A project was undertaken by Yadav (2013) to study the curriculum structure and practice of M.Ed. programme still following the one year M.Ed. curriculum recommended by UGC, 2001. This is worthwhile to state that until 2014 NCTE Guidelines for two-year M.Ed. programme no university implemented M.Ed. curriculum in the light of NCFTE-2009. The eligibility criteria for admission in M.Ed were restricted to B.Ed. degree holders. In other words, M.Ed. programme was considered as an extension of B.Ed. degree. It also aimed at teacher educators' preparation for B.Ed. programme having little relevance for D.El.Ed. programme for elementary teachers. As per UGC guidelines, the one year M.Ed. programme had theory papers and dissertation work. The theory papers covered foundation courses and optional or elective courses. The core papers covered foundations of Education, viz. Philosophical or Educational Research was also a core paper. The elective/optional courses had mostly covered 2 to 10 papers. In some of the universities, the clusters of elective papers were offered such as teacher education, educational administration, educational technology etc. The universities mostly followed traditional marking system.

Yadav (2013) found that the curriculum did not mention curriculum transaction process in the M.Ed. curriculum distinctly, except statements covering practicum and assignments. The scope of study of educational technology/ICT was highlighted along with its usage in teaching-learning and evaluation programme. The study also covered the curricular provision for M.Ed. special education.

There was mention of M.Ed. Elementary Education in the case of selective institutions like Regional Institutes of Education and Jamia Millia Islamia. The pattern of curriculum was very much similar to that of M.Ed. general programme (with B.Ed. eligibility). Yadav (2019) concluded that curriculum reform process was of very slow nature. It must be updated in the light of the National Curriculum Framework-2005, RTE-2009 and NCFTE-2009.

NCTE Curriculum Structure and Guidelines

NCTE evolved guidelines for two-year M.Ed. programme and its curriculum structure through a Committee led by its Chairman, Prof. Shyam B. Menon. The two-year M.Ed. programme under revised guidelines has following features:

- *Eligibility:* B.Ed. Integrated B.Ed. and D.El.Ed with Bachelors degree.
- *Credits:* 80 credits in total: 44 for core courses, 20 credits for specialisations, 8 credits for field internship (4 credits in TEI and 4 credits in the area of specialisation/school) and 8 credits for research leading to dissertation.
- *Programme structure:* The curriculum structure with details of course titles is stated in Table 12.1.

Table 12.1: While conceptualising the Choice Based Credit System (CBCS) proposed by the UGC Committee recommended the following curriculum structure

Modality Components	(e) Taught/(f) Practicum/ Workshop/Seminar	(g) Internship	(h) Research Project
(a) Perspectives 24 credits (c+f)	Sociology-History-Political Economy (8 credits); Curriculum Studies (4 credits), Introduction to Education Studies (4 credits), Psychology of Development and Learning (4 credits)		
(b) Tools 12 credits	Research Methods (Introductory) and advanced levels adding-up to 8 credits, Communication skills (including ICT), Expository Writing, and Academic Writing (3 credits); Self Development (focus on: gender and inclusive education, and mental-physical well-being including *Yoga*)(1 credit)		
(c) Teacher Education 12 credits (c+f+g)	Institutions, Systems and Structures; Conceptual basis of Teacher Education; TE Curriculum, Policy and Practice, Continuing Professional Development and In-Service TE (Total 8 credits)	4 credits in a TE institution	
(d) Specialisation 24 (e+f+g)	Choice between Elementary (up to Class VIII) or Secondary and Senior Secondary (Classes VI to XII) Levels [or Early childhood Education, or Higher Educational], each having: Core courses within elementary/ secondary stage and theme based electives: Curriculum, Pedagogy and Assessment; Policy, Economics, Administration and Learning, Inclusive Education; Education Technology etc. (20 Credits for both the components)	4 credits based on the choice of specialisation cluster	8 credits (preferably in specialization area or in foundation)
Total Credits = 80 (c+f+g+h)	64+8=72		8

Source: NCTE Document 2014.

Components of the Curriculum Structure

(a) Perspective course cover broad knowledge base of education. It includes Introduction to Education studies, Philosophy of Education, Psychology of Education, Sociology, History and Political economy courses and curriculum studies. All these areas address to the issues in school education as well as teacher education.

(b) Tool courses cover research method courses at introductory level and at advanced level; Communication skills and self-development workshops are also included as tool courses.

(c) *Teacher Education course.* It includes classroom activity based programmes on pre-service and in-service teacher education and perspectives, research and issues in teacher education. Besides classroom based programmes four credits are allotted to internship programme in TEIs.

(d) *Specialisations:*

  (i) *Stage based specialisations:* The students may be enrolled in Elementary Education or secondary/senior secondary level teacher education specialisation.

  (ii) Further specialisation under Elementary or secondary level can be listed under following as examples:

  - Curriculum, pedagogy and assessment.
  - Education policy, economics and planning.
  - Educational management, administration and leadership.
  - Inclusive education.
  - Other theme based courses.
  - Modality of transacting curriculum:

    (i) More emphasis be lead on classroom interactions, practicum, workshop and seminars. They are different from internship. ICT can be used for getting learning experiences of varied nature.

    (ii) *Internship:* It covers two types of activities, such as (1) Compulsory attachments with a teacher education institution and (2) Interning at/

associating with a field site relevant to the area of specialisation. Both these internships will be organised 3 to 4 weeks each.

(iii) Research Dissertation: From semester 2 onwards the process may begin. Different processes covering developing a research proposal, presenting it, conducting the study, analysis and interpretation of data, report writing, finalising and presenting in a *viva voce* examination. Different stage activities may be incorporated in assessment process.

(iv) Relationship among specialisation, internship and dissertation. The elementary and secondary stage specialisations can focus on specific issues concerning each stages for research. Internship should be linked with concerned sites and teacher education institutions. The activities can be related to areas of studies like curriculum and pedagogy, Administration and Management, ET/ICT respectively.

Curriculum and Programme Implementation Guidelines of NCTE (2014)

On the basis of recommendations of M.Ed. curriculum committee, NCTE (2014) issued guidelines for M.Ed. programme of TEIs in the country. The guideline highlighted four key features of two year M.Ed. programme such as:

(i) A common core consisting of perspectives courses, tool courses, teacher education courses, and a self-development component,

(ii) Specialisation branches where students choose to specialise in any one of the school levels/areas (such as elementary, or Secondary and Senior Secondary);

(iii) Research leading to dissertation; and

(iv) Field immersion/attachment/internship: There shall be core courses (which shall be of 60% of total credits) and specialised course in elementary education and dissertation with about 40 per cent of credits.

As per recommendation of curriculum committee the NCTE (2014) guideline covered theory courses, practicum, and internship and attachment as different elements of the course for smooth implementation of the course activities. NCTE guideline insisted on preparation of a calendar of all activities including internship and field attachment. The academic calendar must synchronise with that of internship institution. Structure engagement of M.Ed. students with educational sites/fields must be ensured for at least four weeks duration. The fields notes and reflective report shall cover different engagements in pre-service teacher education programme, in-service teacher education programme, curriculum design, development of course materials etc. Periodic workshops, seminars, debates and discussion sessions must be considered as essential course input for M.Ed. programme. NCTE (2014) guidelines also prescribed assessment procedures consisting of at least 30 per cent weightage for continuous internal assessment and 70 per cent for examination conducted by the examining body. The bases of internal assessment may include individual and/or group assignments, seminar presentations, field study appraisal reports etc. One-fourth of the total marks/credits/weightage shall be assigned to practicum, internship, field attachment and dissertation.

Rationale of the Study

As mentioned above teacher educators are considered as one of the key input of teacher development programme. The review of literature reveals that the reforms in teacher education programme have taken into consideration quality education for professional teacher educators. Even though research studies have been conducted on quality improvement of teacher education curriculum and strategies, least attention has been paid to conducting researches on professionalism among teacher educators. Especially curriculum research is essential for preparation of teacher educators and professional development of TE. In the context of quality enhancement of teacher educators system, there have been experiences of curriculum interventions and programme evaluation studies of in-service education for teacher educators through agencies like DIETs, UGC Academic Staff Colleges, IGNOU, CEMCA, NCERT and SCERT. A major breakthrough has been made by NCTE in making two years M.Ed. programme as a mandatory requirement for teacher educators at elementary and secondary level. Besides other qualifications, the NCTE (2014) Norms were implemented in teacher education institutions from the sessions 2015 onwards. And understanding of curriculum reforms in M.Ed. programme all-over the country can provide us input about the feasibility, acceptability and usability of such reforms at M.Ed. level in different TEIs of the country. In this regard, the perception of the students and teacher educators will act as a basis for developing the understanding about implementation of revised structure and process of M.Ed. curriculum so far the researches reveal programme evaluation study results about preparatory teacher education programme and the output of in-service teacher education programme of teachers. No studies has been conducted except (Yadav, 2013) about the status of teacher educators preparatory (TEP) in the country. Especially, no research evidence is available so far about implementation of new curriculum of M.Ed. The present study is of first kind to explore the perception of students (would-be teacher educators and teacher educators (M.Ed. programme) towards curriculum reform in preparatory education for teacher educators. The present study is conducted with the following objectives:

Objectives of the Study

1. To study the perception of students and teacher educators about preparatory education of teacher educators (M.Ed.) programme on different dimensions of curriculum.
2. To study the association between the category of respondents and their perception about different dimensions of curriculum reform in M.Ed. programme.

Hypothesis

There is no significant association between the category of respondents and their perception about different dimension of curriculum reform in M.Ed. programme.

Methods and Procedures

The population of the present study includes all the student-teachers and teacher educators from different teacher education institutions (TEIs) of U.P. It covered government/government-aided and self-financing institutions of teacher education in Uttar Pradesh offering M.Ed. Descriptive survey method was used to conduct the study. The study included 650 student-teachers and 100 teacher educators as sample of the study. The cluster sampling technique was used for sample selection. The institutions were selected randomly. Questionnaire for student-teachers and teacher educators was used for data collection purpose. The questionnaire had six sections viz.: (1) Structural reform; (2) Perspectives in education; (3) Practical and Field based experiences; (4) Internship and Dissertation; (5) Time Table; and (6) Project/Assignments. The respondents responded on a three-point scale, such as agree, disagree and not decided respectively.

Analysis and Interpretation

Data have been analysed by making use of chi-square test for testing the null hypotheses. The analysis and interpretation of the study have been presented in the following:

Perception of Students and Teacher Educators towards Structural Reform in M.Ed. Programme

This is evident from Table 12.2 that there was significant association between the category of respondents and their perception towards structural reforms in M.Ed. programme. A large majority of M.Ed. students (77 to 86%) favoured the reforms concerning 2 years duration of M.Ed. programme, B.Ed. and M.Ed.

Table 12.2: Chi-square test of association between category of respondents and perception towards structural reform

Sl. No.	Items	Respondents	Agree	Disagree	Not Decided	Total	Chi-Square
1.	Two-year teacher education programmes like B.Ed. and M.Ed. are more comprehensive to deal theoretical and practical components of teacher education	Students	556(85.53)	85(13.07)	9(1.30)	650	79.3*
		Teacher educators	57(57.0)	26(26.0)	17(17.0)	100	
2.	B.Ed./M.Ed. integrated courses provides us opportunity to gain ability of school teacher and teacher trainees	Students	547(84.15)	90(13.84)	13(2.0)	650	65.2*
		Teacher educators	59(59.0)	23(23.0)	18(18.0)	100	
		Total	**606(80.80)**	**113(15.06)**	**31(4.13)**	**750**	
3.	Teacher Education programmes at elementary and secondary level are upgraded to higher education stage through composite institutions	Students	500(76.90)	118(18.10)	32(4.90)	650	24.7*
		Teacher educators	57(57.00)	27(27.00)	16(16.00)	100	
		Total	**557(74.26)**	**145(19.33)**	**48(6.40)**	**750**	

Note: *Significant at .01 level.
Figures in Parentheses indicate percentage.

Integrated programme and the provision of composite teacher education institution brought into the fold of higher education. Comparatively, the teacher educators' response towards these items was less encouraging, since 56 to 59 per cent teacher educators gave favourable opinion. A sizable number of teacher educators (41 to 44%) were either neutral or negative about their perception of two years duration. Majority (76-84%) students agreed that B.Ed./M.Ed. integrated courses provides us opportunity to gain ability of school teacher and teacher trainees and teacher education programmes at elementary and secondary level are upgraded to higher education stage through composite institutions than that teacher educators counterparts.

Perception of Students and Teacher Educators towards Perspectives in Education in M.Ed. Programme

Table 12.3 reveals that there was significant association between the category of perspectives and their perception towards curricular perspectives of M.Ed. programme. The students' perception towards different areas of perspective courses were found more encouraging than that of their teacher educator counterparts. A large majority of M.Ed. students (79 to 91%) gave favourable opinion on provision of perspective courses on sociological, philosophical, economic political and psychological foundations of education, education and curriculum studies, critical reflection on various issues concerning social inclusion, Research methods, Teacher education, ICT and Educational Technology and specialisation in elementary teacher education and secondary teacher education level. A perusal of teacher educators' response reveal that comparatively lower percentage of respondents (61 to 68%) gave favourable response on above areas of M.Ed. curriculum, simultaneously. It was noticed that a sizable number of teacher educators (32 to 39%) were neutral or negative towards the curricular perspectives. This is also alarming to note that a large majority of students (88%) and teacher educators (64%) were critical towards the limited role of foundation courses in providing

Table 12.3: Chi-square test of association between category of respondents and perception towards curricular perspectives in education

Sl. No.	Perspectives in education	Respondents	Agree	Disagree	Not Decided	Total	χ^2-value
1.	Perspectives courses in the area of Philosophy education, Sociology, History political economy of education, psychology of education, develop theoretical background of education discipline	Students	560 (86.10)	77 (11.80)	13 (2.00)	650	76.9*
		Teacher educators	62 (62.0)	17 (17.0)	21 (21.0)	100	
		Total	**622** **(82.93)**	**94** **(12.53)**	**34** **(4.53)**	**750**	
2.	Education studies and curriculum studies are most appropriately covered to understand professional background of teacher education	Students	511 (78.60)	108 (16.60)	31 (4.70)	650	39.3*
		Teacher educators	63 (63.00)	15 (15.00)	22 (22.00)	100	
		Total	**574** **(76.53)**	**123** **(16.40)**	**53** **(7.06)**	**750**	

(*Contd.*)

Sl. No.	Perspectives in education	Respondents	Agree	Disagree	Not Decided	Total	χ^2-value
3.	Critical reflection ongender, childhood, disability and marginalization in relation to education are properly designed to meet the masters degree level objectives	Students	590 (90.70)	54 (8.30)	6 (0.90)	650	90.7*
		Teacher educators	61 (61.0)	24 (24.0)	15 (15.0)	100	
		Total	**651** **(86.80)**	**78** **(10.40)**	**21** **(2.80)**	**750**	
4.	Research method course develop proper understanding about different areas of educational research	Students	564 (86.70)	79 (12.10)	7 (1.07)	650	69.6*
		Teacher educators	66 (66.0)	18 (18.0)	16 (16.0)	100	
		Total	**630** **(84.00)**	**97** **(12.93)**	**23** **(3.06)**	**750**	
5.	Division of basic and advanced level foundation courses are relevant to the integrated programme students background of PG level students	Students	592 (91.07)	51 (7.80)	7 (0.90)	650	74.0*
		Teacher educators	65 (65.0)	21 (21.0)	14 (14.0)	100	
		Total	**657** **(87.60)**	**72** **(9.60)**	**20** **(2.66)**	**750**	

(Contd.)

Sl. No.	Perspectives in education	Respondents	Agree	Disagree	Not Decided	Total	χ^2-value
6.	Perspectives or foundation courses does not provide in-depth study of processes of child development and learning concepts and perspectives in education	Students	571 (87.80)	63 (9.60)	16 (2.40)	650	43.2*
		Teacher educators	66 (66.0)	22 (22.0)	12 (12.0)	100	
		Total	**637** **(84.93)**	**84** **(11.20)**	**30** **(4.00)**	**750**	
7.	Teacher Education as a compulsory subject in M.Ed. curriculum included to prepare teacher educators for both theory and practice	Students	548 (84.30)	86 (13.20)	16 (2.40)	650	36.4*
		Teacher educators	65 (65.0)	21 (21.0)	14 (14.0)	100	
		Total	**613** **(81.73)**	**107** **(14.26)**	**30** **(4.00)**	**750**	

(Contd.)

Sl. No.	Perspectives in education	Respondents	Agree	Disagree	Not Decided	Total	χ^2-value
8.	Teacher trainees related ability are develop for the effective execution of the programme	Students	591(90.90)	53(8.10)	6(0.90)	650	90.8*
		Teacher educators	64(64.0)	19(19.0)	17(17.0)	100	
		Total	**655**	**72**	**23**	**750**	
			(87.33)	**(9.60)**	**(3.06)**		
9.	Skills pertaining to ICT and Educational technology integrated in various courses contribute to develop teaching competency of student teachers	Students	576(88.61)	63(9.60)	11(1.60)	650	49.2*
		Teacher educators	68(68.0)	18(18.0)	14(14.0)	100	
		Total	**644**	**81**	**25**	**750**	
			(85.86)	**(10.80)**	**(3.33)**		

Note: *—Significant at .01 level.
Figures in Parentheses indicate percentage.

in-depth study of processes of child development, learning concepts and educational perspectives. The response pattern reveal mixed perception of the stakeholders towards curricular perspectives of theory papers in M.Ed. programme.

Perception of Students and Teacher Educators towards Practical and Fields based Experiences Related to Theory Courses in M.Ed. Programme

Table 12.4 reveals that there was significant association between the category of respondents and perception towards Practical and Fields based experiences related to theory courses in M.Ed. programme. This can be noticed that a large majority of students (81 to 90%) expressed positive responses about the uses of curricular practices of theory papers adopted in M.Ed. programme, such as: organization of seminars workshops, practicum and projects enhancing professional skills and understanding; practicum activities enabling students' understanding of theory related to school situations, fields based activities developed reflective thinking on different educational issues concerning school system; the field studies clarified the complexities of teacher education process and *yoga* practices was useful for personality development of students. Even though majority of teacher educators (62 to 67%) expressed positive opinion on the uses of above processes concerning theory papers comparatively their percentage was lower than that of their student counterparts. A sizable number of teacher educators (33 to 38%) were either negative or neutral about their views on curricular process of theory courses of M.Ed. programme. Such results revealed mixed pattern of response of teacher educators towards practicum and field experiences concerning theory papers.

Perception of Students and Teacher Educators towards Internship and Dissertation in M.Ed. Programme

Table 12.5 indicates significant association between category of respondents and perception towards internship and dissertation work. The students' response was very much encouraging towards

Table 12.4: Chi-square test of association between category of respondents and perception towards Practical and Fields-based experiences related to theory courses

Sl. No.	Practical and Fields-based experiences related to theory	Respondents	Agree	Disagree	Not Decided	Total	χ^2-value
1.	Organization of workshops, practicum activities, projects and seminars enhance professional skills and understanding of the Students	Students	529 (81.3)	104 (16.0)	17 (2.60)	650	48.9*
		Teacher educators	62 (62.0)	20 (20.0)	18 (18.0)	100	
		Total	**591** **(78.80)**	**124** **(16.53)**	**35** **(4.66)**	**750**	
2.	The practicum programme contribute to understand the ground reality at school stage as well as at teacher education level	Students	558 (85.80)	79 (12.10)	13 (2.00)	650	52.6*
		Teacher educators	62 (62.0)	23 (23.0)	15 (15.0)	100	
		Total	**620** **(82.66)**	**102** **(13.60)**	**28** **(3.73)**	**750**	
3.	Field-based activities develop reflective thinking of students on different educational issues concerning school system	Students	564 (86.70)	67 (10.30)	19 (2.90)	650	31.6*
		Teacher educators	67 (67.0)	20 (20.0)	13 (13.0)	100	
		Total	**631** **(84.13)**	**87** **(11.60)**	**32** **(4.26)**	**750**	

(Contd.)

Sl. No.	Practical and Fields based experiences related to theory	Respondents	Agree	Disagree	Not Decided	Total	χ^2-value
4.	Working in a field situation related to the thematic or focus area specialization develop in-depth understanding of complexities of teacher education practices	Students	585 (90.00)	54 (8.30)	11 (1.60)	650	76.6*
		Teacher educators	65 (65.0)	16 (16.0)	19 (19.0)	100	
		Total	**650** **(86.66)**	**70** **(9.33)**	**30** **(4.00)**	**750**	
5.	*Yoga* practices as an integral part of the curriculum is useful for personality development of students	Students	584 (89.80)	60 (9.20)	6 (0.90)	650	61.8*
		Teacher educators	65 (65.0)	24 (24.0)	11 (11.0)	100	
		Total	**649** **(86.53)**	**84** **(11.20)**	**17** **(2.26)**	**750**	

Note: *—Significant at. 01 level.
Figures in Parentheses indicate percentage.

Table 12.5: Chi-square test of association between category of respondents and perception towards Internship and Dissertation

Sl. No.	Internship and Dissertation	Respondents	Agree	Disagree	Not Decided	Total	χ^2-value
1.	Engaging students with teacher education institutions help students to establish Linkage of theory with the ground reality	Students	520 (80.0)	113 (17.30)	17 (2.60)	650	47.9*
		Teacher Educators	62 (62.0)	20 (20.0)	18 (18.0)	100	
		Total	**582** **(77.60)**	**133** **(17.73)**	**35** **(4.66)**	**750**	
2.	Engaging students with teacher education institutions help students to establish Linkage with theoretical courses will promote quality education	Students	565 (86.90)	69 (10.60)	16 (2.40)	650	67.4*
		Teacher Educators	58 (58.0)	24 (24.0)	18 (18.0)	100	
		Total	**623** **(83.06)**	**93** **(12.40)**	**34** **(4.53)**	**750**	

(Contd.)

Sl. No.	Internship and Dissertation	Respondents	Agree	Disagree	Not Decided	Total	χ^2-value
3.	Dissertation in specialized area at elementary/secondary level develop research problem solving skills among the students of concerned stage	Students	559 (86.0)	75 (50.0)	16 (10.60)	650	35.7*
		Teacher Educators	67 (67.0)	18 (18.0)	14 (14.0)	100	
		Total	**626** **(83.46)**	**93** **(12.4)**	**30** **(4.00)**	**750**	
4.	School based attachment as per the school-level specialization provide opportunities for organizing relevant teaching-learning activities	Students	515 (79.23)	110 (16.92)	11 (1.69)	650	66.4*
		Teacher Educators	64 (64.0)	17 (17.0)	19 (19.0)	100	
		Total	**579** **(77.20)**	**127** **(16.93)**	**30** **(4.00)**	**750**	

Note: *—Significant at. 01 level.
Figures in Parentheses indicate percentages.

different items than that of their teach educator counterparts. It is revealed that 79 to 86 per cent students expressed high opinion on internship and dissertation process, such as (i) Engaging students with teacher education institutions help students to establish linkage of theory with the ground reality, (ii) Engaging students with teacher education institutions help students to establish linkage with theoretical courses will promote quality education, (iii) school based attachment as per the school-level specialization provide opportunities for organising relevant teaching-learning activities, and (iv) dissertation concerned stage. The teacher educators expressing positive views on these items varied from 58 to 67 per cent. It was revealed that large size of teacher educator respondents (33 to 42%) were either negative or neutral on these areas of curricular practices. This fact indicates lack of clarity of many teacher educators to adjust with their new responsibilities regarding internship and specialised area specific dissertation work.

Perception of Students and Teacher Educators towards Time-Table in M.Ed. Programme

From Table 12.6, this can be noticed that there was significant association between the category of respondents and their perception towards different items covered under the heading of academic resource support for M.Ed. programme. Regarding timetable matter, a majority of M.Ed. students (74.46%) were critical about time allotment to each area of curriculum. Of course, around 57 per cent teacher educators agreed on this point. As a matter of positive appreciation of semester system and proper management of internship and school based activities, a large majority of students (80 to 83%) and teacher educators (55 to 60%) agreed on these aspects of M.Ed. programme. Regarding teaching-learning support system this can be noticed from Table 12.6 that a large majority of students (67 to 87%) expressed positive views about encouragement of team teaching, creation of conductive learning environment. Of course 63 to 64 per cent teacher educators were in agreement on these facilities. A sizable

Table 12.6: Chi-square test of association between category of respondents and perception towards timetable

Sl. No.	Timetable	Respondents	Agree	Disagree	Not Decided	Total	χ^2-value
1.	Not Enough time is allotted to cover each and every area of curriculum	Students	484 (74.46)	144 (22.10)	22 (3.30)	650	38.6*
		Teacher Educators	57 (57.0)	25 (25.0)	18 (18.0)	100	
		Total	**541**	**169**	**40**	**750**	
			(72.13)	**(22.53)**	**(5.33)**		
2.	Proper arrangements are made for the internship as well as other school based activities of the programme	Students	518 (79.60)	107 (16.46)	25 (3.80)	650	22.4*
		Teacher Educators	60 (60.0)	28 (28.0)	12 (12.0)	100	
		Total	**578**	**135**	**37**	**750**	
			(77.06)	**(18.00)**	**(4.93)**		
3.	Semester system reduces the burden of course requirement	Students	541 (83.23)	99 (15.23)	10 (1.53)	650	78.7*
		Teacher Educators	55 (55.0)	27 (27.0)	18 (18.0)	100	
		Total	**596**	**126**	**28**	**750**	
			(79.46)	**(16.80)**	**(3.73)**		

(*Contd.*)

Sl. No.	Timetable	Respondents	Agree	Disagree	Not Decided	Total	χ^2-value
4.	Team teaching is encouraged by teachers to provide exposure to expertize in different fields	Students	565 (86.90)	67 (10.30)	18 (2.70)	650	55.1*
		Teacher Educators	64 (64.0)	17 (17.0)	19 (19.0)	100	
		Total	**629** **(83.86)**	**84** **(11.20)**	**37** **(4.93)**	**750**	
5.	Teachers develop conducive environment for learning in the institution	Students	496 (67.07)	130 (20.00)	24 (3.60)	650	23.5*
		Teacher Educators	63 (63.00)	22 (22.00)	15 (15.00)	100	
		Total	**599** **(79.86)**	**152** **(20.26)**	**39** **(5.20)**	**750**	
6.	Teachers do not appreciate students' ideas in teaching-learning process	Students	531 (81.60)	94 (14.40)	25 (3.80)	650	45.7*
		Teacher Educators	59 (59.0)	21 (21.0)	20 (20.0)	100	
		Total	**590** **(78.66)**	**115** **(15.33)**	**45** **(6.00)**	**750**	

(Contd.)

Sl. No.	Timetable	Respondents	Agree	Disagree	Not Decided	Total	χ^2-value
7.	Teacher provide timely guidance to students individually as well as in group	Students	521 (80.10)	109 (16.70)	20 (3.07)	650	20.2*
		Teacher Educators	72 (72.00)	15 (15.00)	13 (13.00)	100	
		Total	**593** **(79.06)**	**124** **(16.53)**	**33** **(4.40)**	**750**	
8.	Enough resources are provided for self-study	Students	522 (80.30)	105 (16.15)	23 (3.50)	650	23.0*
		Teacher Educators	65 (65.0)	21 (21.0)	14 (14.0)	100	
		Total	**587** **(78.26)**	**126** (16.80)	37 (4.93)	**750**	

(Contd.)

Sl. No.	Timetable	Respondents	Agree	Disagree	Not Decided	Total	χ^2-value
9.	Collaborative learning is encouraged	Students	494 (76.0)	137 (21.07)	19 (2.90)	650	26.8*
		Teacher Educators	62 (62.00)	24 (24.00)	14 (14.00)	100	
		Total	**556** **(74.13)**	**161** **(21.46)**	**33** **(4.40)**	**750**	
10.	Teacher does not solve the students' problems in teaching-learning process actively	Students	555 (85.30)	76 (11.69)	**19** **(2.90)**	**650**	62.1*
		Teacher Educators	56 (56.0)	**26** **(26.0)**	**18** **(18.0)**	**100**	
		Total	611 (81.46)	**102** (13.60)	**37** (4.93)	**750**	

Note: *—Significant at. 01 level.
Figures in Parentheses indicate percentages.

number of teacher educators (36 to 37%) were either negative or in decision about these opportunities. This can also be observed that a large majority of students (82%) as well as teacher educators (59%) stated about teacher educators that they did not appreciate students' ideas in teaching-learning process. It indicates about teacher centric teaching in M.Ed. programme. This can also be noticed that while a large majority of students (76 to 80%) expressed positive views about provision of self-study and collaborative learning, 85 per cent of them were critical about active role of teacher educators in solving students' problems in teaching-learning process. A large number of teacher educators (56%) agreed on this item with their students' views. Moreover, a sizable number of teacher educators (26 to 35%) were either critical or neutral about the provision of self-study and collaborative learning facilities in M.Ed.

Perception of Students and Teacher Educators towards Project/ Assignments in M.Ed. Programme

From Table 12.7 it can be observed there was significant association between respondents' category and perception towards evaluation practices of M.Ed. programme. There was a significant difference in perception of M.Ed. students and teacher educators on all the items concerning evaluation system. It can be noticed that majority of student respondents (65-88%) gave positive response on allotment of projects as per students' interest, students' involvement in the projects and assignments are well designed, continuous internal assessment encouraged active learning weightage given to practicum and internship was appropriate and engagement of the students with fieldwork as well as project works were evaluated properly. However, a large majority of students (86%) gave critical remarks on teachers' limited feedback during internship. While these expressions reveal mixed response of students on evaluation practices, the teacher educators' remarks were also perceived to be of mixed nature in comparison to students' response pattern comparatively 4 internships. A large number of teachers (36 to 46%) were either

Table 12.7: Chi-square test of association between category of respondents and perception towards timetable

Sl. No.	Project/Assignments	Respondents	Agree	Disagree	Not Decided	Total	χ^2-value
1.	Assignments are given to students on all the areas timely	Students	559(86.0)	79(12.10)	12(1.80)	650	115.3*
		Teacher Educators	57(57.0)	16(16.0)	27(27.0)	100	
		Total	**616**	**95**	**39**	**750**	
			(82.13)	**(12.66)**	**(5.20)**		
2.	Students, involvement in the projects and assignments are well designed	Students	559 (86.0)	73 (11.23)	18 (2.70)	650	80.9*
		Teacher Educators	62(62.0)	13(13.0)	25(25.0)	100	
		Total	**621**	**86**	**43**	**750**	
			(82.80)	**(11.46)**	**(5.73)**		
3.	Continuous internal assessment to encourage active learning	Students	512(78.70)	107(16.40)	31(4.70)	650	28.2*
		Teacher Educators	66(66.00)	15(15.00)	19(19.00)	100	
		Total	**578**	**122**	**50**	**750**	
			(77.06)	**(16.26)**	**(6.66)**		

(Contd.)

Sl. No.	Project/Assignments	Respondents	Agree	Disagree	Not Decided	Total	χ^2-value
4.	Weightage given to practice teaching and internship is appropriate	Students	502(77.23)	128(19.60)	20(3.07)	650	69.9*
		Teacher Educators	56(56.0)	20(20.0)	24(24.0)	100	
		Total	**558**	**148**	**44**	**750**	
			(74.40)	**(19.73)**	**(5.86)**		
5.	Engagement of the learner with fieldwork as well as project works are evaluated properly	Students	420(64.60)	192(29.50)	38(5.80)	650	9.6*
		Teacher Educators	63(63.00)	23(23.00)	14(14.00)	100	
		Total	**483**	**215**	**52**	**750**	
			(64.40)	**(28.66)**	**(6.93)**		
6.	There is not enough scope for teachers to provide feedback for Internship	Students	561(86.30)	75(11.50)	14(2.10)	650	75.5*
		Teacher Educators	61(61.0)	18(18.0)	21(21.0)	100	
		Total	**622**	**93**	**35**	**750**	
			(82.93)	**(12.40)**	**(4.66)**		

Note: *—Significant at. 01 level.
Figures in Parentheses indicate percentages.

neutral or negative towards existing evaluation practices of M.Ed. programme. Such expressions reveal disappointed perception of a large number of teacher educators towards this component.

Conclusion

The findings of the study reveal that a large majority of students (would be teacher educators) of M.Ed. programme have expressed very high opinion about different dimension of M.Ed. programme such as structural reform, curricular perspectives, practicum and field based practices related to theory courses, internship, dissertation work, academic research support and evaluation practices.

While the students are very much enthusiastic about these areas of M.Ed. programme there teacher education counterparts have expressed positive responses, of course, with cautions comparatively lesser percentage of teachers than that of their students have expressed positive used about curriculum reform in M.Ed. This is also rewarded that a large chunk of teacher educators with a range of 35-45 per cent have not expressed positive opinion about M.Ed. programme structure and implementation. In other words, their found to be either neutral or ever seen about different elements of curriculum reform such kind of mixed response TE gives a hint about less preparedness of Teacher Education Institutions in general and teacher education in specific about the implementation of revised M.Ed. programme while it is considered as a significant initiative to bring quality reform in M.Ed. programme. The stakeholders involvement must be encouraged to make the reforms functional. The initial experiences of reform in teacher educators' education programme may be useful in accommodating contextual issues and constraints in this process the findings of the study, certainly indicate a positive appreciation of reform in teacher educators' education necessary improvements may be brought into the curriculum design and implementation with more scope for flexibility at university level and teacher education institutions.

REFERENCES

NCERT (2005). *National Curriculum Framework*, New Delhi: NCERT.

NCTE (2009). *National Curriculum Framework of Teacher Education,* New Delhi: NCTE.

NCTE (2014). *Regulations of Teacher Education in India*, New Delhi: NCTE.

Sharma, P. (2020). *A Study of Stakeholders' Perception towards Curriculum Reforms in Teacher Education*, Unpublished Thesis, University of Allahabad.

Yadav, S.K. (2013). *Preparing Teacher Educators M.Ed. Curriculum Review and Reconstruction,* Department of Teacher Education, NCERT, New Delhi.

13

Student-Teachers' Involvement in Teacher Education Programmes of Open Universities

P.K. Sahoo and *Chandan Prasad*

Teacher Education Programmes through ODL mode is considered as an integral part of higher education in India, over five decades. The National Curriculum Framework for Teacher Education (NCTE, 2009) emphasized on use of context specific constructivist approach in teacher education programmes. It emphasized on active participation of student-teachers in learning and encouraging them to construct knowledge by integrating contextual experiences with structured knowledge system in their own workplaces. The philosophy of open distance learning highlights learners' autonomy in knowledge generation process by making optimum use of learning opportunities provided through various means. Different components of ODL mode, viz. curriculum design, curriculum transaction, learner support services and evaluation process may influence learners' involvement in instructional system. The extent to which student-teachers' involvement is encouraged in teacher preparation practices shall indicate the relevance and quality of ODL system. The contextual framework of gender, locale and discipline may influence student-teachers' involvement in instructional system having interaction with different ODL components. There have been related studies on exploring openness of ODL mode teacher education in India in the context of learning opportunities and decision making of learners. However, the effect of contextual variables and ODL mode components on learners' involvement need further exploration. Hence, it was justified to examine the scope of learners' involvement in ODL mode TEP practices in the context of demographic like: gender, locale and discipline. The major objectives of this study were: (i) To study the effect of ODL components on learners' involvement in instructional system in the context of demographic variables; gender, locale and discipline, and (ii) To study the effect of interaction of ODL mode components with gender, locale and discipline on learners' involvement in instructional system. 2×4 Factorial design was adopted to conduct the study. The population of the study covered ODL mode B.Ed. student-teachers enrolled in U.P. region of IGNOU and UPRTOU. 400 sample respondents of IGNOU (UP region) and UPRTOU (U.P. region) were included in the study. ODL mode student-teachers involvement scale having 40 items developed by the researchers was used for data collection. The student involvement scores were converted into the standard (z) scores. Data were analyzed by using ANOVA followed by t-tests. The study revealed high level of involvement of students in curriculum transaction, assessment and evaluation process irrespective of demographic factors. Learners' involvement was lowest in curriculum design and moderate in LSS respectively indicating centralizations of ODL mode teacher education curriculum. There was significant interaction effect of locale and ODL components on learners' involvement. The scope for student-teachers' higher involvement must be wider with a view to strengthen the basis of openness in teacher development system.

Open Distance Learning (ODL) mode connotes to promotion of openness in learning through distance education. Distance education incorporates multiple educational opportunities for distance learners through learner friendly course materials, media and technology based delivery facilities, ICT based interactive learning opportunities, learner support services and continuous evaluation process. Such provisions emphasis on learners self-initiated participation in their learning and development. The open universities adopt alternative strategies to promote open learning of diversified groups of learners. ODL system is based on humanistic philosophy of education by insisting on holistic development of human beings through liberal and democratic approach. The supremacy of learners is recognized in teaching-learning process. Student-teachers' involvement in educational decision making is ensured through open learning resources and learner support system. Democratic and pluralistic values are interlinked with educational practices by enhancement of learner friendly approaches (Yadav & Lakshmi, 2003). In such system, learning is considered as experiential in nature where learners engage themselves in gaining learning experiences through individual and group efforts. The interpersonal relationships are also promoted for development of academic concepts, life skills and human values. Learner autonomy is promoted in deciding 'What' is to be learnt, 'How' learning will take place, 'Where' learning will occur, 'Who' will assist them for learning, with 'Whom' they will interact for enrichment of learning experiences, 'Which' experiences are valuable and meaningful for them, 'Whether' learning experiences have lead to their development and 'Where' to move after completion of studies. Open learning system encourages student-teachers' involvement in different stages of education in curriculum design, curriculum transaction process, learner support system and evaluation processes. Learner participation is encouraged in social cultural context to develop meaningful experiences related to different walks of life. The 'constructivist' perspective of learning is encouraged by facilitating different learning opportunities for independent inquiry as well as co-operative and collaborative experiences. Hence, open distance learning mode makes its presence for promoting democratization of education in contrast to traditional conservative mode of education.

Teacher Education Programme (TEP) is to be understood as provision of participatory learning opportunities for experienced distance teacher learners by which professional knowledge, values and skills can be developed in their own workplaces. The student-teachers' autonomy is valued in choosing meaningful individual and group learning experiences from alternative learning resources available through open universities. The experienced student-teachers make use of open learning course wares for gaining professional knowledge developing skills and attitudes suiting to their socio-cultural ethoes of school system in general and classroom teaching situations in specific. Such features of open learning system have been highlighted by Lewis (1986) where learners take own responsibility of choosing the content matter, methods of learning, learning support sources and assessment of own progress in studies according to their own expectations. Open learning system's responsibility is also viewed in empowerment of student-teachers to recognize their own potentials and capabilities and to manage their own learning and development through ODL mode.

Thorpe and Grugeon (1987) had also thrown light on openness closeness continuum in educational institutions in the context of learners' autonomy. They identified different areas of learners' autonomy in the context of deciding the curriculum inputs, entrance system, course contents, methods and approaches of learning, study situation, pace of studies, mechanism of assessment, feedback and course end evaluation etc. Such contributions to the literature of open learning paved the way for making distance education more learner friendly in contrast to the industrialized framework of distance education programme. Sahoo (1994) had highlighted the characteristics of open learning system of Indian universities in the context of learners' participation in teaching-learning system of distance institutions of India. Researches had conducted to explore openness of Indian system of distance education in the context of learners' autonomy in educational practices. The Indian system of Distance Education, since its inception, had promoted teacher education programmes for working teachers at schools located in far-flung areas of the country. Since, the school curriculum has been redesigned (NCERT, 2005) to promote constructive learning opportunities, teacher education strategies must be geared to need such requirements. Accordingly, National Council of Teacher Education, developed curriculum framework for teacher education giving emphasis on hands on experience based professional development (NCTE, 2009). Open distance learning based teacher education must prove its worth by incorporating experiential learning based strategies for teachers' preparation in their own workplaces.

Rationale of the Study

There have been researches in the area of ODL mode teacher education in India like Management of different forms of distance education at higher education stage (Patil, 1996); Future expansion and instructional system of distance education at higher education stage (Patri, 1996); Process of B.Ed. programmes in open universities (Kumar, 2011); Students' learning style and instructional inputs in teacher education programme of IGNOU (Sahoo & Chandra, 2014); Comparative study of teacher education programme through open distance learning mode in Thailand and India (Seebal, 2017); Learning style and processes of development of professional skills among Students of professional courses of open universities (Chandra, 2018); Academic motivation and academic problems among minority students studying in general and professional streams (Taufiq, 2018); Involvement of stakeholders in decision making in B.Ed. programmes in university system (Prasad, 2019). Openness in open university system and dual mode system have been studied by (Patil, 1996 & Patri, 1996). They explored learners' autonomy to moderate level in open universities. Prasad (2019) had found learners having lower decision making than their teacher counterparts on curriculum design and entrance matters, whereas learners' autonomy were found higher in Instructional process and assessment and evaluation. So far, the contextual variables affecting learners' involvement in instructional system of teacher education through ODL mode have not been explored in the Indian studies. The extent to which student-teachers' involvement is encouraged in teaching-learning processes of open universities in India will exhibit its relevance and meaningfulness in the education system.

In the Indian context, researches have explored moderate level openness of distance education programmes offered by open universities as well as dual mode universities. Student-teachers' involvement in open learning process can be understood well in the contextual framework. The socio-cultural factors like gender and locale may have influence on student-teachers' involvement level in Instructional system. Similarly, their discipline orientation like science and arts streams may affect their participation pattern in open learning system. Besides contextual variables, the ODL components, like curriculum design, curriculum transaction, learner support services and evaluation system may influence student-teachers' involvement in instructional system. The contextual variables and the ODL components may have interaction effect on student-teachers' involvement, since participation in individual learning activities and group experience processes are linked with the nature of instructional system and contextual factors in interactive form. On the basis of such rationale, the present study has been conducted by the researchers with following objectives.

Objectives of the Study

(i) To study the differences in student-teachers' involvement in instructional system of teacher education programme (TEP) in relation to demographic variables: gender, locale and discipline.

(ii) To study the differences in student-teachers' involvement in instructional system of TEP in the context of ODL components.

(iii) To study the interactive effect of gender and ODL components on student-teachers' involvement in instructional system of TEP.

(iv) To study the interactive effect of locale and ODL components on student-teachers' involvement in instructional system of TEP.

(v) To study the interactive effect of discipline and ODL components on student-teachers' involvement in instructional system of TEP.

Hypotheses of the Study

The following null hypotheses were formulated in the context of objectives of the study:

Null Hypotheses (1)

1.1 There is no significant effect of gender on student-teachers' involvement in instructional system of TEP.

1.2 There is no significant effect of ODL components on student-teachers' involvement in instructional system of TEP.

1.3 There is no significant interactive effect of gender and ODL components on student-teachers' involvement in instructional system of TEP.

Null Hypotheses (2)

2.1 There is no significant effect of locale on student-teachers' involvement in instructional system of TEP.

2.2 There is no significant effect of ODL components on student-teachers' involvement in instructional system of TEP.

2.3 There is no significant interactive effect of locale and ODL components on student-teachers' involvement in instructional system of TEP.

Null Hypotheses (3)

3.1 There is no significant effect of discipline on student-teachers' involvement in Instructional system of TEP.

3.2 There is no significant effect of ODL components on

student-teachers' involvement in instructional system of TEP.

3.3 There is no significant interactive effect of discipline and ODL components on student-teachers' involvement in instructional system of TEP.

Operational Definition of the Terms used in the Study

(i) **Student-teachers' involvement** in instructional system means self-initiated engagement of learners in instructional system of ODL mode as incorporated in the student-teachers' involvement scale developed by the authors.

(ii) **ODL mode components** refer to Curriculum design (CD), Curriculum transaction (CT), Learner support services (LSS) and Assessment & Evaluation (A&E).

(iii) **Gender** classificationis delimited to Men and Women.

(iv) **Locale** means Urban and Rural area residence of student-teachers.

(v) **Discipline** means Arts and Science stream opted by the student-teachers at graduation level.

Methods and Procedures of the Study

Ex-post-Facto research method was used in this study. Population of the study covered all the ODL mode B.Ed. student-teachers enrolled at study centres of IGNOU and UPRTOU located in the state of Uttar Pradesh (UP), India. The sample covered 400 student-teachers (200 each from IGNOU and UPRTOU) enrolled in the study centres at four places of eastern, central and western U.P., India. The ODL mode student-teacher involvement scale was developed by the researchers for collection of data. The tool covered 40 items on four dimensions of open learning system, viz. Curriculum design (CD); Curriculum Transaction (CT); Learner Support Service (LSS) and Assessment and Evaluation (A&E). The content validity of the tool was established on the basis of judgment of the experts of ODL mode system from different universities of India. The items with correlation values .30 to 1 with total scores were included in the tool. The split half reliability co-efficient of items was calculated as 0.97. Each item of the tool was scored on a three point scale; maximum involvement—3; average involvement—2; and neglegible— 1. The raw scores obtained by each respondent on student-teachers' involvement scale were converted to standard scores, z with mean= 50 and SD= 10. The 2×4 ANOVA and 't' tests were used to test the null hypotheses of the study.

Analysis and Interpretation of Data

Analysis and interpretation of data have been presented in the following objective-wise.

Table 13.1: Summary of 2×4 ANOVA on effect of gender and ODL mode components on student-teachers' involvement in instructional system

Source of Variation	SS	df	MS	F	P-value	F crit
Gender	7.14	1	7.14	0.40	0.52	3.85
ODL mode Components	5077.94	3	1692.65	95.84	5.01	2.61
Interaction	49.96	3	16.65	0.94	0.42	2.61
Within	28115.50	1592	17.66			
Total	**33250.54**	**1599**				

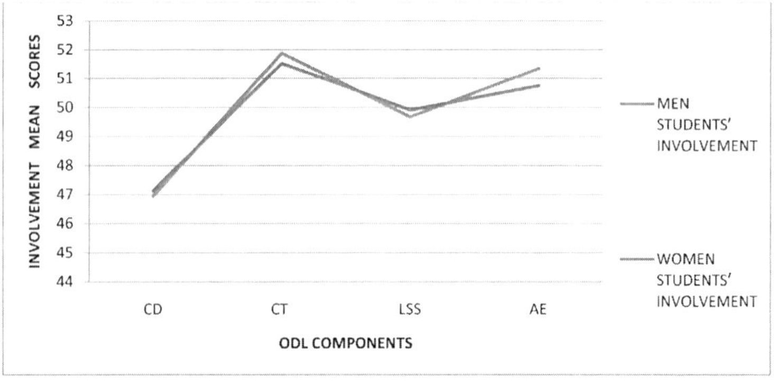

Fig. 13.1: Interactive effect of gender and ODL components on student-teachers' involvement in instructional system.

From Table 13.1, it can be observed that the calculated 'F' value on effect of gender on student-teachers' involvement in instructional system was 0.40, which was not significant at 0.05 level of significance. In the case of effect of ODL components on student-teachers' involvement in instructional system, the 'F' value was found 95.84, which was found to be significant at 0.01 level of significance. However, in the case of interactive effect of gender and ODL components on student-teachers' involvement in instructional system, the 'F' value was found 0.94, which was not significant at 0.05 level. Hence, it can be concluded that the null hypothesis of no significant effect of gender on student-teachers' involvement in instructional system was not rejected. However, the null hypothesis of no significant effect of ODL components on student-teachers' involvement in instructional system was rejected at 0.01 level of significance. It means, there was significant effect of ODL components on student-teachers' involvement in instructional system. This can also be concluded that there was no interaction effect of gender and ODL components on student-teachers' involvement in instructional system (see Fig. 13.1). This is indicative of the fact that effects of gender and ODL components are independent of each other to explain student-teachers' involvement in instructional system. It may be stated that ODL components affect student-teachers' involvement in instructional system irrespective of gender of student-teachers.

Table 13.2: Summary of 2×4 ANOVA on effect of locale and ODL mode components on student-teachers' involvement in instructional system

Source of Variation	**SS**	**df**	**MS**	**F**	**P-value**	**F crit**
Locale	2.46	1	2.46	0.16	0.69	3.85
ODL mode components	4551.38	3	1517	100.62	1.20	2.61
Interaction	181.07	3	60.36	4.00	0.007	2.61
Within	24003.04	1592	15.08			
Total	**28737.95**	**1599**				

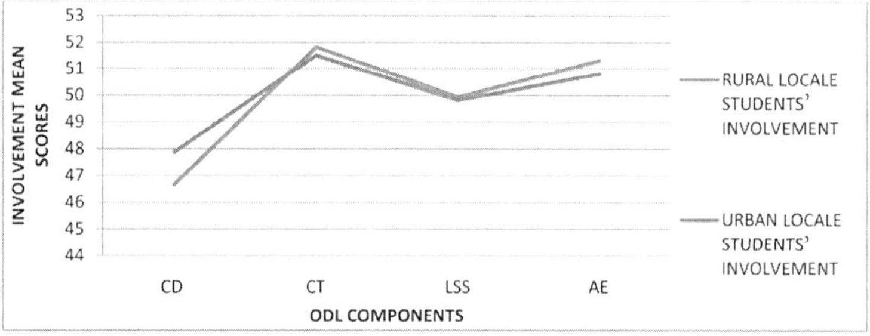

Fig. 13.2: Interactive effect of locale and ODL components on student-teachers' involvement in instructional system.

From Table 13.2, it can be observed that the calculated 'F' value on effect of locale on student-teachers' involvement in instructional system was found 0.16 which was not significant at 0.05 level of significance. In the case of effect of ODL components on student-teachers' involvement in instructional system, the 'F' value was found 100.62, which was found to be significant at 0.01 level of significance. However, in the case of interactive effect of locale and ODL components on student-teachers' involvement in instructional system, the 'F' value was found 4.0, which was significant at 0.01 level. This can be concluded that there was significant interactive effect of locale and ODL components on student-teachers' involvement in instructional system (see Fig. 13.2). This shows that locale and ODL components are dependent upon each other to explain student-teachers' involvement in instructional system.

Table 13.3: Summary of 2×4 ANOVA on effect of discipline and ODL mode components on student-teachers' involvement instructional system

Source of Variation	SS	df	MS	F	P-value	F crit
Discipline	0.21	1	0.21	0.013	0.91	3.85
ODL mode Components	4414.62	3	1471.54	97.88	3.84	2.61
Interaction	39.36	3	13.12	0.87	0.45	2.61
Within	23935.23	1592	15.03			
Total	**28389.42**	**1599**				

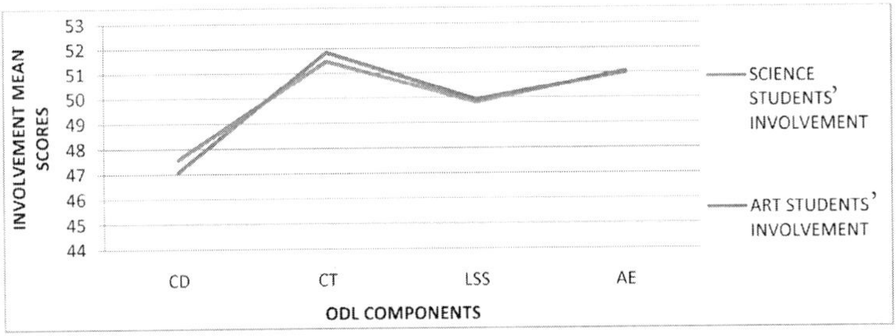

Fig. 13.3: Interactive effect of discipline and ODL components on student-teachers' involvement in instructional system.

From Table 13.3, it can be observed that the calculated 'F' value on effect of discipline on student-teachers' involvement in instructional system was found 0.01 which was not significant at 0.05 level of significance. In the case of effect of ODL components on student-teachers' involvement in instructional system, the 'F' value was found 97.88, which was found to be significant at 0.01 level of significance. However, in the case of interactive effect of discipline and ODL components on learners' involvement in instructional system, the 'F' value was found 0.87, which was not significant at 0.05 level. Hence, it can be concluded that the null hypothesis of no significant effect of discipline on student-teachers' involvement in instructional system was not rejected. However, the null hypothesis of no significant effect of ODL components on student-teachers' involvement in instructional system was rejected at 0.01 level of significance. It means, there was significant effect of ODL components on student-teachers' involvement in instructional system. This can be also concluded that there was no significant interaction effect of discipline and ODL components on student-teachers' involvement in instructional system. This is indicative of the fact that effects of discipline and ODL components are independent of each other to explain student-teachers' involvement in instructional system (see Fig. 13.3). It may be stated that ODL components affect student-teachers' involvement in instructional system irrespective of discipline of student-teachers.

Post Hoc 't' Test

In order to determine significance of difference in the mean involvement scores corresponding to different pair of groups of ODL components (CD-CT, CD-LSS, CD-AE, CT-LSS, CT-AE and LSS-AE); the post hoc analysis was performed by applying 't' test. The results have been presented in Table 13.4.

Table 13.4: Post hoc 't' test on student-teachers' involvement mean difference on ODL components in different pairs

	M1 (CD) 46.95	**M2 (CT) 51.86**	**M3 (LSS) 49.65**	**M4 (AE) 51.33**
M1 (CD) 46.95	-	4.90	2.70	4.38
M2 (CT) 51.86	-	-	2.21	0.53
M3 (LSS) 49.65	-	-	-	1.68
M4 (AE) 51.33	-	-	-	-

The Post hoc test of mean differences by use of 't' was adopted to determine critical mean difference between different pairs of ODL components (Aggarwal, 2013). The 't' values were calculated with the help of MSw from ANOVA summary Table 13.1. The 't' values to be significant differences of mean scores pair were calculated by multiplying SED with 2.58 for 0.01 level and 1.96 for 0.05 respectively. The table of mean differences of student-teacher involvement scores ODL components-wise revealed that all the mean differences, other than student-teachers' involvement with regard to CT and AE are larger than the critical mean difference 1.09 values at 0.01 levels. It can be observed from Table 13.4 that the mean scores of student-teachers' involvement with regard to CT (51.81) was found higher than the mean scores of ODL components CD (46.65), LSS (49.92) and A&E (51.30) respectively.

This difference revealed students' highest involvement in curriculum transaction over student-teachers' involvement in two ODL components, viz. CD and LSS, whereas, there was no significant difference in student-teachers' involvement with regard to CT and A&E. In other words, it can be said that the student-teachers' involvement level with regard to CT and A&E were of high order. It can be noticed from Table 13.4 that student-teachers' involvement in LSS (49.92) was higher than the first component of ODL, viz. CD (46.65) whereas it was lower than the 4th component of ODL A&E (51.30). The involvement level in A&E (51.30) was also found higher than the first component of instruction, CD (46.65). The test of differences of mean scores of student-teachers' involvement in TEP component-wise revealed the order of preferences, as (i) CT (51.50), (ii) A&E (51.30), (iii) LSS (49.92), and (iv) CD (46.65). These findings revealed that curriculum transaction and assessment and evaluation promote higher level of student-teachers' involvement, whereas, student-teachers' involvement with regard to curriculum design was found negligible. Their involvement in instructional system with regard to LSS was found to be of moderate nature.

Conclusion

The findings revealed that curriculum design part did not ensure involvement of learners, thereby indicating centralized system. The student-teachers' involvement have not been valued to develop learner friendly curriculum by taking into consideration their problems in school situation, professional needs and priorities. Moreover, learner support services, which are supposed to be of learner friendly nature, have not been valued properly by ODL system. They appear to be of structured nature. The dominance of regional directors and programme coordinators over management of learner support activities are clearly visible in ODL system. Student-teachers' moderate involvement indicates lessor openness of learner support system. Special affection of the open universities is sought to make it context-specific and problem-oriented in nature. The learner support system must incorporate flexibility and encourage learners' involvement in solving problems in decentralized form. The results are found to be encouraging with regard to learners' involvement in curriculum transaction process and assessment and evaluation process. There is scope for promoting more learner-specific activities with the provision of ICT based learning and collaborative efforts for learning and development in teachers' workplaces. Appropriate networking and monitoring of curriculum transaction and evaluation practices must be encouraged in TEP of open universities. This will lead to establish credentials of TEP of ODL system.

REFERENCES

Aggarwal, Y.P. (2013). *Statistical Methods: concepts application and computation*, third revised edition, Sterling Publishers Pvt. Ltd. New Delhi, ISSN: 9788120720022.

Chandra, S. (2018). *A Study of Learning Styles and Process of Development of Professional Skills among Students of Professional Courses of Open Universities*, Unpublished D.Phil. Education thesis, Allahabad University, Allahabad.

Kumar, S. (2011). *A Study of Process of B.Ed. Programmes in Open Universities.* Unpublished D.Phil. (Education) Thesis, University of Allahabad, Allahabad.

Lewis, R. (1986). *What is Open Learning?* Open Learning, Vol. 2.

NCERT (2005). *National Curriculum Framework-2005*, New Delhi: NCERT.

NCTE (2009). *National Curriculum Framework for Teacher Education*, New Delhi: NCTE.

Patil, S.S. (1996). *Management of Different form of Distance Education at Higher Education Stage in Karnataka and its Futures towards 2005.* Unpublished Ph.D. (Education) thesis, DAVV, Indore.

Patri, K. (1996). *A Study of Future Expansion and Instructional System of Distance Education at Higher Education in Orissa (by 2005)*, Unpublished Ph.D. (Education) thesis, DAVV, Indore.

Prasad, C. (2019). A Study of the Involvement of Stakeholders in Decision Making in B.Ed. Programmes in Open University System, Unpublished D.Phil. Education thesis, Allahabad University, Allahabad.

Sahoo, P.K. and Chandra, S. (2014). A Study of the Relationship between Students' Learning Style and Instructional Inputs in a Teacher Education Programme of IGNOU, *Asian Association of Open Universities Journal, 9*(1): 17-34, https://doi.org/10.1108/AAOUJ-09-01-2014-B003Permanent link to this document:https://doi.org/10.1108/AAOUJ-09-01-2014-B003.

Sahoo, P.K. and Prasad, C. (2018), *Decision Making Level of Students and Teacher Educators in Secondary Teacher Degree Programme of Open University. AAOU 2018, Conference Proceeding.*https://aaou2018.hou.edu.vn/wplogin.php?redirect_to=https://aaou2018.hou.edu.vn/%2Fconference-proceeding-download%2F.

Sahoo P.K. (1994). *Open Learning System*, New Delhi: Uppal Publication.

Seebal, P.K. (2017). *Teacher Education Programme Through Open Distance Learning Mode in Thailand and India: A Comparative Study.* Unpublished D.Phil. (Education) Thesis, University of Allahabad, Allahabad, UP.

Taufiq, S. (2018). *A Study on Academic Motivation and Academic Problem Among Minority Students Studying in General and Professional Streams.* Unpublished D.Phil. education thesis, University of Allahabad, Allahabad, UP.

Throp, M. and Grugeon, D. (Eds.)(1987). *Open Learning for Adults*, Essex: Longman Orient Ltd.

Yadav, M.S. and Lakshmi, S. (Eds.)(2003). *Conceptual Inputs for Secondary Teacher Education*, New Delhi: NCTE.

Section III
TECHNOLOGY INTEGRATED TEACHER EDUCATION

14

Effectiveness of TPACK Teaching Practice

B.C. Das, P.B. Binjha, Ashok Dansana and *Bijay Kumar Das*

The educational landscape outlined in the National Education Policy (NEP) 2020 emphasizes the integration of technology in teaching and learning processes to facilitate holistic development and adaptive learning methodologies. This policy underscores the imperative for educators to possess robust TPACK to navigate the complexities of modern education effectively. Consequently, there is a pressing need for pre-service teacher education programmes to align with these principles and equip educators with the requisite skills and knowledge to leverage technology for enhanced pedagogical practices.

The Information and Communication Technology (ICT) Competency Standards for Teachers, as delineated by UNESCO in 2008, underscore the critical need for educators to adeptly employ ICT to bolster constructivist learning methodologies. Constructivist learning, encompassing activities such as knowledge construction and problem-solving within authentic contexts (Airasian & Walsh, 1997; Duffy & Cunningham, 1996), aligns with the notion of Technological Pedagogical Content Knowledge

(TPACK) introduced by Mishra and Koehler (2006). This framework encapsulates teachers' proficiency in integrating information and communication technology into their pedagogical practices. However, contemporary research suggests that many educators fail to fully leverage the potential of ICT tools for constructivist teaching (Lim & Chai, 2008; Starkey, 2010; Webb & Cox, 2004), indicating a significant challenge in developing constructivist-oriented TPACK among teachers. Moreover, studies have demonstrated that teachers' perceptions of their own efficacy significantly influence their adoption of ICT (Wozney, Venkatesh, & Abrami, 2006). Consequently, enhancing teachers' professional development in ICT necessitates a deeper understanding of their perceptions regarding constructivist-oriented TPACK and the factors that shape these perceptions. However, existing literature primarily focuses on teachers' TPACK perceptions in specific subject areas, such as science education, e-learning facilitation, social studies, and mathematics (e.g. Archambault & Barnett, 2010; Graham et al., 2009; Lee & Tsai, 2010; Schmidt *et al.,* 2009), leaving gaps in our understanding of teachers' perceived knowledge gaps in constructivist-oriented TPACK.

TPACK is widely recognized as a crucial framework for enhancing the instructional competency of teachers in the twentieth-first century. It encompasses the intersection of technological, pedagogical, and content knowledge required for effective technology integration in teaching. Teaching with technology involves a multifaceted understanding, including the representation of concepts using technology, employing pedagogical techniques that utilize technology constructively, addressing learning difficulties with technology, understanding epistemological theories, and utilizing technology to build on existing knowledge (Koehler *et al.*, 2007). Integrating technology into pedagogy extends pedagogical and content knowledge (PCK) into a domain that encompasses technology (Shulman, 1986, 1987). However, it is crucial to recognize that technological integration affects pedagogical processes rather than altering the content itself.

Mishra and Koehler (2006) proposed a hybrid concept of teachers' knowledge, incorporating technology, pedagogy, and content, along with contextual influences on learning. Harris and Hofer (2011) further explored how this knowledge influences instructional planning, activities, and ultimately, technology integration for enhanced student learning and classroom engagement. Pre-service teachers require comprehensive knowledge of effective technology integration into their teaching practices (Schmidt *et al.*, 2009; Tokmak *et al.*, 2013), emphasizing the necessity for a symbiotic development of technological, pedagogical, and content knowledge to meet the demands of modern education.

The prevailing situation in pre-service teacher education is undergoing rapid transformation amidst a deluge of innovations. Consequently, there is a need for clear guidance to navigate these changes effectively and ensure that educators are adequately prepared to address the diverse challenges inherent in teaching and learning. This project aims to explore various possibilities to guide the adoption of appropriate technological and pedagogical approaches to address content-related challenges. Key questions to be addressed include:

1. What are the current TPACK practices observed in practice teaching among pre-service teachers?
2. What are the existing levels of Technological Pedagogical and Content Knowledge among pre-service teachers?
3. To what extent do pre-service teachers require Technological Pedagogical and Content Knowledge?
4. How effective could TPACK-based practice teaching be?
5. What are the reactions of pre-service teachers, particularly those in science and social science disciplines, towards TPACK-based practice teaching?

This study endeavours to shed light on potential strategies for enhancing the practice teaching programme through the integration of TPACK principles.

Objectives and Methods

1. To study the effectiveness of TPACK based practice teaching in science and social science with reference to learning achievement of students.

Hypotheses

1.1 There exists no significant difference between the mean pre-test learning achievement score obtained by both experimental group-1 and control group-1 of science and social science students.

1.2 There exists no significant difference between the mean post-test learning achievement score obtained by both experimental group-1 and control group-1 of science and social science students.

1.3 There exists no significant difference between the mean post-test learning achievement score obtained by both experimental group-2 and control group-2 of science and social science students.

1.4 There exists no significant difference between the mean post-test learning achievement score obtained by both experimental group-1 and experimental group-2 of science and social science students.

1.5 There exists no significant difference between the mean post-test learning achievement score obtained by both control group-1 and control group-2 of science and social science students.

Methodology

The project team led the experiment conducted by 40 pre-service teachers out of which 20 (10 science + 10 social science) pre-service teachers carried out practice teaching experiments in two experiment group schools. In each school there were 5 science and 5 social science pre-service teachers. Likewise, 20 (10 science + 10 social science) pre-service teachers carried out practice teaching in two control group schools. In each school there were 5 science and 5 social science pre-service teachers. The scheme of experiment was carried out following Solomon Four Group Design. The pre-service teachers administered pre- and post-test as instructed by Solomon Four Group Design to collect data related to learning achievement by using self-developed achievement tests.

Analysis and Interpretation

The effectiveness of TPACK based practice teaching in science and social science with reference to learning achievement of students and competencies of pre-service teachers were analysed and interpreted variable-wise.

Effectiveness of TPACK-based Practice Teaching in Science and Social Science with Reference to Learning Achievement of Students

The effectiveness of TPACK-based practice teaching with reference to learning achievement of students were analysed and interpreted in following tables and figures discipline-wise.

Effectiveness of TPACK-based Practice Teaching in Science with Reference to Learning Achievement of Students

Table 14.1: Pre-test of Experimental group and Control group in Science (N=95)

Group Statistics				
	Group	**N**	**Mean**	**Std. Deviation**
Pre-Test	Experimental Group 1	60	14.0354	1.09967
	Control Group 1	35	15.2386	2.54784

It was intended to study the effectiveness of TPACK-based practice teaching in science with reference to learning achievement. There were two levels of group, namely experimental and control group. The data were analysed with the help of t-test and results are given in Table. From the Table, it is evident that the t-value is not significant. It shows that the mean score of learning achievement of experimental group-1 and control group-1 of science students did not differ significantly. Thus, the null hypothesis that there exists no significant difference between the mean pre-test learning

Table 14.2: Independent sample t-test for pre-test of Experimental Group-1 and Control Group-1 in science

Independent Samples Test								
		Levene's Test for Equality of Variances		t-test for Equality of Means				
		F	Sig.	t	df	Sig. (2-tailed)	Mean Difference	Std. Error Difference
Pre-Test	Equal variances assumed	16.889	.000	-3.192	93	.002**	-1.2031	.37692
	Equal variances not assumed			-2.653	41.508	.011**	-1.2031	.45346

**Not Significant

achievement score obtained by both experimental group-1 and control group-1 of science students is not rejected. It may therefore, be said that the science students of experimental group-1 and control group-1 were found to believe to the same extent in their learning achievement.

Table 14.3: Descriptive Statistics of Experimental and control group belonging to science

Groups	N	Mean	Std. Deviation	Std. Error	Minimum	Maximum
Experimental Group 1	60	21.25	.94	.12	19.50	23.38
Experimental Group 2	39	22.01	1.21	.19	19.50	24.10
Control Group 1	35	17.71	1.28	.21	15.67	21.00
Control Group 2	36	16.20	1.81	.30	12.00	19.75
Total	**170**	**19.63**	**2.67**	**.20**	**12.00**	**24.10**

Table 14.4: Summary of ANOVA (Science Groups)

Post-Test					
	Sum of Squares	**df**	**Mean Square**	**F**	**Sig.**
Between Groups	929.831	3	309.944	183.513	.000*
Within Groups	280.366	166	1.689		
Total	**1210.197**	**169**			

*Significant at 0.05 level.

Table 14.5: Post Hoc Tests (Science Groups)

	(I) Group	(J) Group	Mean Difference (I-J)	Std. Error	Sig.
Games-Howell	Experimental Group 1	Experimental Group 2	-.75647*	.23004	.009
		Control Group 1	3.54126*	.24953	**.000***
		Control Group 2	5.04750*	.32569	**.000***

(Contd.)

	(I) Group	(J) Group	Mean Difference (I-J)	Std. Error	Sig.
	Experimental Group 2	Experimental Group 1	.75647*	.23004	.009
		Control Group 1	4.29774*	.29244	**.000***
		Control Group 2	5.80397*	.35963	**.000***
	Control Group 1	Experimental Group 1	-3.54126*	.24953	**.000***
		Experimental Group 2	-4.29774*	.29244	**.000***
		Control Group 2	1.50624*	.37240	.001
	Control Group 2	Experimental Group 1	-5.04750*	.32569	**.000***
		Experimental Group 2	-5.80397*	.35963	**.000***
		Control Group 1	-1.50624*	.37240	.001

*Significant at the 0.05 level.

- It was intended to compare the mean post-test learning achievement score obtained by both experimental group-1 and control group-1 of science students. From Table 14.5, it is evident that it is significant at 0.05 level with df= 3/166. It shows that the mean score of learning achievement of science students of experimental group-1 and control group-1 differ significantly. Thus, the null hypothesis that there exists no significant difference between the mean post-test learning achievement score obtained by both experimental group-1 and control group-1 of science students is rejected. In other words, it can be said that the experimental group-1 taught by TPACK based practice teaching found superior to their counterpart control group-1 taught by traditional approach-based practice teaching.
- It was intended to compare the mean post-test learning achievement score obtained by both experimental group-2 and control group-2 of science students. From Table 14.5, it is evident that it is significant at 0.05 level with df= 3/166. It shows that the mean score of learning achievement of science students of experimental group-2 and control group-2 differ

significantly. Thus, the null hypothesis that there exists no significant difference between the mean post-test learning achievement score obtained by both experimental group-2 and control group-2 of science students is rejected. In other words, it can be said that the experimental group-2 taught by TPACK-based practice teaching found superior to their counterpart control group-2 taught by traditional approach-based practice teaching.

- It was intended to compare the mean post-test learning achievement score obtained by both experimental group-1 and experimental group-2 of science students. From Table 14.5, it is evident that it is not significant at 0.05 level with df = 3/166. It shows that the mean score of learning achievement of science students of experimental group-1 and Experimental group-2 did not differ significantly. Thus, the null hypothesis that there exists no significant difference between the mean post-test learning achievement score obtained by both experimental group-1 and experimental group-2 of science students is not rejected. In other words, it can be said that the experimental group-1 taught by TPACK-based practice teaching found equal to their counterpart experimental group-2 taught by same TPACK-based practice teaching.
- It was intended to compare the mean post-test learning achievement score obtained by both control group-1 and control group-2 of science students. From Table 14.5, it is evident that it is not significant at 0.05 level with df= 3/166. It shows that the mean score of learning achievement of science students of control group-1 and control group-2 did not differ significantly. Thus, the null hypothesis that there exists no significant difference between the mean post-test learning achievement score obtained by both control group-1 and control group-2 of science students is not rejected. In other words, it can be said that the control group-1 taught by traditional approach-based practice teaching found equal to their counterpart control group-2 taught by same traditional approach-based practice teaching.

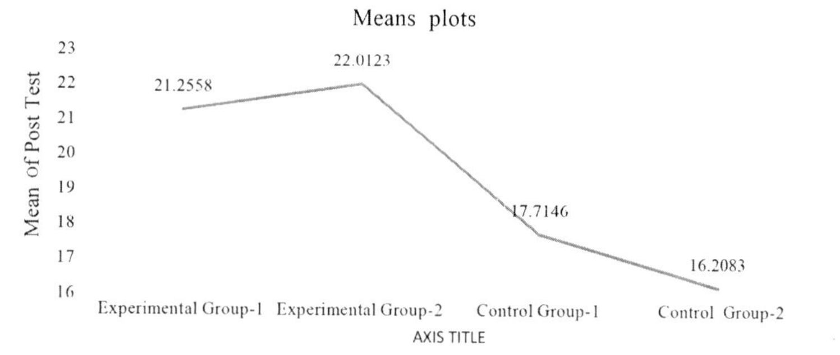

Fig 14.1: Mean of Post-test in Experimental and Control group (Science Groups)

It is evident from the above Table and Figure that there is significant difference between the experimental Group-1 and control Group-1. Further there is significant difference between the experimental Group-2 and control Group-2. In both the experiments mean score of experimental Group-1 & 2 was found higher than the mean score of control Group-1 & 2. Further, there is a negligible difference is found between the experimental Group-1 & 2 and control Group-1 & 2 as well. In other words, it can be said that TPACK-based practice teaching was found superior to traditional based practice teaching.

Effectiveness of TPACK-based Practice Teaching in Social Science with Reference to Learning Achievement of Students

Table 14.6: Pre-test of Experimental group and Control group in Social Science (N=98)

Group Statistics					
Group		**N**	**Mean**	**Std. Deviation**	**Std. Error Mean**
Pre-Test	Experimental Group 1	60	17.09	12.45	1.60
	Control Group 1	38	13.89	2.41	.39

(*Contd.*)

It was intended to study the effectiveness of TPACK-based practice teaching in social science with reference to learning achievement. There were two levels of group, namely experimental and control group. The data were analysed with the help of t-test and results are given in Table. From the Table, it is evident that the t-value is not significant. It shows that the mean score of learning achievement of experimental Group-1 and control Group-1 of social science students did not differ significantly. Thus, the null hypothesis that there exists no significant difference between the mean pre-test learning achievement score obtained by both experimental Group-1 and control Group-1 of social science students is not rejected. It may therefore, be said that the social science students of experimental Group-1 and control Group-1 were found to believe to the same extent in their learning achievement score.

Table 14.7: Independent sample t-test for pre-test of Experimental Group-1 and Control Group-1 in Social Science

Group		Levene's Test for Equality of Variances		t-test for Equality of Means				
		F	Sig.	t	df	Sig. (2-tailed)	Mean Diffe-rence	Std. Error Diffe-rence
Pre-Test	Equal variances assumed	10.764	.001	3.329	96	.001	1.227	.3688
	Equal variances not assumed			3.031	.001	**.004**	1.227	.4049

*Not Significant

Table 14.8: Descriptive Statistics of Experimental and control group belonging to social science

Group	Post Test					
	N	Mean	Std. Deviation	Std. Error	Minimum	Maximum
Experimental Group 1	60	22.2722	1.20056	.15499	19.75	24.50
Experimental Group 2	39	22.1538	1.88538	.30190	18.00	25.00
Control Group 1	38	17.5895	1.98967	.32277	13.00	20.50
Control Group 2	34	17.0200	2.31714	.39739	12.67	22.00
Total	**171**	**20.1603**	**3.02229**	**.23112**	**12.67**	**25.00**

Table 14.9: Test of Homogeneity of Variances (social science)

Post Test			
Levene Statistic	df1	df2	Sig.
7.791	3	167	**.000**

It is evident that the given data in Table is normal for use of parametric statistics.

Table 14.10: Summary of ANOVA (Social Science Groups)

Post-Test					
	Sum of Squares	df	Mean Square	F	Sig.
Between Groups	1009.046	3	336.349	103.297	**.000**
Within Groups	543.775	167	3.256		
Total	**1552.821**	**170**			

*Significant at 0.05 level.

Table 14.11: Post Hoc Test (Social Science Group)

	(I) Group	**(J) Group**	**Mean Difference (I-J)**	**Std. Error**	**Sig.**
Games-Howell	Experimental Group 1	Experimental Group 2	.11	.33	.985
		Control Group 1	4.68*	.35	**.000***
		Control Group 2	5.25*	.42	**.000***
	Experimental Group 2	Experimental Group 1	-.11	.33	.985
		Control Group 1	4.56*	.44	**.000***
		Control Group 2	5.13*	.49	**.000***
	Control Group 1	Experimental Group 1	-4.68*	.35	**.000***
		Experimental Group 2	-4.56*	.44	**.000***
		Control Group 2	.56	.51	.683
	Control Group 2	Experimental Group 1	-5.25*	.42	**.000***
		Experimental Group 2	-5.13*	.49	**.000***
		Control Group 1	-.56	.51	.683

*The mean difference is significant at the 0.05 level.

- It was intended to compare the mean post-test learning achievement score obtained by both experimental Group-1 and control Group-1 of social science students. From the Table, it is evident that it is significant at 0.05 level with df = 3/167. It shows that the mean score of learning achievement of social science students of experimental Group-1 and control Group-1 differ significantly. Thus, the null hypothesis that there exists no significant difference between the mean post-test learning achievement score obtained by both experimental Group-1 and control Group-1 of social science students is rejected. In other words, it can be said that the experimental Group-1 taught by TPACK-based practice teaching found superior to their counterpart control Group-1 taught by traditional approach-based practice teaching.

- It was intended to compare the mean post-test learning achievement score obtained by both experimental Group-2 and control Group-2 of social science students. From the table, it is evident that it is significant at 0.05 level with df = 3/167. It shows that the mean score of learning achievement of social science students of experimental Group-2 and control Group-2 differ significantly. Thus, the null hypothesis that there exists no significant difference between the mean post-test learning achievement score obtained by both experimental Group-2 and control Group-2 of social science students is rejected. In other words, it can be said that the experimental Group-2 taught by TPACK-based practice teaching found superior to their counterpart control Group-2 taught by traditional approach-based practice teaching.
- It was intended to compare the mean post-test learning achievement score obtained by both experimental Group-1 and experimental Group-2 of social science students. From the table, it is evident that it is not significant at 0.05 level with df = 3/167. It shows that the mean score of learning achievement of social science students of experimental Group-1 and experimental Group-2 did not differ significantly. Thus, the null hypothesis that there exists no significant difference between the mean post-test learning achievement score obtained by both experimental Group-1 and experimental Group-2 of social science students is not rejected. In other words, it can be said that the experimental Group-1 taught by TPACK-based practice teaching found equal to their counterpart experimental Group-2 taught by same TPACK-based practice teaching.

- It was intended to compare the mean post-test learning achievement score obtained by both control Group-1 and control Group-2 of social science students. From the Table, it is evident that it is not significant at 0.05 level with df = 3/167. It shows that the mean score of learning achievement of social science students of control Group-1 and control Group-2 did not differ significantly. Thus, the null hypothesis that there exists no significant difference between the mean post-test learning achievement score obtained by both experimental Group-1 and experimental Group-2 of social science students is not rejected. In other words, it can be said that the control Group-1 taught by traditional approach-based practice teaching found equal to their counterpart control Group-2 taught by same traditional approach-based practice teaching.

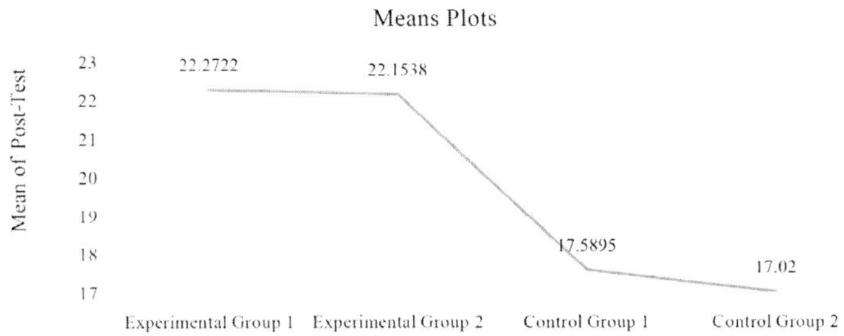

Fig. 14.2: Mean of post-test in Experimental and Control group (Social Science Groups)

It is evident from the above figure and that there is significant difference between the experimental Group-1 and control Group-1. Further, there is significant difference between the experimental Group-2 and control Group-2. In both the experiments mean score of experimental Group-1 & 2 was found higher than the mean score of control Group-1 & 2. Further, there is a negligible difference found between the experimental Group-1 & 2 and control Group-1 & 2 as well. In other words, it can be said that

TPACK-based practice teaching was found superior to traditional approach-based practice teaching.

Effectiveness of TPACK-based Practice Teaching in Science and Social Science with Reference to Learning Achievement of Students

Effectiveness of TPACK-based Practice Teaching in Science with Reference to Learning Achievement of Students

1. *Hypothesis:* There exists no significant difference between the mean post-test learning achievement score obtained by both experimental Group-1 and control Group-1 of science students. The mean score of learning achievement of science students of experimental Group-1 and control Group-1 differs significantly at 0.05 level. In other words, it can be said that the experimental Group-1 taught by TPACK-based practice teaching found superior to their counterpart control Group-1 taught by traditional approach-based practice teaching.
2. *Hypothesis:* There exists no significant difference between the mean post-test learning achievement score obtained by both experimental Group-2 and control Group-2 of science students. The mean score of learning achievement of science students of experimental Group-2 and control Group-2 differs significantly at 0.05 level. In other words, it can be said that the experimental Group-2 taught by TPACK-based practice teaching found superior to their counterpart control Group-2 taught by traditional approach-based practice teaching.
3. *Hypothesis:* There exists no significant difference between the mean post-test learning achievement score obtained by both experimental Group-1 and experimental Group-2 of science students. The mean score of learning achievement of science students of experimental Group-1 and experimental Group-2 did not differ significantly. In other words, it can be said that the experimental Group-1 taught by TPACK-

based practice teaching found equal to their counterpart experimental Group-2 taught by same TPACK-based practice teaching.

4. *Hypothesis:* There exists no significant difference between the mean post-test learning achievement score obtained by both control Group-1 and control Group-2 of science students. The mean score of learning achievement of science students of control Group-1 and control Group-2 did not differ significantly. In other words, it can be said that the control Group-1 taught by traditional approach-based practice teaching found equal to their counterpart control Group-2 taught by same traditional approach-based practice teaching.

Effectiveness of TPACK-based Practice Teaching in Social Science with Reference to Learning Achievement of Students

1. *Hypothesis:* There exists no significant difference between the mean post-test learning achievement score obtained by both experimental Group-1 and control Group-1 of social science students. The mean score of learning achievement of social science students of experimental Group-1 and control Group-1 differs significantly. In other words, it can be said that the experimental Group-1 taught by TPACK-based practice teaching found superior to their counterpart control Group-1 taught by traditional approach-based practice teaching.
2. *Hypothesis:* There exists no significant difference between the mean post-test learning achievement score obtained by both experimental Group-2 and control Group-2 of social science students. The mean score of learning achievement of social science students of experimental Group-2 and control Group-2 differs significantly. In other words, it can be said that the experimental Group-2 taught by TPACK-based practice teaching found superior to their counterpart control Group-2 taught by traditional approach-based practice teaching.

3. *Hypothesis:* There exists no significant difference between the mean post-test learning achievement score obtained by both experimental Group-1 and experimental Group-2 of social science students. The mean score of learning achievement of social science students of experimental Group-1 and experimental Group-2 did not differ significantly. In other words, it can be said that the experimental Group-1 taught by TPACK-based practice teaching found equal to their counterpart experimental Group-2 taught by same TPACK based practice teaching.
4. *Hypothesis:* There exists no significant difference between the mean post-test learning achievement score obtained by both experimental Group-1 and Experimental Group-2 of social science students. The mean score of learning achievement of social science students of control Group-1 and control Group-2 did not differ significantly. In other words, it can be said that the control Group-1 taught by traditional approach-based practice teaching found equal to their counterpart control Group-2 taught by same traditional approach-based practice teaching.

Conclusions and Implications

1. There is significant difference between the experimental Group-1 and control Group-1. Further, there is significant difference between the experimental Group-2 and control Group-2. In both the experiments mean score of learning achievement of experimental Group-1 & 2 was found higher than the mean score of learning achievement of control Group-1 & 2. Further, there is a negligible difference found between the experimental Group-1 & 2 and control Group-1 & 2 as well. In other words, it can be said that TPACK-based practice teaching was found superior to traditional approach-based practice teaching.

2. The study reveals that TPACK-based practice teaching was found superior to traditional approach-based practice teaching with reference to learning achievement of students. It is imperative therefore to provide rigorous orientation exposure on TPACK practices and development and use of TPACK-based Lesson Plans for pre-service teachers facilitated by the teacher educators and concerned teacher education institutions.
3. It was also revealed that TPACK-based practice teaching was found effective in both science and social science teaching. Therefore, research and training may be undertaken to experiment TPACK-based practice teaching effectiveness in other subjects like languages and mathematics.
4. At policy level the NCTE, NCERT, SCERT, DIET and the PMMMNMTT need to conduct a greater number of project experiments and formulate necessary guidelines for TPACK practices at pre-service practice teaching level. Also, the government agencies like state level school and mass education departments need to conduct in-service training on TPACK-based teaching to empower teachers at school level. The government must provide technology infrastructure at school level and teacher education institution level to make TPACK-based teaching successful and useful.

REFERENCES

Airasian, P.W. & Walsh, M.E. (1997). Cautions for Classroom Constructivists. *Education Digest, 62*(8): 62-69.

Airasian, P. & Walsh, M. (1997). Constructivist Cautions. *Educational Measurement: Issues and Practice, 16*(4), 4-7.

Archambault, L. & Barnett, J. (2010). Revisiting Technological Pedagogical Content Knowledge: Exploring the TPACK Framework. *Computers & Education, 55*(4): 1656-62.

Duffy, T.M. & Cunningham, D.J. (1996). "Constructivism: Implications for the Design and Delivery of Instruction". In D.H. Jonassen (Ed.),

Handbook of Research for Educational Communications and Technology. NY: Macmillan Library Reference, USA.

Graham, C.R., Burgoyne, N., Cantrell, P., Smith, L., Clair, L.S. & Harris, R. (2009). "TPACK Development in Science Teaching: Measuring the TPACK Confidence of Inservice Science Teachers". *TechTrends*, *53*(5): 70-79.

Harish, J.B. & Hofer, M.J. (2011). "Technological Pedagogical and Content Knowledge (TPACK) in Action: A Descriptive Study of Secondary Teacher's Curriculum-based, Technology related Instructional Planning". *Journal of Research on Technology in Education, 43*(3): 211-29.

Koehler, M.J., Mishra, P. & Yahya, K. (2007). "Tracing the Development of Teacher Knowledge in a Design Seminar: Integrating Content, Pedagogy and Technology". *Computers & Education*, *49*(3): 740-62.

Lee, M.H. & Tsai, C.C. (2010). "Exploring Teachers' Perceived Self-efficacy and Technological Pedagogical Content Knowledge with Respect to Educational Use of the World Wide Web". *Instructional Science: An International Journal of the Learning Sciences, 38*(1): 1-21.

Lim, C.P. & Chai, C.S. (2008). "Teachers' Pedagogical Beliefs and Their Planning and Conduct of Computer-Mediated Classroom Lessons". *British Journal of Educational Technology*, *39*(5): 807-28.

Mishra, P. & Koehler, M.J. (2006). "Technological Pedagogical Content Knowledge: A Framework for Teacher Knowledge". *Teachers College Record*, *108*(6): 1017-54.

Schmidt, D.A., Baran, E., Thompson, A.D., Mishra, P., Koehler, M.J. & Shin, T.S. (2009). "Technological Pedagogical Content Knowledge (T-pack): The Development and Validation of an Assessment Instrument for Pre-service Teachers". *Journal of Research on Technology in Education*, *42*(2): 123-49.

Schmidt, D.A., Baran, E., Thompson, A.M., Mishra, P., Koehler, M.J. & Shin, T.S. (2006). "Between In-service Teachers' Technology and Non-Technology Related Knowledge of TPACK". In B. Chang, S.C. Tan, T. Matsui, G. Biswas, L.H. Wong, T. Hirashima & W. Chen (Eds.), *Workshop Proceedings of the 20th International Conference on Computers in Education* (pp. 258-62). Singapore: Asia-Pacific Society for Computers in Education.

Shulman, L.S. (1986). "Those Who Understand: Knowledge Growth in Teaching". *Educational Researcher*, *15*: 4-14.

Starkey, L. (2010). "Supporting the Digitally able Beginning Teacher". *Teaching and Teacher Education: An International Journal of Research and Studies*, *26*(7).

Tokmak, H.S., Surmeli, H. & Ozgelen, S. (2013). "Pre-service Science Teachers Perception of their TPACK Development after Creating Digital Stories". *International Journal of Environmental and Science Education,* 9: 247-64.

Tsai, P.S., Chai, C.S., Koh, J.H.L., & Yang, S.J.H. (2012). Examining the relationships UNESCO (2003) UNESCO Report: *Information and Communication Technologies in Teacher Education-A planning Guide*. Division of Higher Education, UNESCO.

Webb, M. & Cox, M. (2004). "A Review of Pedagogy Related to Information and Communications Technology". *Technology, Pedagogy and Education, 13*(3): 235-86.

Wozney, L., Venkatesh, V. & Abrami, P. (2006). "Implementing Computer Technologies: Teachers' Perceptions and Practices". *Journal of Technology and Teacher Education, 14*: 173-207.

15

Blended Learning in Teacher Education

A. Muthumanickam

Education is the process of facilitating learning, or the acquisition of knowledge, skills, values, beliefs, and habits. (Wikipedia). It can also be defined as, "Education is an act or process of acquiring and imparting knowledge." We can explain this in the teachers' point of view since the teachers are already having existing knowledge through their studies. In addition to that on the basis of the syllabus, they can collect information from various sources like the reference books, journals, articles and also browsing internet etc. Then the collected information can be disseminated to their students. To simplify this one can say that the information collected by the teachers from the different sources, can be imparted to the students. Alternatively we can also explain this in students' point of view that students can get information from the teachers in the classrooms, in addition to that they have to collect information from other sources like visiting libraries, referring suggested references books, journals, getting information from internet, discussing peer groups and also other sources.

Here I would like to mention the aim of education as follows: It aims to modify the behaviour of the children/students, so that they can become as good citizens and they can contribute to the maximum towards the welfare of the society.

There are two important components in Education. One is Process and another one is Product. Education is the process of helping the child to adjust to this changing world. That means, according to the current development in the World, we have to provide information to our children. Otherwise, they will not be in a position to adjust/cooperate with the current global development. Education is a product of experience, i.e. knowledge, skill and attitude are transmitted to the members of the community. Education concerns both the components which are indispensable. Without the process, the product cannot be assessed. Without product, there is no use of the process.

Importance of Teaching

Generally, teaching helps the children to adjust themselves to their environment and also provides appropriate learning activities (curricular, co-curricular and extra-curricular activities) and experience for learning.

We can interpret the twenty-first century as the information age, digital era and more importantly knowledge age. The late twentieth century was a period of major social, economic and political changes. Erich Asbey (1967) stated that the current development in electronics (radio, television and computer etc.) stated as fourth educational revolution. Further he mentioned that the task of education shifted from parents to teacher/from home to school that considered as the first educational revolution; the second revolution is the adoption of written word as a tool of education and the third revolution is the invention of printing and availability of books and other teaching-learning material. At present, the students are having more media exposure. The role of teachers is a highly challenging one. Two decades ago, the teacher was the only source of disseminating information to the students in the classroom. Now-a-days, the teacher is considered as the one of the sources to provide information to the students. So the students' expectations are more. The teacher alone cannot fulfil the students' expectations. The teachers can decide how to utilize digital gadgets in their class rooms to supplement or to complement.

The Importance of Blended Learning

In the present context, Blended learning is playing vital role in Higher Education, especially in Teacher Education. Blended learning refers to the combination of on-line learning and off-line learning. Google defines it, "as a style of education in which students learn *via* electronic and online media as well as traditional face-to-face teaching." We can understand the concept of blended learning in a class room situation very easily. For example, if the teacher wants to deliver the information to thirty students she can ask each student to have a computer with internet facility in the class room. The teacher will deliver the concept of a subject to the students for an hour. This is called as *Off-line Learning*. The teacher can suggest useful websites to the students for the already delivered concept of the subject which may be allowed for another hour. This is called as On-line Learning which is even often referred to as e-learning. After that, the teacher can clarify the doubts of the students from the websites. This approach both off-line and on-line learning is called as *Blended Learning*.

Purposes of Blended Learning

- It provides lively atmosphere and ensures active participation of the students.
- It increases motivation towards learning.
- It increases reading habits among the students.
- It provides real learning situations which look to be quite real and actual.
- It receives the current, recent and up to date information.
- It provides collaborative learning practices by the students from the teachers.
- It helps the learning situation, which is quite vivid.

- It is possible to provide more illustrations of all the learning situations.
- It has the scope of immediate feedback.
- It has the provision of tireless repetition.
- It gives an opportunity for selecting the right speed for providing information for individual learners.

Different Approaches to Blended Learning

Instructor-led E-learning

Learning happens in the presence of teacher, whose delivery method is supported by electronic media in the class room situation, where the teacher delivers the information to the learners. After that, the teacher can decide when and where to use the media. For example, when the teacher is delivering the concept to the learners, s/e decides the use of video clippings related to the concept that the learners—particularly average and below average can easily understand the concept. In the modern era, the role of teacher is changed to be as facilitators, which means, there are more number of institutions that come forward to develop a subject related software materials and host them in different web sites. The students will have an opportunity to visit the web sites to get the software materials. If the students need any clarification/doubts about the software materials, the teacher can do so. Regarding this e-learning refers to online delivery of information, communication, education and training. In a simple way we say that it is the instructional material delivered by electronic media. One can get the e-learning materials anytime, anywhere and any combination as required. E-learning is a process and E-content is a product. E-content refers to the web based instruction developed for individual's auto learning on any subject required by the learners. The variety of technologies can be used for retrieving materials for e-learning. Anyone of the technologies can be used to deliver an instruction at a time. E-content is based on the prescribed syllabus.

Facilitated E-learning

Learning happens from a remote location through direct interaction with the teachers, viz. electronic media (such as e-mail, telephone, video-conferencing, mobile phone, interactive television, multimedia etc.) is called facilitated e-learning. In online programmes, the students can join any programmes and also they have to get software materials through online. After they go through the online materials, the students can clarify their doubts related online materials through anyone of the electronic media with the teachers. This is called as facilitated e-learning.

Self-paced E-learning

An important contribution of the educational technology in the individualized instruction is the learner learning in his/her own pace. The current development is related to technology as the individualized instruction. Self-paced e-learning is also the same, which means independent learning *via* an electronic medium with access to online support. It is a self-instructional programme, where the students have to get the information on the basis of their personal requirement without getting assistance from others.

The Role of Teacher in Blended Learning

In blended learning, after the delivering of information to the students by the teachers, they have to provide useful websites to the students to get further information. If any doubts raised by the students, the teachers have to clear them all. In addition to that the role of the teacher is highly required to develop content learning material as software materials and as supplement material to the learners which are tested and also hosted in the website for anyone to access the materials easily. Many institutions are extending their services to the teachers to provide training to develop software materials.

The following roles for the teachers are essential in blended learning:

Training on Blended Learning

Before introducing the blended learning for the students, the teachers must be familiarized with the programme. In this regard, the teachers must attend the training on how to use blended learning in the class room setting; what are the problems that will occur before, during and after the programme and also know how to solve those problems.

Essentials for Online Environment

The teachers have to create conducive online learning environment in the class room situation. The frequency of contact and also familiarity with online course material and the liveliness of the discussion with the students are all influenced by the teachers. The main responsibility of the teachers is to create and also to maintain an online environment where each student feels secured and respected.

Establishment of Good Rapport

The teachers must maintain a very good rapport with the students. The teachers must familiarize about the students' knowledge and understanding level, which will be helpful to provide suitable online materials to the students.

Needs of the Learners

The teachers must analyze the needs of the learners on blended learning, which will be helpful in selecting and providing appropriate online materials to them.

Explaining the Objectives of Blended Learning

The blended learning is a combination of both off-line and on-line learning. The teacher must explain the objectives of the blended learning in the beginning of the learning time so that the learners can understand and cooperate throughout the entire programme meaningfully.

Research Attitude

The teachers must have research attitude to conduct an experiment for online learning. The research will reflect the students' learning, utility of online materials, the findings of collaborative learning, understanding level of the students and feedback about the materials etc.

Include Effective Assessment in the Programme

In the programme, the students' assessment must be included in the program. The teacher must ensure the final outcome of the programme in terms of comparison between the entry and exit behaviour of the learners. This exercise will be helpful to further programme. This is a continuous one.

Proper Planning and Execution

Proper Planning and Execution must be carried out meticulously. The success of the blended learning is based on effective planning, organizing, and synchronization of online programme, feedback and evaluation. The teacher must concentrate and also effectively monitor the whole event. The problems that may arise frequently during the programme must be solved then and there by the teachers.

Conclusion

Education is keeping itself abreast of the materialistic advancement globally. Hence, need to look for ways and means to deliver the learning in a more digitally cumbersome way. The aid comes in the form of Blended Learning. It is advancement to the teachers at the same time a participatory learning platform for the learners. If teachers take this tool in their hands, it can promote deeper learning, reduce stress, and increase student satisfaction. Teachers can become more engaged with their students. Blended Learning presents an increased opportunity for students to connect with their professors and teachers.

REFERENCES

Agarwal, J.C. (1999). *Essentials of Educational Technology*, Delhi: Vikas Publishing House Pvt. Ltd.

ww.en.wikipedia.org/e-learning

www.en.wikipedia.org/blended learning

www.en.wikipedia.org/wiki/education

16

Blended Teaching-Learning through Traditional and Advanced Digital Technology

Sujeet Kumar

We can understand the education as process and as system. When we see that a teacher is teaching any subject at any standard/class to students than it means education process is going on for transforming the concern subject knowledge and for smooth processing of above process of knowledge, the education system has been developed in various aspects like level of education, level of courses and examinations, infrastructure, institutions, teaching, specific area. As above description of the process of transforming the subject knowledge, teaching is prime concern of education sector and teaching is related to teacher and curriculum.

For smooth processing of transforming the subject knowledge the education system has been developed in various aspects, i.e. level of education-wise (primary, secondary and higher), level of courses and examinations-wise (Kindergarten, Montessori, class 1 to 9, Secondary Board, Sr. Secondary Board, Diploma, Certificates, Graduation, post-Graduation, M.Phil., Ph.D. etc.) Class,

Laboretories, Offices, Sport facilities and Building Infrastructure-wise (primary schools, secondary schools, polytechnics, ITIs, universities and colleges, medical universities and colleges, agriculture universities and colleges, teachers' education university and colleges, Hindi university, Urdu university, English University, Sanskrit university, Tribal university, Hindu university, Muslim university, Christian university, Technical university (IITs, NITs, IIITs, IIMs and AIIMS), Human resource-wise (teachers, administrative officers, non-teachers, doctors, nursing staff, vehicle staff etc.), Governing policy and Funding-wise (Central Government, State Government, Statutory Agencies, Trusts and Private Bodies).

Here, we will discuss about secondary education and teaching-learning in school standard because secondary education is a kind of education system which is given after primary education and before higher education. It is second stage in the system of public education usually beginning with class IX and ending in class XII. This secondary education spreads over the age of almost from 13 to 18 years and these are years of adolescence. It is well known fact that these years of transaction, indeed are most crucial years of life. At this stage, the bodily changes take final shape and stabilize. This is also the stage of emotional transformation and maturity that swing between joy and trauma. Secondary education essentially has to be education of the adolescence. Experiences in schooling have to be designed to be responsive to the need of transaction and stabilization. Since, larger number of students are likely to transit from education to the world of work, it is also stage of transaction to work. Secondary education must foster skills of transaction that is why teacher aims to encourage students with singular interests and/or talents in the classroom by giving them supplementary enrichment material and guidance and encouragement, and will help them to organize such Topic-centred Clubs and Circles through specific funding allocated for this purpose. For the teachers, UNESCO suggests a business-like approach in the organization of class activities impartiality and willingness to adapt the class room situation, objectivity, resourcefulness and interest in teaching as the hallmark of a good teacher.

We know that our education system keeps fluid nature in itself because Indian education is growing from ancient era to till present era. So that we have traditional mode of teaching and their system but now-a-days advance digital technology is emerging as a major driving force for global education system. It is going to be vehicle of the technologies revolution in every aspect of education in present millennium. Our teaching and learning perception and goals have driven the need for innovative and productive learning situations. Schools can no longer prepare students in digital era by teaching in the conventional manner.

The conventional teaching-learning process is classroom model because it is such a familiar and accepted environment. However, the classroom model of teaching and learning has numerous weaknesses. A significant weakness is that classroom teaching and learning is separated from life and has little relevance to work based tasks. The conventional teaching-learning process reaches till students with very limited in term of numbers. The quality of content teaching depends upon teacher and teaching often in variety from excellent to poor. In this context, an urgent need to find a solution, some of the points are given below:

- Instructions are not held by geographic boundaries.
- Faster delivery of appropriate teaching is applicable in schools.
- Flexibility to modify or change content and to make it accessible on demand.
- Reduce time away from work for students.

Teaching with the help of advance digital technology has crossed classroom borders and has opened up a world of opportunities for students. From easy sharing of information to collaboration with the help of e-mail and cloud applications to instant access to learning programmes anytime, anywhere, here is how technology is altering in teaching-learning process. The link between digital technology and education is unique and complimentary. Today, schools' students will decide the future direction of digital technology as they are going to be the innovators of tomorrow. So, equipping is key to success in any field of life of our students. We are already a digital society and are moving towards the knowledge society. Hence, the task is cut out for students and teachers. It is time for learning, relearning and unlearning. Over the years, technology has outdated our conventional theories and practices in teaching. Blackboards, chalks, textbooks and ink pens are fast turning into the things of the past. Traditional classrooms are giving way to smart classrooms. Students are smart enough to swim with the current trends and they are constantly on the learning curve. This learning will surely continue. But, for teachers, it is time for relearning, whether it is pedagogical tools, content or dissemination. They need to update themselves to catch up with students. A few examples of advance technology are discussed in brief below:

3D Printing

3D printing is a process whereby a 3D design is turned into a real object. First, software is used to slice the 3D design into layers, and then the design is printed layer by layer on a 3D printer. A 3D printer works by "printing" objects—but instead of using ink, it uses more substantive materials—plastics, metal, rubber, and the like. It scans an object—or takes an existing scan of an object—and slices it into layers it can then convert into a physical object.

There are a handful of schools that have invested in this, mainly because they are yet to understand the overall scope of such technology and have funds to afford such technology.

(Contd.)

These schools having a structured 3D Printing curriculum adds a new dimension to the classroom by integrating into learning. Curriculum supported learning tools make learning fun and teaching concepts of science, technology, engineering and math (STEM) concepts very easy. In a few schools in India, 3D printing curriculum is specially integrated into the curriculum to help the students in their academics and boost their all-round performance. 3D pens and 3D printed subject models and run the curriculum for one year from class III-VIII.

3D printers can be extremely helpful in teaching subjects like geography, mathematics, history and biology. School students are learning more complicated subjects than the past generation. With the comprehensive use of 3D scanners, printers and software, learning can be made fun and interactive.

Augmented & Virtual Reality

Augmented reality (AR) is an interactive experience of a real-world environment where the objects that reside in the real-world are "augmented" by computer-generated perceptual information,

(Contd.)

sometimes across multiple sensory modalities, including visual, auditory, Haptic, Somatosensory, and Olfactory. Augmented and Virtual reality alters one's ongoing perception of a real world environment, whereas virtual reality completely replaces the user's real world environment with a simulated one.

When a mobile phone with the right app installed is pointed at an object like a picture, which has a trigger connected to it, additional material will be loaded on to the mobile device. So you may have a picture on the wall of the classroom of various famous tourist sites around the world. Pointing the mobile phone at the picture will bring up additional information.

Artificial Intelligence

Artificial intelligence is the simulation of human intelligence processes by machines, especially computer systems. These

(*Contd.*)

processes include learning (the acquisition of information and rules for using the information), reasoning (using rules to reach approximate or definite conclusions) and self-correction. Artificial intelligence is well placed to provide sophisticated pedagogical models and target children's academic weaknesses surgically. So far, the Indian Government think tank NITI Aayog has already organized two international hackathons on artificial intelligence. Artificial intelligence would be used more to supplement the best ways of teaching and learning that exist already.

Digital Repositories & Libraries

Digital Repositories offer a convenient infrastructure through which to store, manage, re-use and curate digital materials. Repositories must be sustainable, trusted, well-supported and well-managed in order to function properly. The Digital Libraries have emerged as a crucial component of global information infrastructure, adopting the latest Information and Communication Technology (ICT) to promote an organizational structure that encourages communication and resource sharing between the academician and scholars across the nations. In India, a number of digital library initiatives and digitization programmes have been initiated across the country. Few digital library names category-wise are given below:

1. ***Digital Library of Books: Digital Library of India*** (http://www.dli.ernet.in/,)
   Vigyan Prasar Digital Library (http://www.vigyanprasar.gov.in/digilib/,)
   NCERT Online Text Books (http://www.ncert.nic.in/textbooks/testing/Index.htm)
2. ***Digital Library of Manuscripts***: *Kalasampada: Digital Library Resources for Indian Cultural Heritage* (http://www.ignca.nic.in/dlrich.html)
   National Mission for Manuscripts (http://www.namami.org/index.htm)

Shodh Ganga: Indian ETD Repository (http://shodhganga.inflibnet.ac.in/)
Vidyanidhi Digital Library (http://www.vidyanidhi.org.in/)

3. ***Open Journal System***: Indianjournals.com (www.indianjournals.com)
Indian Academy of Sciences (www.ias.ac.in/pubs/journals/)
3.5.2 Indian National Science Academy (www.insa.ac.in)

These above examples are related to advance digital technology and these are an alternative to the traditional classroom mode of teaching-learning rather than attending conventional class students receive their learning digitally at a time and place that is more convenient for their schedule. Much of justification for the implementing technology based teaching-learning is based on reducing time away from the job, reducing travel expenses and shortening the amount of time students spend in their learning experiences.

A major weakness of digital technologies based on teaching-learning in particular remote area of every region of India is that little consideration is given delivering effective instructions with the medium. Second important thing is that the teachers who are teaching in conventional classroom to the concerned subject with traditionally, they are not trained or aware in rapid changing digital technology. Another significant weakness of digital technology based teaching-learning is its failure to provide effective social transactions for students while in conventional classroom, students are able to interact with other classmates and their teachers to socially construct their knowledge.

Now we are moving to blended teaching-learning environment emanates from the power of technology to simulate conventional classroom and build the strengths and yet overcome the limitations that exit in the digital technology based teaching-learning model. In the classroom, the teacher provides familiar teaching methods such as lecture, discussion, demonstration, social recitation, dialogue, experiments, problem solving with old techniques like audio, visuals, picture, chart, diagram, laboratory experiments etc. Students in the classroom learn through social interaction by having discussion, exchange of ideas and sharing their experience with their classmates. The concept of blended teaching-learning is to maintain our tradition as well as go to with rapid changes scenario. The blended teaching-learning environment has made collaborative learning a reality of today. Another side of the blended teaching-learning environment attempts to bring together aspects of classroom teaching with the advanced digital technology.

As an example in a blended teaching-learning course of study with component of blended solutions points:

- Lecture/Discussion/Problem solving/Social recitation with Smart class/Board.
- Lecture/Discussion/Problem solving/Social recitation with 3D Printer/Artificial Intelligence.
- Lecture/Discussion/Problem solving/Social recitation with augmented with virtual reality.
- Lecture/Discussion/Problem solving/Social recitation with digital Repositories and Libraries.

The above mix model or blended teaching-learning will be success in our changed scenario because according to a recent report by Google, KPMG, Online education in India will see approximately eight times growth in the next five years. This will have a significant impact on the Edtech market that has a potential to touch $1.96 billion by 2021.

REFERENCES

Gupta, S.P. & Gupta, Alka (2001). *Problem, Development and History of Education.* Sharda Pustak Bhawan, Allahabad.

Kujur, Neelam Sandhya (2016). *A Study of Teaching Effectiveness of Secondary School Teachers with Reference to Teaching and Non-teaching Background of Fathers.* Unpublished Ph.D. Thesis, Department of Education, Banasthali Vidyapith Rajasthan.

Kumar, Sujeet (2017). *Glorious Past of Indian Higher Education System and Present with 3Cs (Conflict, Complexity and Challenges to Development)*, Seminar paper in international seminar on Bharat Rejuvenation at Guru Ghasidas Vishwavidyalaya, October 15-17, 2017.

Kumar, Sujeet (2017). *Requirment of Pre Service Teacher Education Programme in Higher Education with Reference to UGC-HRDCs*, Seminar paper in international seminar on New Education Policy and NAMODI Framework at IGNTU, Amarkantak, July 12-14, 2016.

MHRD (2015-16). *Report of All India Survey of Higher Education*, http://mhrd.gov.in 26/2/2018.

MHRD (2016). *Report of New Education Policy*, http://mhrd.gov.in 26/2/2018.

RAMSA Framework MHRD (2009).

Sahoo, P.K., Yadav, D. and Das, B.C. (2014). *Quality Education in India: Inputs and Initiatives*, New Delhi: Concept Publishing Company Pvt. Ltd.

Tyagi, Depali (2019). *A Study of Neo-ICT and Pedagogy Symbiosis in Teacher Education Programs for Next Generation Teacher,* Unpublished Post Doctoral Thesis of ICSSR, New Delhi funded PDF, Department of Education, Bilaspur: Guru Ghasidas Vishwavidyalay.

www.dailyo.in/technology/artificial-intelligence-education-india-teachers-research-machine/story.

17

Students' Awareness of MOOC and Usefulness of Teacher Education Course Offered through SWAYAM

P.K. Sahoo, Namita Sahoo and *Usha Devi*

Indian higher education system is being geared towards digitalized learning movement. The initiative of University Grants Commission (UGC) in lunching MOOC Programmes at higher education stage through SWAYAM (Studying Webs of Active Learning for Young Aspiring Minds) portal is an eye opener for providing ample opportunities for higher Learning to the learners in different nooks and corners of the country. Systematic efforts have been made for development and production of multimedia technology based course wares on different branches of university education. Appropriate care is taken to develop quality material; integrating advanced technology based learning system for self-study, interactive learning activity and provisions for self-assessment and course end examination. MOOC provides opportunities for education of youth with high passion for self-study and earning credits for higher education stage certificates, diplomas and degrees through CBCS system. The joint efforts of UGC, MHRD, Govt. of India, INFLIBNET, leading Universities and Institutions of higher education have resulted in programme development, delivery, execution and evaluation of various credit based courses in different disciplines. So far, SWAYAM covered 36 four to six credits modular courses developed and operated by 14 Universities and Institutions of Higher learning. Students registered in different courses get opportunity to study e-lessons having four quadrants: Textual documents, Video and Audio content, Multiple choice questions and related links like open content on Internet, Articles, case studies and Wikipaedia development of course.

The learners get timely feedback on their studies. They appear in course end examinations to earn credit through CBCS system. Such programme has been gaining ground through well co-ordinated networking of universities and the nodal centre at UGC level. Since, the programme is considered as an eye opener for digitalized learning in India, it is worthwhile to explore the awareness of university and college students about SWAYAM courses in general and to study its usefulness as perceived by the user students in specific.

With this rationale, the present study has been conducted with following objectives:

1. To explore the awareness of university and college students about UGC MOOC programme and in the context of level of higher education and stream of education.
2. To study the usefulness of MOOC programme as perceived by the student participants.

The study employed descriptive survey-*cum-ex post facto* design of research. For objective one 400 sample students were chosen from University of Allahabad and its constituents colleges. For objective two 30 user students of one MOOC course on India Educational Administration, Management and Leadership were included in the sample.

One self made MOOC Awareness Test, one Reaction Scale and one student's perception questionnaire were used to collect data. Data were analysed quantitatively using 't' test and chi square tests. The findings of the study revealed a mixed response of students about MOOC. Below average level awareness was noticed among traditional course students. There existed differences of awareness in the context of their level of education and steams of education. The PG students and professional course students had edge over awareness of UG and non-professional. The reaction of user students was found positive towards MOOC courses. The participants found very much useful the MOOC programme on "Educational Administration, Management and Leadership."

The implications of the study hint at motivating higher education students to avail the opportunity of digital learning at PG and UG stages and monitoring the progress of students through proper institutional leadership.

MOOC broadly aims at providing open learning opportunities to diversified groups of learners at different stages of education. It aims at catering to educational needs of students already studying inside the framework of formal education as well as pursuing education for lifelong learning. MOOC incorporates multimedia learning opportunities suitably designed to achieve instructional objectives of different courses at higher education stage. Learners of different professional as well as general education streams get additional opportunities for availing IFT support courses which could not have been possible to opt for in formal education institutions. The motivated learners, aspiring for life skill oriented education of different nature may find MOOC as best alternative for open learning. Of late, different institutionalized efforts have been made to promote MOOC facilities at higher education stage in India. The Indian initiative for MOOC at higher education stage provides opportunities for blended learning to the students enrolled in different kinds of higher education courses. The interdisciplinary/multidisciplinary nature of courses has been encouraged through SWAYAM (Study Webs of Active Learning for Young Aspiring Minds) portal of MHRD, Government of India. Opportunities have been provided for blended learning by means of choice based credit system (CBCS) at university stage. Different kinds of core, elective or minor or soft skilled programmes can be opted by higher education students through cafeteria approach. The University Grants Commission (UGC) has launched a massive programme open learning in the Indian Universities through MOOC (MHRD, 2015). The non-technology post-graduation courses have been launched by UGC directly on SWAYAM portal. Other programmes for under-graduate students are covered through consortium for education communication (CEC). Besides such initiatives, MOOC programmes cover a wide range of stakeholders belonging to technical education, teacher education, management education and school education (Jain and Singh, 2018). Launching such massive programme at national level require appropriate management system involving planning for course design, development and delivery; organizational collaborations and involvement of expertise with academic discipline background and technology system; co-ordination of programmes by involving educational institutions and manpower; timely implementation of academic programmes in consonance with academic calendars of the university and monitoring and evaluation of programmes to ensure quality of education and its impact on the stakeholders. In this context, empirical data based studies can be of great use to fulfil the mission of open learning through MOOC.

MOOC Programme on Education at PG Level

(i) The MOOC uses courseware e-content developed for different PG subjects through e-PG Pathshala project of UGC. Currently, UGC is offering/running 147 credit programmes in 36 subject areas at PG level through MOOC on SWAYAM platform. The main author act as PI of e-PG Pathshala course ware development in education subject. Education subject has 16 modular programmes of 4 credits. Each course has 36 to 40 lessons of E-text. Each lesson has four quadrants, viz. text, (i) video/self-learning, (ii) self-assessment, (iii) and learn more. The textual document is supplemented with multimedia and self-check exercises. Each question is supplemented with answer to assist learners for assessment of own progress in studies. The textual document of each lesson consists of 8 pages write up of around 3000 words. The format follows semi-programmed instructional material with division of content into sub-contents. Different maxims of teaching like simple to complex, concrete to abstract, known to unknown etc. are included in organisation of course content. Mostly, the pictorials, PPTs and key points are included/interlinked with the write up. The topics of each module are built in logical manner, of course, in modular form. A summary at the end is given for quick review of each unit.

(ii) Video and audio content is presented systematically in the context of e-text. The teacher video presentation supplemented with PPTs, demonstration of practicals, case study, documentary etc. The PPT presentations are made in the form of bulleted points.

(iii) As presented above, the self-assessment questions are highlighted in the e-content. Minimum 8 multiple choice questions/problems are incorporated in each lesson.

(iv) Learn more: Related links, open content in internet etc. are suggested for references and further studies by the students.

One of the programmes in Education, viz. on Educational Administration, Management and Leadership in School Education: four credit courses are currently being offered under MOOC for PG level students. The MOOC programme on this course includes six areas, viz. Concepts and approaches in educational administration; Educational administration in India, Supervision and Monitoring in Education System, Decentralization and Local Management and Governance in Education, Emerging Issues and Problems of Educational Administration. The programme was developed by the experts from three leading organizations of the country—University of Allahabad, Khalsa College of Education, Amritsar and Central Institute of Educational Technology (CIET), NCERT, New Delhi.

The Audio and Video were developed in collaboration with CIET studio, the programme is being offered by MOOC, since 2017. So far more than 3000 learners have been registered for this course. The examinations are conducted by UGC for the course at the end of each semester. The qualified students get certificates by the controller of examination of University of Allahabad.

Rationale of the Study

MOOC is characterized as ICT based open learning programme encouraging learners' participation in deciding the objectives of own learning (why), course contents (what), self-feedback (what extent), place and pace of study (where), sources of learning (which) and learning experiences through use of appropriate means, methods and media through own learning strategies (how). Exercise of learners' autonomy in self-study are associated with learners' awareness of own academic potentials and prioritizing academic needs, own learning skills and learning opportunities available in different forms through different means. They keep themselves engaged in learning experiences and sustaining motivation to continue with studies. They adopt appropriate learning strategies for self-study by making use of available learning support services. They follow suitable assessment and evaluation procedures to complete the online course. MOOC must take care of learners' awareness level, learners' motivation in studies and their involvement in studies with suitable learner support facilities and adequate evaluation mechanisms. While course wares count a lot for quality of any academic programmme learners' participation, programme implementation and evaluation strategies play significant role in establishing its credibility in higher education system.

Empirical studies on different aspects of online learning programme have been conducted abroad like students' engagement in studies, learners' support facilities and outcome of online studies. In a study on student engagement and blended learning (Vaughan, 2014), the students perceived high value of using collaborative learning applications through online education, Martin and Parker

(2014) revealed that the instructors of online education adopted virtual classroom strategies to reach distance learners and to promote interactivity in teaching-learning activities. Maboe (2016) highlighted the interactive learning facilities of student to student contact and student to teacher contact through online education. Only 3.8 per cent students had participated in online discussion. Regarding teachers' role in online education (Duncan and Barnett, 2009), it was revealed that there was rare engagement in pedagogical dialogue in online education. Tello (2007) revealed that absence of social interaction and presence of the instructors came on the way of students completing online studies. Levy (2003) highlighted the need for learner support activities beyond an instructor or help desk through online programme. In the Indian context, some efforts have been made to conduct programme evaluation studies of online programmes of IGNOU (Sharma, 2019). She revealed positive aspects of IGNOU online programmes perceived by learners and teachers regarding curriculum design, delivery system, learning styles, technology system and assessment and evaluation. MOOC programmes for elementary teachers designed by NIOS was, also evaluated by Singh (2018) indicating favourable status of blending television with MOOCs. So far, MOOC (SWAYAM)'s status at traditional higher education system has not been explored.

Hence, it is significant to explore learners' awareness about MOOC programmes at UG and PG level and to study learners' reaction about course inputs, process and outcomes of a MOOC programme.

Objectives of the Study

1. To explore awareness of traditional regular university and college students about MOOC (SWAYAM) programme in the context of stages of higher education (UG and PG) and nature of courses (professional and non-professional).

2. To study the reaction of traditional regular university and college students about the role of MOOC (SWAYAM) in higher education.
3. To study the usefulness of a MOOC (SWAYAM) programme in Education as perceived by the MOOC student participants.

Hypotheses of the Study

The following null hypotheses were formulated in the context of above objectives:

1. There was no significant difference in the mean awareness of scores of MOOCs (SWAYAM) obtained by (i) UG and PG students; (ii) professional course and non-professional course students; (iii) UG professional and PG professional students; (iv) UG non-professional and PG non-professional students; (v) UG professional and PG non-professional students; and (vi) PG professional and PG non-professional students, respectively.
2. The response given by the students against different alternatives of reaction scale about the role of MOOC in higher education have equal cell values.
3. The perception of user students towards usefulness of MOOC programme expressed on different alternatives of the questionnaire items have equal cell values.

Methods and Procedures of the Study

The study was of descriptive survey-*cum-ex post-facto* nature. The population of the study covered all the students enrolled in traditional regular courses of University of Allahabad as well as all the students registered in one MOOC course on Educational Administration and Management. For objective one and two, the sample of the study covered 400 students from UG and PG programmes of University of Allahabad (including teaching departments and colleges). For objective three, 30 students who completed the MOOC (SWAYAM) course in Educational Administration and Management were included in the study.

The researcher used three self-made tools to collect data:

1. Awareness test for students on MOOC (SWAYAM);
2. Students' reaction scale on MOOC: Its role in higher education; and
3. Questionnaire on usefulness of MOOC programme on Educational Administration and Management.

The face validity of tools was established by the experts of educational technology in the context of objectives of MOOC (SWAYAM) programme. Data were collected from traditional regular mode students by administrating the tools in the classroom situation. For objective three, data were collected from contacting all enrolled students (2018 Session) in MOOC course on Educational Administration and Management by e-mail. Out of 500 total registered students contacted by e-mail, only 30 students responded to the online questionnaire. Data were analysed by using t-test, chi-square test and percentages.

Analysis and Interpretation of Data

Study of Awareness of Traditional Regular Students about MOOC (SWAYAM)

Table 17.1: Comparison of mean awareness scores of MOOC (SWAYAM) PG and UG course students of Allahabad University

Groups	Mean	SD	N	t-vaue
PG	6.38(42.53%)	3.55	200	2.33*
UG	5.49(36.60%)	4.05	200	

Note: *—Significant at .05 level.
Figures in Parentheses indicate percentages.

From Table 17.1, it can be observed that the obtained 't' value is found to be 2.33, which is significant at .05 level with df 398. Hence, the null hypothesis of no significant difference between awareness of UG and PG students towards MOOC (SWAYAM) was rejected. The mean scores of PG students (42.53%) was found higher than that of UG students. The PG students were more aware of MOOC (SWAYAM) than their UG counterparts. It may be due to the direct effort of UGC for incorporation of subject based PG programmes in CBCS pattern at University level. The UG programmes at university level have yet to adopt CBCS programme. Moreover, the subject based MOOC credit courses may not be popular at UG level. As a whole, it can be noticed that even though the PG students had an edge over their UG counterparts on awareness of MOOC, their awareness was of moderate level.

Table 17.2: Comparison of mean awareness scores of MOOC (SWAYAM) professional course and non-professional course students of Allahabad University

Groups	Mean	SD	N	t-vaue
Professional	6.20 (41.33%)	2.37	230	3.24*
Non-Professional	5.32 (35.46%)	2.89	170	

Note: *—Significant at .01 level.
Figures in Parentheses indicate percentages.

From Table 17.2, it can be noticed that the obtained 't' value is found to be 3.24, which is significant at .01 level with df 396. Hence, the null hypothesis of no significant difference between awareness of professional and non-professional course students towards MOOC (SWAYAM) was rejected. The mean scores of professional course students (6.20) was found higher than that of their non-professional course counterparts. The professional course students were more aware of MOOC than their non-professional counterparts. Professional, it may be due to students' high acquaintance with technological developments and ICT. As a whole, it can be noticed that the professional course students had moderate (41.3%) level of awareness.

Table 17.3: Comparison of mean awareness scores of MOOC (SWAYAM) UG professional and UG non-professional course students of Allahabad University

Groups	Mean	SD	N	t-vaue
UG professional	5.51 (36.60%)	4.72	130	1.28 N.S.
UG non-professional	6.20 (41.33%)	2.86	70	

Note: *—Significant at .05 level.
N.S. —Not Significant.
Figures in Parentheses indicate percentages.

From Table 17.3, it can be noticed that the obtained 't' value is found to be 1.28, which is not significant at .05 level with df 198. Hence, the null hypothesis of no significant difference between awareness of UG professional and UG non-professional students towards MOOC (SWAYAM) was not rejected. The mean scores of PG professional course students (36.73) and the mean scores of UG non-professional is found (6.20). The level of course did not exert effect on professional students' awareness.

Table 17.4: Comparison of mean awareness scores of MOOC (SWAYAM) PG professional and PG non-professional course students of Allahabad University

Groups	Mean	SD	N	t-vaue
UG professional	6.23(41.53%)	2.30	100	2.75* S.
UG non-professional	5.23(34.86%)	2.81	100	

Note: *—Significant at .05 level.
S. —Not Significant.
Figures in Parentheses indicate percentages.

From Table 17.4, it can be noticed that the obtained 't' value is found to be 2.75, which is significant at .05 level with df 198. Hence, the null hypothesis of no significant difference between awareness of PG professional and PG non-professional course students towards MOOC (SWAYAM) was rejected. The mean scores of PG professional course students (6.23) was found higher than that of their PG non-professional course counterparts. The PG professional course students were more aware of MOOC than their

PG non-professional counterparts. As a whole, it can be noticed that the PG professional course students had moderate (41.53%) level of awareness.

Table 17.5: Comparison of mean awareness scores of MOOC (SWAYAM) UG non-professional and PG non-professional course students of Allahabad University

Groups	Mean	SD	N	t-vaue
UG professional	6.20 (41.33%)	2.86	70	2.19*
UG non-professional	5.23 (44.06%)	3.11	100	

Note: *—Significant at .05 level.
Figures in Parentheses indicate percentages.

From Table 17.5, it can be noticed that the obtained 't' value is found to be 2.19, which is significant at .05 level with df 168. Hence, the null hypothesis of no significant difference between awareness of PG professional and PG non-professional course students towards MOOC (SWAYAM) was rejected. The mean scores of UG non-professional course students (5.46) was found higher than that of their PG non-professional course counterparts. The PG non-professional course students were more aware of MOOC than their UG non-professional counterparts. As a whole, it can be noticed that the PG non-professional course students had moderate (44.06%) level of awareness.

Table 17.6: Comparison of mean awareness scores of MOOC (SWAYAM) UG professional and PG professional course students of Allahabad University

Groups	Mean	SD	N	t-vaue
UG professional	5.51 (36.60%)	4.72	130	1.52 N.S.
UG non-professional	6.15 (41.53%)	2.30	100	

N.S.—Not Significant.
Figures in Parentheses indicate percentages.

From Table 17.6, it can be noticed that the obtained 't' value is found to be 1.52, which is not significant at .05 level with df 228. Hence, the null hypothesis of no significant difference between awareness of UG professional and PG professional students towards MOOC (SWAYAM) was not rejected. The mean scores of UG professional course students and the mean scores PG professional course students are not found significantly different from each other. It reveals that the professional course students had moderate level of awareness of MOOC irrespective of the stage of higher education.

Table 17.7: Reaction of students towards MOOC (SWAYAM)'s role in higher studies (Chi-square of equal appearance of responses)

Sl. No.	Item	Agree	Disagree	Total	Chi-square value
1.	SWAYAM platform provides alternative opportunities for higher studies to university students	274 (68.5%)	126 (31.5%)	400	54.76*
2.	Students are self-motivated to use SWAYAM platform	163 (40.75%)	237 (59.25%)	400	13.68*
3.	I am keen to use MOOC for completing my studies	293 (73.25%)	107 (26.75%)	400	86.49*
4.	I agree that MOOC can get equal status with traditional formal education	328 (82%)	72 (18%)	400	163.84*
5.	I am willing to pursue my futures studies through MOOC	303 (75.75%)	97 (24.25%)	400	106.09*
6.	MHRD, Govt. of India must make MOOC as a mission of higher education of equal appearance of cell values	301 (75.25%)	99 (24.75%)	400	102.01*

Note: *—Significant at .05 level.

From Table 17.7, it can be observed that in the case of all the items, the chi-square values were found significant at level df 1. A large number of traditional course students (69 to 82%) expressed positive reaction towards in terms of:

- I agree that MOOC can get equal status with traditional formal education.
- I am willing to pursue my future studies through MOOC.
- MHRD, Government of India must make MOOC as a mission of higher education of equal appearance of cell values.
- I am keen to use MOOC for completing my studies.
- SWAYAM platform provides alternative opportunities for higher studies to university students. Only in one case, majority of students (59%) did not agree that students were self-motivated to use SWAYAM programme.

Table 17.8: Traditional regular course students' preference to MOOC (SWAYAM) programmes

Sl. No.	Reasons	F
1.	MOOC (SWAYAM) is most appropriate source for open learning	111 (27.90%)
2.	MOOC (SWAYAM) facilitates self-study of learner.	92 (23.00%)
3.	Blended learning is encouraged because of MOOC (SWAYAM)	42 (10.45%)
4.	MOOC (SWAYAM) can support enhancement of learners' achievement	29 (7.25%)
5	Not sure	126 (31.50%)

From Table 17.8, it can be observed that almost two-third (68.50%) of traditional UG and PG course sample students from different streams gave preference to MOOC (SWAYAM) programme. They appreciated the open learning (28%) and self-study nature of MOOC programmes (23%) at higher education stage. It portrays an encouraging status of open learning nature of MOOC in traditional system.

With regard to successful implementation of MOOC (SWAYAM) programme, the traditional course students gave emphasis on learner support facilities (Table 17.9) by (i) classroom teaching linked with MOOC (SWAYAM) presentations (42%), (ii) appropriate guidance for learners using MOOC (21%), (iii) encouragement of student level interactions (19%), and (iv) due emphasis on coverage of MOOC courses in university examinations (13%).Theses views matter a lot for promotion of MOOC programme at Higher Education Institutions.

Table 17.9: Traditional regular students' opinion on learner support facilities concerning MOOC

Sl. No.	Reasons	F
1.	Teacher must link MOOC programme with classroom teaching	167 (41.75%)
2.	Appropriate guidance be provided to students to use MOOC programmes	167 (41.75%)
3.	Students' level of interaction be encouraged	76 (19%)
4.	MOOC courses must be covered by university examination	53 (13.25%)

N=400

Table 17.10: Traditional regular course students' expectations about integration of MOOC in university curriculum

Sl. No.	Reasons	F
1.	MOOC should be kept optional to students	113 (28.20%)
2.	Provision for minimum six credit course of MOOC be opted by every student	111 (27.90)
3.	Mandatory provision for every course	50 (12.50%)
4.	MOOC results be mentioned in degree certificate	36 (9.0%)
5.	Not sure	90 (22.50%)

N=400

From Table 17.10, it can be observed that around 28 per cent students favoured optional status of MOOC courses for regular students whereas almost similar (28%) number of students have favoured the provision for minimum 6 credit MOOC course for every student. As an extreme suggestion around 13 per cent students suggest for mandatory provision for MOOC programmes in traditional courses.

Table 17.11: User students' perception of usefulness of MOOC course on Educational Administration and Management

Sl. No.	Item	Strongly agree	Agree	Disagree	Total	Chi-square
1.	The Course is useful to develop understanding of educational, administration and management	16 (53.33%)	13 (43.33%)	1 (3.33%)	30	12.6*
2.	The course enables me to develop management skills in school education	9 (30%)	20 (66.6%)	1 (3.33%)	30	18.2*
3.	The course is valuable for inculcating professional ethics among school level managers and administrators	16 (53.33%)	13 (43.3%)	1 (3.33%)	30	12.6*
4.	MOOC is the best source of providing quality input to self-study	17 (56.6%)	12 (40.0%)	1 (3.33%)	30	13.4*
5	MOOC is beneficial to varied interest group of learners	14 (46.6%)	15 (50%)	1 (3.33%)	30	12.2*
6.	MOOC is the best alternative of higher education for students opting modular courses	11 (36.6%)	17 (56.6%)	2 (6.66%)	30	11.4*
7.	I can learn at my own time and pace through SWAYAM Portal.	16 (53.3%)	13 (43.3%)	1 (3.33%)	30	12.6*
8.	The written materials cover whole course	14 (46.6%)	15 (50.0%)	1 (3.33%)	30	12.2*
9.	The language used in the text is simple	10 (33.3%)	19 (63.3%)	1 (3.33%)	30	16.2*
10.	The concepts are clarified with suitable examples	5 (16.6%)	23 (76.6%)	2 (6.66%)	30	27.5*

(Contd.)

Sl. No.	Item	Strongly agree	Agree	Disagree	Total	Chi-square
11.	The course content is relevant to understand context specific issues	6 (20.0%)	23 (76.6%)	1 (3.33%)	30	26.6*
12.	The learners' activities specified in each module are useful for active learning	9 (30.0%)	18 (60.0%)	3 (10.0%)	30	11.4*
13.	Viewing of video lessons provided clarity of concepts	11 (36.6%)	18 (60.0%)	1 (3.33%)	30	14.6*
14.	Major learning points were suitably projected through captions	7 (23.3%)	23 (76.66%)	1 (3.33%)	30	25.9*
15.	The visual images were useful in learning the concepts with clarity	10 (33.33%)	7 (23.33%)	1 (3.33%)	30	16.2*
16.	I felt my presence in classroom teaching while viewing video lessons	8 (26.66%)	15 (50.0%)	7 (23.3%)	30	12.2*
17.	The questions asked towards the end of each unit were useful to judge my progress in studies	9 (30.0%)	20 (66.66%)	1 (3.33%)	30	18.2*
18.	The question answer exercises helped me to get self-feedback	8 (26.6%)	21 (70.0%)	1 (3.33%)	30	20.6*
19.	The suggestions given for further reading made my study more comprehensive	8 (26.66%)	21 (70.0%)	1 (3.33%)	30	20.6*
20.	The on-line study programme suited my study schedule	13 (43.3%)	15 (50.0%)	2 (6.66%)	30	9.80*
21.	I enjoyed my studies through on-line written text, video lectures and learning exercises	12 (40.0%)	17 (56.66%)	1 (3.33%)	30	13.4*
22.	Blended approach of written text, video lesson and learning exercises are effective means for self-study	13 (43.33%)	16 (53.33%)	1 (3.33%)	30	12.6*

(Contd.)

Sl. No.	Item	Strongly agree	Agree	Disagree	Total	Chi-square
23.	MOOC programme is useful to earn additional credits in my PG Course	13 (43.33%)	16 (53.33%)	1 (3.33%)	30	12.6*
24.	MOOC facilitates my studies through choice based credit system at higher education	12 (40.0%)	17 (56.66%)	1 (3.33%)	30	13.4*
25.	I will prefer to join more number of MOOC courses available on SWAYAM portal	17 (56.6%)	12 (40.0%)	1 (3.33%)	30	13.4*

Note: *—Significant at .05 level and .01 level.

From Table 17.11, it can be observed that the chi-square test values of equal appearance of responses in three cells for all the 25 items were found significant at .01 level with df 2. Hence, the null hypothesis of equal appearance of responses in different cells were rejected at .01 level of significance. The figures indicating the students' responses in percentages reveal two major patterns. First, it can be noticed from Table 3 that in the case of all the items large majority of students (93 to 97%) expressed positive views except one item, viz. "I felt my presence in classroom teaching while viewing video lessons" (77%). Second, majority of students expressed strong agreement (53 to 56%) on following item:

- The Course is useful to develop understanding of educational administration and management.
- The course is valuable for inculcating professional ethics among school level managers and administrators.
- MOOC is the best source of providing quality input to self-study.
- I will prefer to join more number of MOOC courses available on SWAYAM portal.

In the case of following items majority of user student respondents expressed moderate views (53-77%) about the usefulness of MOOC course, such as:

- The course enables me to develop management skills in school education.
- MOOC is the best alternative of higher education for students opting modular courses.
- The language used in the text is simple.
- The concepts are clarified with suitable examples.
- The course content is relevant to understand context specific issues.
- The learners' activities specified in each module are useful for active learning.
- Viewing of video lessons provided clarity of concepts.
- Major learning points were suitably projected through captions.
- The visual images were useful in learning the concepts with clarity.
- The questions asked towards the end of each unit were useful to judge my progress in studies.
- The question answer exercises helped me to get self-feedback.
- The suggestions given for further reading made my study more comprehensive.
- The on-line study programme suited my study schedule.
- I enjoyed my studies through on-line written text, video lectures and learning exercises.
- Blended approach of written text, video lesson and learning exercises are effective means for self-study.
- MOOC programme is useful to earn additional credits in my PG Course.
- MOOC facilitates my studies through choice based credit system at higher education.

In rest of the cases, majority of user students expressed moderate as well as high opinion (93 to 97%):

- MOOC is beneficial to varied interest group of learners.
- The written materials cover whole course.

- I felt my presence in classroom teaching while viewing video lessons.
- The on-line study programme suited my study schedule.

As a whole, it can be concluded that the user student respondents expressed satisfaction over MOOC course on educational administration and management programme. It reveals the usefulness of the course as per perception of students who completed the course.

Conclusion

The findings of the revealed below average awareness of traditional regular course students towards MOOC (SWAYAM) programme. There was significant effect of level of higher education and streams of higher education on students awareness, indicating higher awareness of PG students as well as professional course students. This may be due to UGC's encouragement of MOOC (SWAYAM) programmes at PG stage as well as in professional education streams. The result implies proper guidance to students at UG as well as PG level. The students of general education streams must be aware of blended mode learning opportunities through CBCS at PG and UG levels. The students have expressed high positive reaction towards MOOC (SWAYAM) except one point, i.e. the students are not self-motivated to join MOOC (SWAYAM) programme as a component of regular mode studies under CBCS. The online education programme of SWAYAM in different subject areas are very well appreciated by the user students. The participant students' response towards MOOC course completion stage perceived its usefulness to a large extent. They may be provided support services by the facilitator experts from different streams of higher education. The study has indicated about appropriate steps to be taken for learners' motivation and learners' high participation in learning situations. There must be well co-ordinated efforts between course ware design and development, delivery system, instructional activities, learner support services and evaluation strategies. The MOOC initiatives by UGC at national level must be interlinked with every stage of higher education with a view to provision of alternative and multiple opportunities for open learning to the students. Special emphasis be given on students' orientation and teachers' orientation at higher education institutions about implementation of MOOC programmes as an integral component of higher education

REFERENCES

Jain, R. and Singh, A.K. (2018). "Exploring MOOC Development Methodology for SWAYAM", *University News, 56*(31). July 30-August 5.

Levy, S. (2003). "Six factors to Consider when Planning Online Distance Learning Programmes in Higher Education". Online *Journal of Distance Learning Administration*, 6U.

Maboe, K.A. (2016). *Online Communication of Health Studies Students: Perspective of Open Distance Learning*, Health SA Gesonheid.

MHRD (2015). *Annual Report 2014-15*. Department of Higher Education, MHRD, Government of India. Retrieved from http://mhrd.gov.in/sites/upload_files/document-reports/Part1.pdf.

Martiny, F. and Parker, M.A. (2014). "Use of Synchronous Virtual Classrooms: Why, Who, and How?" *MERLOT Journal of Online Learning and Teaching, 10*(2).

Singh, G. (2018). "Blended Television with MOOCs: An Experiment in Elementary Teacher Education in India" in Phuong Tran Thi (Ed.) *Open Education in Human Resource Development in Asia's Period of Integration*, Vol. z, Hanoi: Bach Khoa Publishing House.

Sharma, M. (2019). *A Comprehensive Evaluation of online Programme at IGNOU: Towards Developing a Framework for IGNOU Online Programme*, Unpublished Ph.D. Distance Education.

Tello, S.F. (2007). "An Analysis of Student Persistence in Online Education", *International Journal of Information and Communication Technology Education, 3*(3).

Vaughan, N. (2014). "Student Engagement and Blended Learning: Making the Assessment Connection", *EDU. Sci.*, 4.

18

Technological Pedagogical and Content Knowledge of Pre-Service Teachers

B.C. Das and *Bijay Kumar Das*

The framework of Technological Pedagogical and Content Knowledge (TPACK) has been used to illustrate instructional ideas regarding how teachers integrate technology into their pedagogy and embrace as a theoretical basis for structuring ICT curriculum in teacher education programmes (Chai *et al.*, 2011; Jimoyiannis, 2010). Pre-service teachers' education in particular has shifted its emphasis from transmission-oriented approach to a constructivist approach, where teacher learners focus on what they know instead of what they do, bringing prior knowledge and personal experience to bear on the new learning situations (Cochran-Smith & Lytle, 2001). Through reflection, pre-service teachers become more aware of themselves as would-be teachers and of the pedagogical context that are contingent directly upon teaching and learning. In order to help pre-service teachers gain in enough knowledge and expertise is to motivate both teachers and instructors, and to inform them of their weaknesses and strengths. Furthermore, the intended programmes should be well-designed to meet the standards required of the teachers (Lee, 2007). Pre-Service training programmes of Teacher Education need to be revised at a sight of latest development and changes. The National Council of Educational Research and Training (NCERT) has brought out a National Curriculum Framework for School Education-2000 (NCFSE) with the objective to provide quality education and upgrade the curriculum at the school stage. Pre-service education of teachers is essential for bridging the gap in in-service education and for meeting the demands of the changing education scenario, its context and concerns. Keeping in view the recent trends and utility of information and communication technology, NCTE in its General Body meeting held on 17th August, 2000, decided that 'Information and Communication Technology (ICT) Literacy', shall be made a compulsory part of B.Ed. course. After observations and surveys number of secondary schools it is noted that the existing pattern on teaching methods are not much more effective in classroom interaction and are not creating interest among students at secondary level.

Geer (2002) concluded that upcoming trends changed the present scenario and adopted the constructivist learning approach which is more focused on innovative activities and knowledge acquisition. According to Seimens and Tittenberger (2009), the information cycle is now changing from creation to validation. The approaches to pedagogy is generic or dynamic, as it changes through various aspects of content, context, teaching style, cognitive development stage of child (Piaget, 1954), different learning style (Gardner and Hatch, 1989). Sale (2015) advocated on needs of strong empirical evidence of best pedagogy practice, that teachers adopt in their teaching practice and makes a most significant difference in students' learning attainment levels and lives. Shulman (1986, 1987) emphasized the significance of content and pedagogical knowledge for effective teaching. Similarly, the extension of pedagogical and content knowledge (PCK) with integration of technology became a domain of knowledge for teaching-learning practices. However, technological integration changes the process of pedagogy not the content. Thus, pedagogy that is practically useful in terms of how we teach? Mishra and Koehler (2006) had given a hybrid concept on teacher's knowledge about technology, pedagogy, content and its contextual influence on learning. Harris and Hofer (2011) questioned about how does knowledge about technology, pedagogy and content influence the teacher's instructional planning, activities and in results technology integration in content enhance student's learning and classroom activities. According to Schmidt *et al.* (2009) and Tokmak *et al.* (2013) pre-service teachers need to know the effective integration technology into their teaching practices. Therefore, a symbiotic development in terms of knowledge of technology, pedagogy and content is need and demand of the time. While integrating TPACK model for science teachers increase their confidence and helps in inquiry based teaching (Graham *et al.*, 2009). The use of TPACK model enhances digital pedagogies and encourages students to become reflective learner and to create knowledge collaboratively (Maor, 2013). The prevailed situation in pre-service teacher education has been complex with the flood of innovations around and hence it requires appropriate directions, which appears to be neglected over the recent times. There is need of trained human resources to cope up with given gamut of challenges posed on teaching-learning endeavours.

It is imperative, therefore, to moot the pertinent question such as—What are the existing levels of Technological Pedagogical and Content Knowledge among pre-service teachers. This kind of assessment study can be an attempt to look at certain possibilities which may give a direction on adoption of suitable technological and pedagogical approaches to deal with contents. The prime focus of this study is to explore the existing status of TPACK knowledge among Teacher Education Programme (TEP) and Integrated Teacher Education Programme (ITEP) Pre-Service teachers in teacher education institutions of Odisha.

Objective and Methodology

To study the existing levels of Technological, Pedagogical and

Content Knowledge among pre-service teachers of TEP and ITEP.

Hypothesis

There exists significant difference between the levels of Technological Pedagogical and Content knowledge among Pre-service Teachers in relation to their nature of teacher education programme.

Explorative Descriptive Design was employed to explore the existing status of TPACK knowledge of TEP and ITEP pre-service teachers. The target population of the proposed study comprised the pre-service teachers of secondary teacher education institutions in Odisha. However, the accessible population is the per-service teachers in ITEP and TEP belonging to both Science and Arts from five institutions including state university department of education and teacher education institution. The samples comprise 300 pre-service secondary school teachers selected randomly out of 600 accessible population. Data was collected from the sample institutions through questionnaire. Collected data was analyzed by percentage analysis and chi-square test of independence.

Analysis and Interpretation

TPACK of pre-service teachers covers six dimensions including (i) Pedagogical Knowledge (PK), (ii) Content Knowledge(CK), (iii) Technological Knowledge (TK), (iv) Pedagogical Content Knowledge (PCK), (v) Technological Content Knowledge (TCK), (vi) Technological Pedagogical and Content Knowledge (TPACK). The existing status of TPACK TEP and ITEP of teacher education institutions of Odisha are analyzed and interpreted in the succeeding section.

Pedagogical Knowledge (PK) of Pre-service Teachers

The Pedagogical Knowledge among pre-service teachers TEP and ITEP have been comparatively analyzed and interpreted components-wise on the basis of different knowledge level such as Having Advanced Knowledge (HAK), Having Basic Knowledge

(HBK), and Having Minimum Knowledge (HMK) respectively. On the aspects of Pedagogical Knowledge it is evident from Table 18.1 and related figures that the ITEP pre-Service teachers were found having higher Pedagogical Knowledge than TEP.

Table 18.1: Chi-Square test of Independence between Frequencies of Pedagogical Knowledge components related to nature of teacher education programme

Nature of Teacher Education Programme	Knowledge Level			Total	Chi-Square Value df = 2
	HAK	HBK	HMK		
TEP	154 (20.53)	357 (47.6)	239 (31.87)	750 (100)	86.94*
ITEP	322 (42.93)	261 (34.8)	167 (22.67)	750 (100)	
Total	476 (31.73)	**618** (41.2)	406 (27.06)	**1500** (100)	

Note: *—Significant at 0.01 level.
Numbers in the parentheses indicate percentages.

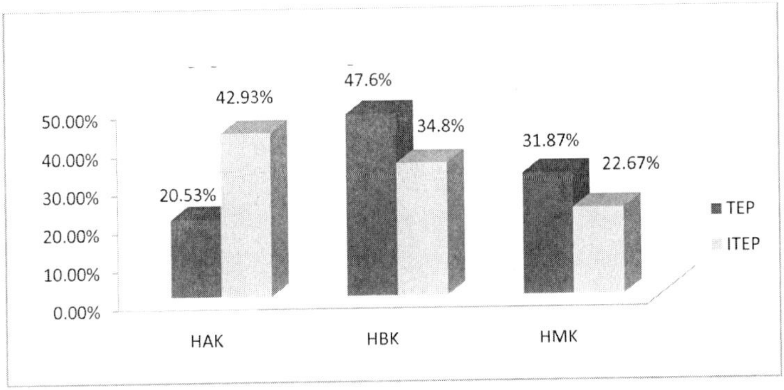

Fig. 18.1: Pedagogical knowledge betweenTEP and ITEP.

Going by the nature of teacher education programme, it is evident that majority of pre-service teachers in ITEP (42.93%) stated about advanced knowledge in pedagogical knowledge components than that of TEP pre-service teachers (20.53%).

From the Table 18.1, it can be observed that advanced knowledge in Pedagogical knowledge components was significantly associated with the nature of teacher education programme at 0.01 level of significance. However, within the significant association from the frequencies of responses it was found that the associations of nature of teacher education programme ITEP pre-service teachers have greater existing level of knowledge in pedagogical perspectives.

Content Knowledge (CK) Among Pre-service Teachers

The Content Knowledge among pre-service teachers TEP and ITEP have been comparatively analyzed and interpreted component-wise on the basis of different knowledge level such as Having Advanced Knowledge (HAK), Having Basic Knowledge (HBK), and Having Minimum Knowledge (HMK) respectively. On the aspects of Content Knowledge, it is evident from the Table 18.2 and related figures that the ITEP pre-Service teachers were found having higher Content Knowledge.

Table 18.2: Chi-Square test of Independence between Frequencies of Content Knowledge components related to nature of teacher education programme

Nature of Teacher Education Programme	CK Knowledge Level			Total	Chi-Square Value df = 2
	HAK	HBK	HMK		
TEP	359 (47.87)	261 (34.8)	130 (17.33)	750 (100)	44.16*
ITEP	259 (34.53)	398 (53.07)	93 (12.4)	750 (100)	
Total	**618 (41.2)**	**659 (43.93)**	**223 (14.87)**	**1500 (100)**	

Note: *—Significant at 0.01 level.
Numbers in the parentheses indicate percentages.

On these aspects of content knowledge components TEP pre-service teachers have more content knowledge with respect to ITEP pre-service teachers. However, both the teacher education programmes were found having basic content knowledge components (43.13%). It can be noticed that majority of respondents from ITEP pre-service teachers (53.07%) possess having basic knowledge than the TEP pre-service teachers (34.8%). From Table 18.2, it can be observed that the content knowledge components was significantly associated with nature teacher education programme at 0.01 level of significance. However, within the significant association from the frequencies of responses, it was found that the association of ITEP was higher than the TEP.

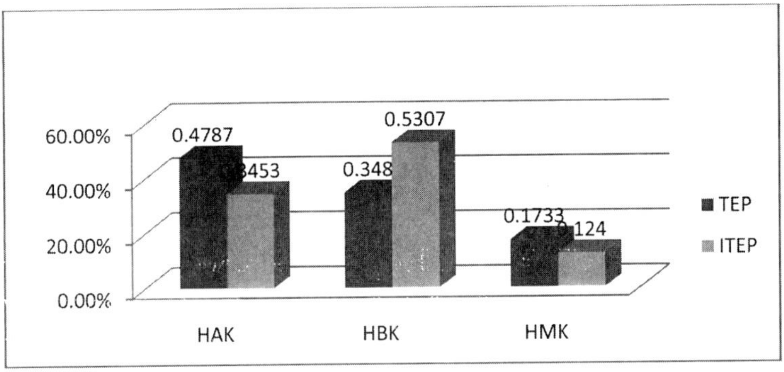

Fig. 18.2: Pedagogical knowledge betweenTEP and ITEP.

Technological Knowledge (TK) Among Pre-service Teachers

The Technological Knowledge among pre-service teachers TEP and ITEP have been comparatively analyzed and interpreted components-wise on the basis of different knowledge level such as Having Advanced Knowledge (HAK), Having Basic Knowledge (HBK), and Having Minimum Knowledge (HMK) respectively. On the aspects of Content knowledge, it is evident from the Table 18.3 and related figures that the ITEP pre-Service teachers were found higher having Technological Knowledge.

Table 18.3 and the related figure reveal that in all-around 37 per cent of respondents having advanced technological knowledge components in both the teacher education programme. It can be noticed that majority of ITEP pre-service teachers (48.13%) stated about advanced technological knowledge in different components where TEP pre-service teachers having basic knowledge in these aspects. From Table 18.3, it can be observed that the technological knowledge components of both the teacher education programmes were significantly associated at 0.01 level of significance. The ITEP pre-service teachers were found to be more advanced in technological knowledge.

Table 18.3: Chi-Square test of Independence between Frequencies of Technological Knowledge components related to nature of teacher education programme

Nature of Teacher Education Programme	Technological Knowledge Level			Total	Chi-Square Value, df = 2
	HAK	HBK	HMK		
TEP	201 (26.8)	300 (40)	249 (33.2)	750 (100)	80.80*
ITEP	361 (48.13)	249 (33.2)	140 (18.67)	750 (100)	
Total	**562 (37.47)**	**549 (36.6)**	**389 (25.93)**	**1500 (100)**	

Note: *—Significant at 0.01 level.
Numbers in the parentheses indicate percentages.

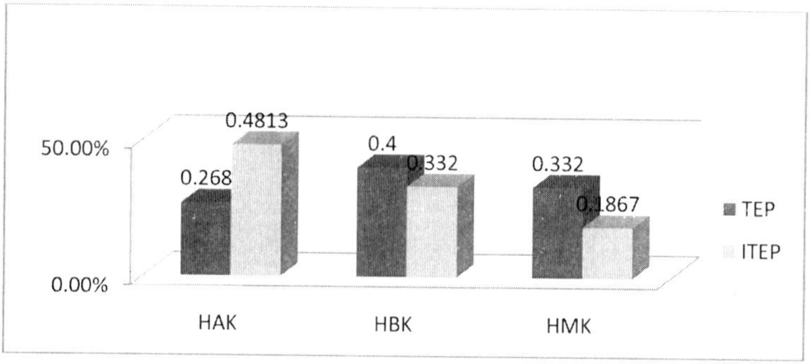

Fig. 18.3: Technological knowledge between TEP and ITEP.

Pedagogical Content Knowledge (PCK) Among Pre-service Teachers

The Pedagogical Content Knowledge among Pre-service teachers

TEP and ITEP have been comparatively analyzed and interpreted component-wise on the basis of different knowledge level such as Having Advanced Knowledge (HAK), Having Basic Knowledge (HBK), and Having Minimum Knowledge (HMK) respectively. On the aspects of Content Knowledge, it is evident from Table 18.4 and related figures that the ITEP pre-Service teachers were found having higher Pedagogical Content Knowledge. Pedagogical Content Knowledge of Teacher Education programmes as practices for professional development of teachers to improve quality of training of teachers.

Table 18.4: Chi-Square test of Independence between Frequencies of Pedagogical Content Knowledge components related to nature of teacher education programme

Nature of Teacher Education Programme	Knowledge Level			Total	Chi-Square Value, df = 2
	HAK	HBK	HMK		
TEP	173 (23.07)	417 (55.6)	160 (21.33)	750 (100)	7.84*
ITEP	220 (29.33)	388 (51.74)	142 (18.93)	750 (100)	
Total	**393 (26.2)**	**805 (53.67)**	**302 (20.13)**	**1500 (100)**	

Note: *—Significant at 0.01 level.
Numbers in the parentheses indicate percentages.

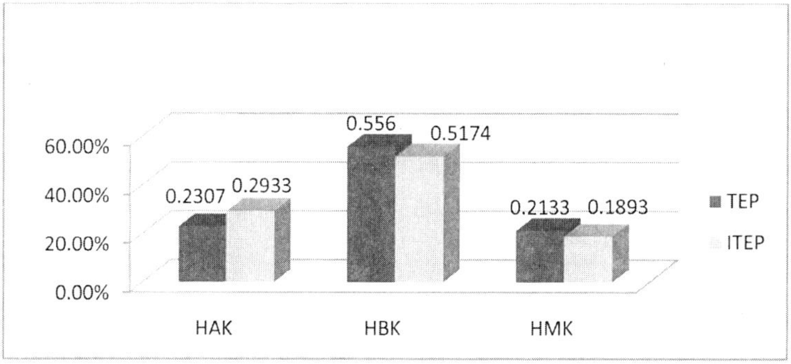

Fig. 18.4: Pedagogical Content Knowledge between TEP and ITEP.

Table 18.4 and the related figure reveals that only 26 per cent of pre-service teachers have advanced knowledge in pedagogical knowledge components in both the teacher education programmes. It can be noticed that ITEP (29.33%) having advanced level of knowledge than the TEP (23.07%) and majority (53.67%) of teachers have basic knowledge in pedagogical content knowledge components and around 20 per cent of both the teachers have minimum levels of pedagogical knowledge. From Table 18.4, it can be observed that pedagogical content knowledge components significantly associated with nature of teacher education programme at 0.05 level of significance. The ITEP pre-service teachers were found to be greater having pedagogical content knowledge.

Technological Content Knowledge (TCK) Among Pre-service Teachers

The Technological Content Knowledge among Pre-service Teachers TEP and ITEP have been comparatively analyzed and interpreted component-wise on the basis of different knowledge level such as Having Advanced Knowledge (HAK), Having Basic Knowledge (HBK), and Having Minimum Knowledge (HMK) respectively. On the aspects of Technological Content Knowledge, it is evident from Table 18.5 and related figure that the ITEP pre-Service teachers were found having higher Technological Content Knowledge. Technological Content Knowledge of Teacher Education programmes as practices for professional development of teachers to improve quality of training for teachers.

Table 18.5 and the related figure reveal that around 42 per cent of pre-service teachers have advanced knowledge in Technological content knowledge components in both the teacher education programmes. It can be noticed that ITEP (51.2%) having advanced level of knowledge than the TEP (33.33%) and about (28%) of teachers have basic knowledge in Technological Content Knowledge components and around 29 per cent of both the teachers have minimum levels of pedagogical knowledge. From Table 18.5, can be observed that Technological Content Knowledge components significantly associated with nature of teacher education programme at 0.01 level of significance. The ITEP pre-service teachers were found having greater technological content knowledge.

Table 18.5: Chi-Square test of Independence between Frequencies of Technological Content Knowledge components related to nature of teacher education programme

Nature of Teacher Education Programme	Technological Content Knowledge Level			Total	Chi-Square Value df = 2
	HAK	HBK	HMK		
TEP	250 (33.33)	211 (28.13)	289 (38.54)	750 (100)	67.38*
ITEP	384 (51.2)	209 (27.87)	157 (20.93)	750 (100)	
Total	**634** (42.27)	**420** (28)	**446** (29.73)	**1500** (100)	

Note: *—Significant at 0.01 level.
Numbers in the parentheses indicate percentages.

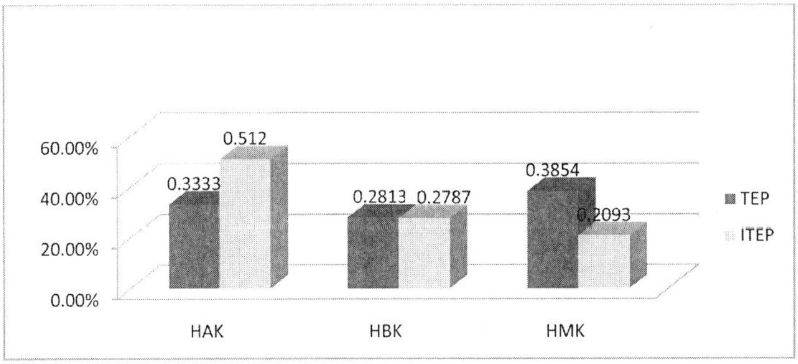

Fig. 18.5: Technological Content Knowledge between TEP and ITEP.

Technological Pedagogical and Content Knowledge (TPACK) among Pre-service Teachers

The Technological, Pedagogical and Content Knowledge among pre-service teachers of TEP and ITEP have been comparatively analyzed and interpreted component-wise on the basis of different knowledge level such as Having Advanced Knowledge

(HAK), Having Basic Knowledge (HBK), and Having Minimum Knowledge (HMK) respectively. On the aspects of Technological, Pedagogical and Content Knowledge, it is evident from Table 18.6 and related figures that the ITEP pre-Service teachers were found having higher Technological, Pedagogical and Content Knowledge. TPACK knowledge of teacher education programmes as practices for professional development of teachers to improve quality of training for teachers.

Table 18.6: Chi-Square test of Independence between Frequencies of Technological Knowledge components related to nature of Teacher Education Programme

Nature of Teacher Education Programme	TPACK Knowledge Level			Total	Chi-Square Value df = 2
	HAK	HBK	HMK		
TEP	33 (4.4)	137 (18.26)	580 (77.33)	750 (100)	
ITEP	81 (10.8)	208 (27.73)	461 (61.47)	750 (100)	48.4*
Total	**114** (7.6)	**345** (23)	**1041** (69.4)	**1500** (100)	

Note: *—Significant at 0.01 level.
Numbers in the parentheses indicate percentages.

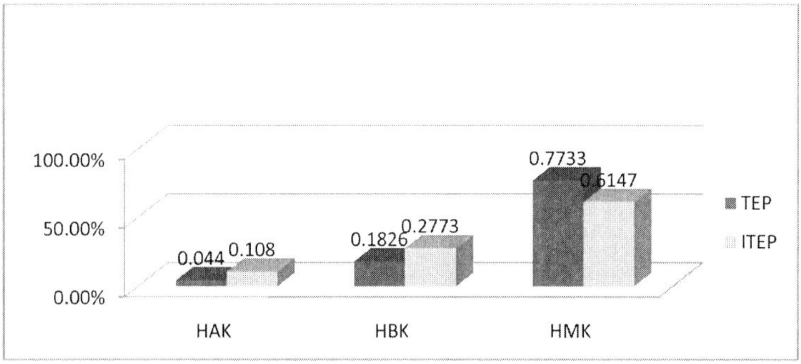

Fig. 18.6: Technological, Pedagogical and Content Knowledge between TEP and ITEP.

Table 18.6 and the related figure reveals that around 7 per cent of pre-service teachers have advanced knowledge in pedagogical knowledge components in both the teacher education programmes. It can be noticed that ITEP (10.8%) having advanced level of knowledge than the TEP (4.4%) and majority (69.4%) of teachers have minimum knowledge in pedagogical content knowledge components and (23%) of both the teachers have basic levels of Technological, Pedagogical and Content Knowledge. From Table 18.6, it can be observed that TPACK knowledge components significantly associated with nature of teacher education programme at 0.01 level of significance. The ITEP pre-service teachers were found having greater Technological, pedagogical and content knowledge than the TEP.

Conclusions and Implications

There is significant difference in the existing level of knowledge between the pre-service teachers pursuing two-year teacher education programme (TEP) and four-year integrated teacher education programme (ITEP). The ITEP pre-service teachers reported that they have more advanced knowledge in technological, pedagogical and content knowledge components in comparison to their counterpart TEP pre-service teachers. Whereas TEP pre-service teachers have reported they have basic knowledge in the technological, pedagogical and content knowledge components. Most of the TEP and ITEP pre-service teachers reported that they have minimum knowledge about the TPACK components. ICT needs to be used for sharing quality training in teacher education institutions. The teacher education curriculum needs to be integrated with TPACK components so that the pre-service teachers will be acquainted with the integration of technologies with pedagogy and contents. In practice teaching programme, the pre-service teachers must be given opportunity to develop TPACK based lesson plans and have its practice in real classroom.

REFERENCES

Guler, M. & Celik, D. (2018). "Uncovering the relation between CK and PCK: An investigation of pre-service elementary mathematics teachers' algebra teaching knowledge". *REDIMAT Journal of Research in Mathematics Education*, *7*(2): 161-94. https://doi.org/10.17583/redimat.2018.2575

Harish, J.B. & Hofer, M.J. (2011). "Technological Pedagogical and Content Knowledge (TPACK) in action: A descriptive study of secondary teacher's curriculum-based, technology related instructional planning". *Journal of Research on Technology in Education. 43*(3): 211-29. Retrieved from https://files.eric.ed.gov/fulltext/EJ918905.pdf

Hofer, Mark. J. & Harris, Judi (2012). "TPACK Research with In-service Teachers: Where's the TCK?" *Book Chapters. Book 9.* http://publish.wm.edu/bookchapters/9

Lee, Y. (2007). "Development and Application of the TPACK-P Education Programme for Pre-Service Teachers' TPACK". *International Journal of Engineering & Technology, 7* (3.34) (2018): 654-62.

Maor, D. (2013). "Does the use of the TPACK model enhances digital pedagogies: we don't understand the present so how can we imagine the future?" *Proceedings of 30th ASCILITE Conference 2013.*

Mishra, P. & Koehler, M.J. (2006). "Technological pedagogical content knowledge: A framework for teacher knowledge". *Teachers College Record, 108*(6): 1017-54

Sale, D. (2015). "The Heuristics of Effective Teaching". *Creative Teaching: An Effective Based Approach,* pp.19-83. Springer-Verlag Singapure Publisher. DOI 10.1007/978-981-287-534-1_2

Schmidt, D.A., Baran, E., Thompson, A.M., Mishra, P., Koehler, M.J., & Shin, T.S. (2006). "Technological Pedagogical Content Knowledge (TPACK): Development and Validation of an Assessment Instrument for Pre-service Teachers". *Journal of Research on Technology in Education, 42*(2): 123-49. *Science.* Advance online publication. Retrieved from https://www.sciencedirect.com/science/article/pii/S2452315118301000

Seimens, G. & Tittenberger, P. (2009). *Handbook of Emerging Technologies for Learning.* University of Manitoba.

Shulman, L.S. (1987). "Knowledge and teaching: Foundations of the New Reform". *Harvard Educational Review, 57*: 1-22.

Shulman, L.S. (1986). "Those Who Understand: Knowledge Growth in Teaching". *Educational Researcher, 15*: 4-14.

Tokmak, H.S., Surmeli, H. & Ozgelen, S. (2013). "Pre-service Science Teachers' Perception of their TPACK Development after Creating Digital Stories". *International Journal of Environmental and Science Education, 9*: 247-64. Doi: 10.12973/ijese.2014.214a

UNESCO (2003). UNESCO Report: *Information and Communication Technologies in Teacher Education—A Planning Guide*. Division of Higher Education, UNESCO.

19

Uses of ICT in Doctoral Research

P.K. Sahoo and *Uzma Khanam*

Use of ICT in knowledge development process is of paramount significance in doctoral research programmes at university stage. Its role in different processes of research must be studied with a view to make research programmes more efficient and effective. The present study aims at exploring the status of use of ICT in different research processes, viz. initial review and identification of problem, research design, sources of research data, data collection, data analysis, interpretation of data and writing report. The online questionnaire survey was conducted on 150 doctoral level research scholars from Arts and Science faculties of University of Allahabad. One of the oldest universities of India. The rating of various uses of ICT was analysed descriptively. 't' test was used to study the effect of discipline and gender on the use of ICT in research process. The study revealed prominent use of ICT facilities in the context of literature review and problem identification, analysis of data and report writing, cutting across the Arts and Science disciplines. There was no significant effect of discipline on use of ICT in research process than their men counterparts. It is concluded that most sustainable efforts must be to promote ICT integrated facilities for different processes of research at university stage in India.

The emergence of Information and communication technology (ICT) in the era of twenty first century has changed the process of acquisition of knowledge as well as generation of knowledge. The paradigm shift on the pedagogy integrated with ICT has brought revolutionary change in teaching-learning process. ICT is no more considered as a tool of procuring and dissemination of the information; rather it is going to transform the nature of education.As a source of learning, ICT has played significant role to facilitate knowledge construction at different stages of education. Increasing availability of open source course content on the internet and provision of collaborative and co-operative learning projects has brought a tremendous change in the teaching-learning process. Moreover, ICT has provided ample scope for learners' decision making in organizing various kinds of inquiry based teaching-learning practices individually as well as groups.

While integrated teaching-learning practices contribute significantly towards subject based curricular activities, there is enough scope for Knowledge Generation Practices cutting across the boundaries of different disciplines. The contribution of ICT through the Knowledge Integration Environment (KIE) and Web-based Inquiry Science Environment (WISE) are some of the examples of facilitating Inquiry based approach in Knowledge Generation (Linn, 2006).

Of late, major transformation has been noticed in teaching-learning process since open sources, on-line-resources and curriculum materials have been available at school stage as well as at high education stage. Open Educational Resources (OER) are understood as any resource available at little or no cost that can be used for teaching, learning contents; simulations, games, and other learning applications; syllabi, quizzes, and assessment tools. Any OER typically refers to electronic resources, including those in multimedia formats and such materials are generally released under a Creative Commons or similar licence that supports open or nearly open use of the contents. OER can originate from colleges and universities, libraries, archival organisations, government agencies etc. who develop educational resources they are willing to share. In the Indian Context, the MHRD, Government of India, NCERT and other research institutions have developed OER repositories. Teachers, learners and researchers can download OER and use them in formal or informal learning situations.

Because of the OER availability the students from different disciplines have been benefited to identify the original documents as well as different kinds of learning texts suiting to different curriculums. This has been rightly stated by Mean's & Roschel (2010), that beyond access to information and artefacts, the Web offers educational resources organized into units of learning activities and increasingly, entire courses that a school or individual may choose to use. There has been a tremendous effort at different countries' level as well as through the International organizations, to provide OER opportunities to the researchers. The open course ware systems have been popularized through open-course materials.

There have been instances of online learning as an integral component of higher education. Online learning has been considered as an integral component of open-distance learning system too. Its advantage in providing access to educational support, cost-effective use of learning facilities and learner support services for quality outcome have been ensured through online learning system. Different kinds of synchronous and asynchronous technologies have been used to promote flexi learning system. Emergence of advanced communication technologies have provided to strengthen various kinds of interaction based experiences conclude. Thus, it can be stated that ICT provides ample scope for locating the sources of learning using multiple information resources and giving information from multiple perspective thus fostering conductive learning environment for the learners. ICT makes complex learning forum easier to learn; through various means. Thus, ICT functions as a facilitator of alternative learning and higher order thinking (Alexander, 1999).

ICTs' contribution to enable students for development competencies of the 21st century has a lot of significance for development of research skills among the young researchers. According to Law (2008), the new set of competency standards for the global community is constructed around three approaches to ICT institution for educational change on the basis of three factors leading to human-capacity-based growth that have been identified by economists: capital deepening, higher-quality labour, and technological innovation. The technology-literacy approach focuses on increasing the technological uptake of students and citizens by incorporating technology skills in the curriculum, a goal suitable for a capital-deepening economy. The knowledge-deepening approach focuses on building up a high-performance workforce by developing the ability of students and citizens to solve complex, real-world problems by applying the knowledge they have learned. The knowledge-creation approach aims to produce a workforce that can innovate, produce, and benefit from new knowledge for a knowledge economy.

In view of strengthening the base of knowledge generation process, ICT plays a major role by providing digital environment that supports the interaction among members of the learning community, as they engage in evolving cycle of idea-improvement and deepening levels of understanding as an important part of the knowledge building process. In this perspective, the researchers' competencies in making optimum use of ICT integrated inquiry systems is very much pertinent to contribute towards knowledge generation in respective fields especially in the case of developing countries.

ICT Related Studies in Education

Review of literature on use of ICT in education by different group of stakeholders in a few cases have been reported below. In the context of Australian Schools, the evidences about the uses of ICT in Queensland College of Teachers Research Digest (2009) revealed that the use of computers is common at home and at school;

ICT learning objects are used mostly in Mathematics, English and Science and Students use ICT in limited ways. Information access and searching are common, but creating, analysing and transforming information are less common in Australian schools.

Shelley S.C. Young and Hsin-Ho Ku (2008) conducted a study on Uses of ICT in Primary Education through Four Winning School Cases in the Taiwan Schools Cyber Fair. The purpose of this study was to understand, describe and interpret the uses of information communication technology (ICT) in primary education in the Taiwan School Cyber Fair as a means to expand and enhance student learning in an extra-curricular setting. Four winning schools with 48 teachers and students involved were purposefully selected for study. The research findings revealed that students in each group were highly motivated through the extensive use of ICT. Through long-term engagement with ICT, students were empowered to conduct both wider and deeper exploration of their selected topics of interest. They reported that participants involved in the ICT-enabled activities contributed to the success of the outstanding performance of the four winning schools at the School cyber fair contest.

Chinwe M.T. Nwezeh (2010) conducted a study on The Use of ICT in Nigerian Universities: A Case Study of Obafemi Awolowo University, Ile-Ife. He stated that internet's seemingly infinite information offers access to up-to-date research reports and global knowledge, so it has become an important component of electronic services in academic institutions. Internet has become an invaluable tool for learning, teaching and research (including collaborative research) in Nigeria. The study revealed that e-mail was the most used Internet technology by both staff and students used in the survey while file transfer protocol was the list used. The respondents made use of search interfaces and discussion groups. Both the staff and students used search interfaces to look for information while they use the resources of the library involved in research. The few staff and students who made use of discussion groups did mainly to be updated on research issues as well as for social reasons.

R.K. Krishnaveni and Meenakumari (2010) conducted a study on Usage of ICT for Information Administration in Higher Education Institutions. They concluded that the integration of ICT helps to reduce the complexity and enhance the overall administration of higher education. They identified various functional areas to which ICT is deployed for information administration in higher education institutions and to found the current extent various factors that contributed to these functional areas were identified as: (a) Universal and individual challenges, (b) Balancing between traditional and modern approaches, (c) Long-term and short-term consideration, and (d) Competition and equity challenges and Extraordinary expansion of knowledge. As a part of strategy, the authors mentioned that these challenges could be overcome with the proper usage of technology. Moreover, many studies revealed the need for ICT integration into administrative activities of higher education institutions.

Kourosh Fathi Vajargah *et al.* (2010) conducted a study on Application of ICTs in Teaching and Learning at University Level: The Case of Shahid Beheshti University. This study was conducted at the National University of Iran, the second largest university in the country. The research population consisted of the university academics and students. A questionnaire was administrated for collection of data. The main results are reported based on the following: (1) The possible domains of using ICT in curriculum decision-making in higher education, (2) Obstacles of using ICT in curriculum development at university level, (3) Facilitating factors and essential supports needed for application of ICT in curriculum development of higher education, and (4) Advantages and disadvantages of using ICT for curricular activities at universities level.

Nitika Tolani-Brown *et al.* (2009) conducted a study on Analysis of the Research and Impact of ICT in Education in Developing Country Contexts. The researchers reviewed relevant literature that investigates the impacts of ICT interventions on student learning outcomes and have highlighted the challenges that hinder rigorous evaluation of such interventions. Their review suggested that the impacts of ICTs on impacts, however, among stakeholders were mostly positive and whether ICTs can meet these expectations is dependent upon how such solutions were implemented.

Panda and Rout (2012) study on attitude of Teacher Trainees towards ICT in Teacher Education revealed their positive attitude towards ICT sex had significant effect on attitude towards ICT with high value of men students. There was significant effect of stream on student-teachers' attitude ICT integration in teaching practice deprived on teachers and teacher educators' motivation, attitude and interest.

The above studies indicate that there have been efforts to popularize ICT in education sector. However, the movement needs to be more comprehensive and dynamic in the context of the developing countries.

ICT in Doctoral Study Programmes

Doctoral Study programmes at university stage aim at sharpening understanding level of researchers in various paradigms of knowledge generation processes and developing the competencies of the researchers in conducting doctoral level projects in specific areas of concerned discipline. In the Indian universities, the University Grants Commission (UGC) made it a compulsory feature to acquire knowledge and skills on use of ICT in different steps of research in its doctoral degree course such as : review of e-literature, computer applications and interactive multimedia based presentations.

This has been observed that in general, the ICT users perform two groups of activities (Anderson and Ainley, 2010), such as:

I. Group of functions is referred to as Internet/entertainment use and is probably close to what is referred to in some literature as social networking. It includes the following items:

- Browsing the Internet for information about people, things or ideas;
- Playing games;
- Using the Internet to collaborate with a group or team;
- Downloading software from the Internet (including games);
- Downloading music from the Internet; and
- Communicating (e-mail or chat rooms).

II. Group of function is referred to as programme/software use and includes the following items:
- Writing documents (e.g. with Word or Word Perfect);
- Using spreadsheet (e.g., Lotus 123 or MS Excel);
- Using educational software such as mathematics programmes; and
- Writing computer programmes.

Besides above functions, the researchers make use of sophisticated software for analysis of quantitative and qualitative data.

The functions of ICT in knowledge generation process cover a wide range of activities, such as analysis of the theoretical bases of knowledge, sharpening research questions, formulation of suitable designs, and collection of evidences in laboratory situation or in natural setting, treatment of data, interpretation of data and writing of reports. Different forms of ICT related functions in research cover computer based data processing, Internet based Communication, use of Web based knowledge repositories, e-library references, Synchronous and Asynchronous mode interactions with experts and co-workers, co-operative ventures in decision making while dealing with complex research questions and critical research process, gathering qualitative and quantitative evidences for answering research questions, analysis of massive data base, employing multivariate designs and predictions of research findings with high accuracy, triangulation of qualitative data for interpretive reporting, literary narratives, writing of reports and sharing of knowledge with the knowledge community. ICT's role in facilitating research work is not just restricted to a tool of gathering evidences and manipulation of data, rather it serves as an expert system to sharpen the inquiry process and generation of knowledge. ICT is considered as a best source of knowledge generation in any branch of knowledge, viz. natural sciences, social sciences and humanities. Hence, it is relevant to make well co-ordinated efforts for use of ICT based teaching-learning strategies for facilitating research programmes at university stage. In this context, understanding the existing practices of ICT by the researchers in doctoral study programmes at university level is considered relevant. The research works conducted so far focus on the area of ICT support learning mainly in school curriculum areas. The studies at higher education stage focus on ICT supported academic management and administrative functions. In view of understanding the major role of ICT in knowledge generation process, it is essential to explore the status of ICT integrated practices of the research programmes in the university stage.

Research process irrespective of differences in knowledge generation paradigms involve seven common components, viz. Literature review, theoretical analysis and sources of Data, Collection of data: Qualitative and Quantitative analysis of data, interpretation of data and report writing. As stated above, ICT integrated activities in pursuing different research processes are considered very much prominent in increasing efficiency and effectiveness of knowledge generation by the researchers. However, there can be different factors influencing uses of ICT in research like nature of discipline and researchers' gender background. For instance, Science field may rely heavily on Positivistic Paradigm whereas Social Science and Humanities may focus more on Interpretive paradigm or mixed paradigm. Moreover, genders' role in knowledge generation processes may play a significant role. The present study has been conducted with a focus on exploring the level of uses of ICT by the doctoral level scholars on different processes of research in the context of their discipline gender. Moreover, the issue of discipline and gender on uses of ICT in research processes have been dealt with in the present study.

Objectives of the Study

1. To study level of uses of ICT in different components of research process by the doctoral level research scholars.
2. To compare the level of uses of ICT on different components of research process by science stream research scholars.
3. To compare the level uses of ICT in research by women and men research scholars.

Hypotheses

1. There will be no significant difference between the mean scores of the use of ICT on different components of research process among Arts and Science discipline research scholars.
2. There will be no significant difference between the mean scores of the use of ICT in research among women and men research scholars.

Methods and Procedure of the Study

The study was confined to the research scholars of the Arts and Science faculties of University of Allahabad. University of Allahabad is one of the oldest teaching and research universities of India. It enrols approximately 1500 students for research studies on residential basis. The ICT facilities are available for research work in the campus in the form of centralised e-library departments and research centres. The present study covered a sample of 150 research scholars drawn randomly from the population. The study was delimited to Arts (including Economics) and Science disciplines. The study did not include Law and Commerce disciplines.

A Likert type rating scale developed by the researchers was used for data collection purpose. The tool consisted of 35 items covering 7 areas of research process with 5 items each, such as:

1. Initial Review and problem identification,
2. Formulating research design, and
3. Identification of relevant and authentic sources of data.

Data Collection

- Data analysis—qualitative and quantitative,
- Interpretation of Data, and
- Writing of Report.

The sample respondents were requested to e-mail the response to the researchers data were analysed with the help of descriptive statistics and t-test. The level of use of ICT was rated by the respondents on a 5-point giving weightage of: to seldom, to sometimes, to average, to frequently and to more frequently.

Analysis and Interpretation

From Table 19.1, it can be observed that there was no significant difference between the mean scores of use ICT among Arts and Science discipline research scholars. It indicated that the discipline background did not affect the use of ICT on different components of research process. The Arts as well as Science stream research scholar's level of use of ICT were at par with each other. From Graph I, it can be observed that researchers of Science and Arts discipline made optimum use of ICT (72-74%) for initial level review, for identification of problem and theoretical analysis. They also made very high level use of ICT (69-74%) for analysis of data. A very high weightage was (70-75%) given to use of ICT for writing the research of data. In the case of other research processes like research design (64-67%) identification of sources of data (65-66%) collecting data (58-68%) and interpretation of data (67-68%), the level use was quite high among Science and Arts faculty research scholars. It shows that the ICT's popularity in research process is gaining ground at university stage in the Indian Subcontinent.

Table 19.1: ‘t’ test for comparison of mean scores of use of ICT among Arts and Science discipline research scholars of AU on different components of research process

Discipline							
Sl. No.	**Sciences (N=40)**			**Arts (N=110)**			**T-Test**
	Mean	**%**	**S.D**	**Mean**	**%**	**S.D**	
1	18.40	73.6	3.26	18.20	72.8	3.42	0.33NS
2	16.10	64.4	3.28	16.70	66.8	4.22	0.40NS
3	16.61	66.44	3.83	16.21	64.84	3.26	0.31NS
4	14.62	58.48	4.19	17.05	68.2	4.92	0.47NS
5	18.52	74.08	2.96	17.30	69.2	3.47	0.34NS
6	16.72	66.9	3.36	17.10	68.4	3.39	0.32NS
7	17.64	70.6	3.36	18.71	74.84	3.47	0.33NS

NS—Not significant at 0.05 level with df=149.

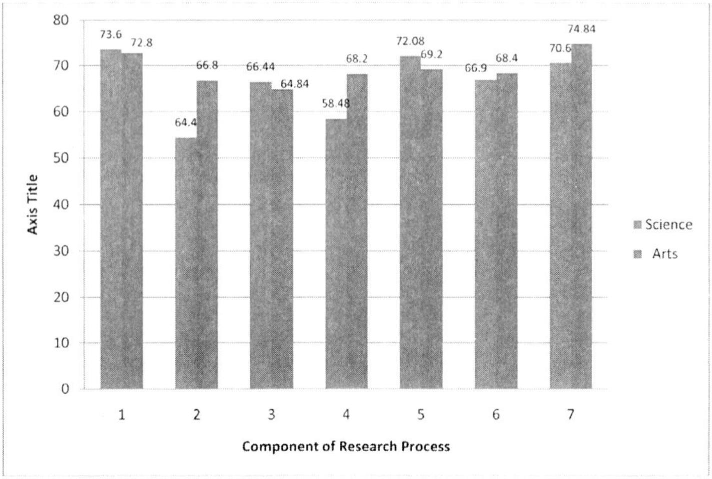

Fig. 19.1: Comparison of mean scores of use of ICT.

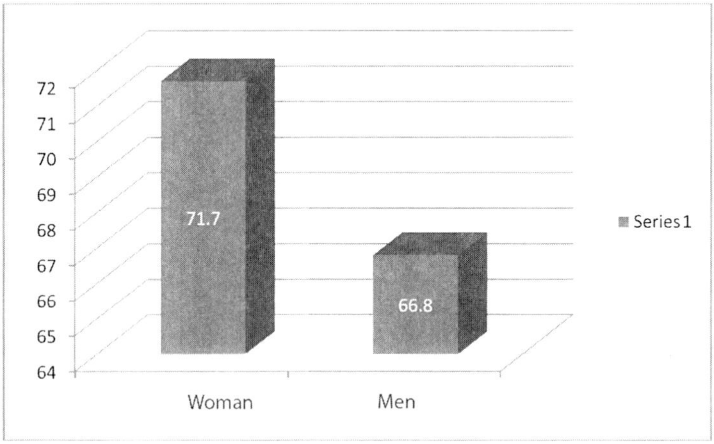

Fig. 19.2: Use of ICT among women and men research scholars in research process.

Research activities be encouraged with blended approach for knowledge generation in a fast rate.

Table 19.2: 't' test for comparison of mean scores of use of ICT among women and men research scholars of AU on research process

Women N=77			**Men N=73**			**df**	**'t' Value**	**Significant**
Mean	**%**	**S.D.**	**Mean**	**%**	**S.D.**			
125.40	71.7	20.08	116.88	66.8	18.37	149	2.15	.05

From Table 19.2, it can be witnessed that there was significant difference between the mean scores of use of ICT among women and men research scholars at 0.05 level of significance. It indicates that gender has significant effect on the use of ICT in research process. From Fig. 19.2, it can be observed that the level of ICT use was higher in the case of women scholars (71.7%) than that of their men counterparts (66.8%). It indicates that the women scholars are more ICT friendly in research process than their men counterparts. ICT has provided more flexible learning environment of research, particularly among women students.

Discussion

The study revealed promising findings on the use of ICT among doctoral students on different processes of research in the Indian University. Knowledge generation process through ICT has given ample opportunity for self-study, interactive mode learning, use of audio and visual presentations, besides print based outputs and guided activities. Collaborative institutional ventures have promoted co-operative learning environment for the researchers. The e-library facilities have facilitated research processes irrespective of discipline background. As noticed above most popular mode of use of ICT has been noticed with regard to review of literature at initial stage, analysis of data and writing of reports respectively. This is influenced mainly because of upgraded e-library facilities, available open educational resources, Web based interaction, use of standard data analysis packages and reporting facilities in written, visual, and audio visual forms. Moreover, there is a formal requirement for submission of doctoral thesis in e-form. The gender difference has indicated feministic appeal of ICT in research work. ICT has been found to be more popular among women scholars on different functions of research than their men counterparts. As a whole, more interactive expert facilities must be provided to the researchers in different functions like formulation of appropriate design of research, locating appropriate and authentic data from reliable sources, conducting laboratory studies with ICT integrated tools, collecting data in natural setting and conducting field studies and interpretation of data with it. ICT facilities must be promoted in the university campus to facilitate above functions of knowledge generation. This is an age of globalization. Higher education sector promoting research activities must be encouraged with blended approach for knowledge generation in a fast rate.

REFERENCES

B. Means & J. Roschelle (2010). *Technology and Learning: An Overview of Technology and Learning International Encyclopaedia of Education.* 3rd Edition, Vol. 8, pp. 1-10.

Chinwe, M.T.N. (2010). *The Use of ICT in Nigerian Universities: A Case Study of Obbafemi,* Awolowo University, Ile–Ife. In Library Philosophy and Practice 2010.

Educause Learning Initiative (2010). *Open Educational Resources.*

Kourosh Fathi Vajargah, *et al.* (2010). *Application of ICTs in Teaching and Learning at University Level: The Case of Shahid Beheshti University.* April, Vol. 9, No. 2.

Law, N. Pelgrum, W.J. & Plomp, T. (2008). *Pedagogy and ICT use in Schools Around the World: Findings from the IEA Sites 2006 Study.* Hong Kong. University of Hong Kong Comparative Education Research Centre.

Linn, M. (2006). "The Knowledge Integration Perspective on Learning and Instruction". In Swayer, R.K. (ed.) *Cambridge Handbook of the Learning Sciences,* pp. 243-64. Cambridge: Cambridge University Press.

Nikita Tolani-Brown *et al.* (2009). *An Analysis of the Research and Impact of ICT in Education in Developing Country Contexts.*

Panda, B.N. and Rout, R.K. (2012). "Attitude of Teacher Trainees Towards the use of ICT in Teacher Education Programmes of Odisha", in Harichandan, D. and Pandya, S.R. (Eds.), *Teacher Education and ICT,* New Delhi: ADH Pub. Corp.

Penelpe Perterson Eva Baker, Barry McGaw (2010). *International Encyclopedia of Education.* 3rd Edition, Vol. 8.

Queensland College of Teachers Research Digest, Vol. 4, April 2009.

R. Andersonn & Ainley (2010). *Technology and Learning: Access in Schools Around the World. Inteernational Encylopedia of Education.* 3rd Edition, Vol. 8, pp. 21-33.

R.K.Veni Krishna & J. Kumari (2010). *Usage of ICT for Information Administration in Higher Education Insstitutions–A Study.*

Young. S.S.C. & Ku, H.H. (2008). "A study of uses in Primary Education through Four Winning School Cases in the Taiwan Schools Cyberfair". *Educational Technology & Society, 11*(3): 52-66.